CHILD TO SOLDIER

Stories from Joseph Kony's Lord's Resistance Army

How and why are children forced to become soldiers, and what are the long-term implications for individual children and a society? Should former child-inducted soldiers be prosecuted for their past criminal activities and conduct? In *Child to Soldier*, Opiyo Oloya addresses these questions by exploring how Acholi children in northern Uganda, abducted by infamous warlord Joseph Kony and his Lord's Resistance Army (LRA), became soldiers.

Oloya – himself an Acholi, a refugee from Idi Amin's rule of Uganda – challenges conventional thinking by demonstrating how child-inducted soldiers in Uganda developed a form of familial loyalty to their captors and comrades within their new surroundings in the bush. Based on interviews with former child combatants, this book provides a cultural context for understanding the process of socializing children into violence. Oloya details how Kony and the LRA exploited and perverted Acholi heritage and pride to control and direct the children in war.

Child to Soldier highlights the tragic political and personal circumstances surrounding the use of child soldiers. It also emphasizes the reality that child-inducted soldiers do not remain children forever but become adults who remain deeply scarred by their experiences. In this eye-opening book, Oloya offers a rare glimpse into the everyday world of the child soldier and at the same time provides a broader understanding of the roots of modern-day ethnic tension and conflict.

OPIYO OLOYA is the superintendent of education for school leadership with the York Catholic District School Board. He writes a weekly column on social issues for the Ugandan newspaper *New Vision*, which is read throughout Africa, and has spent the last three summers working in Somalia with the African Mission in Somalia (AMISOM).

OPIYO OLOYA

Child to Soldier

Stories from Joseph Kony's Lord's Resistance Army

UNIVERSITY OF TORONTO PRESS
Toronto Buffalo London

© University of Toronto Press 2013
Toronto Buffalo London
www.utppublishing.com
Printed in Canada

ISBN 978-1-4426-4604-9 (cloth)
ISBN 978-1-4426-1417-8 (paper)

Printed on acid-free, 100% post-consumer recycled paper with vegetable-based inks.

Library and Archives Canada Cataloguing in Publication

Oloya, Opiyo
Child to soldier: stories from Joseph Kony's Lord's Resistance Army /
Opiyo Oloya.

Includes bibliographical references and index.
ISBN 978-1-4426-4604-9 (bound).   ISBN 978-1-4426-1417-8 (pbk.)

1. Children and war – Uganda.   2. Child soldiers – Uganda – Social conditions.
3. Child soldiers – Uganda – Interviews.   4. Lord's Resistance Army.
5. Acholi (African people) – Uganda – Social conditions.   I. Title.

HQ784.W3046 2012   303.6'4083096761   C2012-907226-5

The author and publisher gratefully acknowledge the estate of Okot P'Bitek for permission to reprint excerpts from *Song of Lowino* (Nairobi: East African Publishing House 1966).

This book has been published with the help of a grant from the Canadian Federation for the Humanities and Social Sciences, through the Aid to Scholarly Publications Program, using funds provided by the Social Sciences and Humanities Research Council of Canada.

University of Toronto Press acknowledges the financial assistance to its publishing program of the Canada Council for the Arts and the Ontario Arts Council.

University of Toronto Press acknowledges the financial support for its publishing activities of the Government of Canada through the Canada Book Fund.

Canada Council   Conseil des Arts
for the Arts   du Canada

ONTARIO ARTS COUNCIL
CONSEIL DES ARTS DE L'ONTARIO
50 YEARS OF ONTARIO GOVERNMENT SUPPORT OF THE ARTS
50 ANS DE SOUTIEN DU GOUVERNEMENT DE L'ONTARIO AUX ARTS

Contents

Acknowledgments

The Acholi have a saying that a child cannot thank his or her mother for the milk she provided when the child was a baby. That is not because the child is ungrateful, but because the mother's sacrifice is immensely priceless. Such is the case with the love and support I received from my wife, Emily, and our sons, Oceng and Ogaba, while writing this book. They gave me enormous space to work, never complaining about the long hours spent away from them.

Still on the family front, I must thank my parents, who inculcated in me a love of learning, a desire to dig beneath the dirt to see what lay down there. My father died two years ago, but he knew about my book and asked often how close it was to being completed.

In a similar vein, I can never be thankful enough for the tremendous support that I received from so many generous people who gave life to this book. I recall the cold morning in March 2000 when I walked into the office of the former director of education for York Catholic District School Board, Susan LaRosa, to ask for time to travel to Uganda to look into the story of children fighting a devastating war. After listening to my pitch, she said, without blinking, 'You go ahead,' Opiyo, this is important.' I am deeply grateful Ms LaRosa, without whom this project would not have started, for recognizing and responding to a problem half a world away with compassion and humanity. I also wish to thank my colleagues and friends at the York Catholic District School Board, including current director Patricia Preston, Mary (Maria) Battista, Andy Disebastiano, Robert Lostracco, Sandra Tuzi-DeCaro, Sue Kralik, Dan Ryan, the staff at All Saints, Divine Mercy, and St Vincent de Paul Catholic elementary schools for their encouragement, warmth, and support.

Furthermore, while researching this book at York University, Toronto, professors Warren Crichlow, Deborah Britzman, and Pablo Idahosa did not hesitate to support the project, nurturing it always and helping to give it the form that it eventually acquired. All through it, there were moments when I faltered but they revived my determination to push on. I am grateful also to Erin Baines (University of British Columbia), who challenged me to find a different way to describe children who fight in wars because the term 'child soldier' was inadequate; Onek Adyanga (Millersville University, Pennsylvania), who worked with me on some difficult Acholi concepts during the writing; Aparna Mishra Tarc (York University), who helped with proofreading; and Curtis Fahey, who edited the book thoroughly until it finally shone.

I sincerely thank the family of the late Okot p'Bitek, especially Jane p'Bitek Langoya and Julie Okot p'Bitek, for allowing me the freedom to quote liberally from the various works of their father, a prolific Acholi poet.

Finally and most importantly, this project would not have been possible without the former child inducted soldiers opening up to me about what they experienced in war, the pain that they endured and the struggles they faced on returning home. Their stories stayed with me during cold and lonely nights when all I wanted was to crawl under blankets and forget in sleep the difficulties I was experiencing with the writing. Their serenity in the face of hardship and, above all, their bravery in staring down the worst that fellow human beings threw at them is the everlasting lesson of what it means to be *dano adana*, a human person.

Opiyo Oloya
Toronto, January 2013

CHILD TO SOLDIER

Stories from Joseph Kony's Lord's Resistance Army

Lanyut (Pointer): War, Culture, and Children in Northern Uganda

Everybody in Gulu town in war-ravaged northern Uganda has a story to tell about the war. In the Acholi oral storytelling tradition, every *labok lok* (storyteller) needs a *lawiny lok* (story-listener).

It is a hot July day in Gulu town. Inside the small room with one large dusty window, located on the second floor of the headquarters of the Gulu Support the Children Organisation (GUSCO), a non-profit reception and counselling centre for demobilized young soldiers, the humidity is suffocating. I am sitting on a rough wooden chair facing Miya Aparo, who occasionally uses a white handkerchief to wipe the sweat off her brow. She is the first in a group of seven former combatants, referred to here as child-inducted (CI) soldiers, who served with the rebel group the Lord's Resistance Movement/Army (LRM/A)[1] and are scheduled to sit down to tell me their stories. Miya Aparo is the teller and I am the listener. We both understand the informal rule of Acholi oral storytelling tradition which abhors *balo boko lok* (spoiling the story telling or interrupting the flow of the story), but I am here to do an interview about her life and that of other former child combatants. As an Acholi, I understand that her role as *labok lok* requires that she draw me into the story with details in such a way that the story will bind me as a listener to her experiences as the storyteller. It is also understood that this is storytelling where I have to probe, ask questions, clarify, and get more details of experiences that Miya Aparo may prefer not to relive. However, while fulfilling my role as a researcher, I cannot forget the role of being a good listener, the near silent witness to what Miya Aparo has gone through in the war that has ravaged this region for two decades. Hers is a story in progress with a definite beginning and middle but no clear end yet in sight. She is the central character in the story she is about to tell me, which, although a personal one, makes up an important part of the stories of child combatants in northern Uganda.

Sitting there in that hot room in Gulu on that first day of the interview, listening to Miya Aparo, I realized that much had changed in the years since I left Uganda on 6 March 1981, first becoming a refugee in neighbouring Kenya and then, three months later, moving to Canada. From that point, I busied myself with my studies, completing my undergraduate degree at Queen's University in Kingston before going on to graduate work in education at the University of Ottawa in 1986. News of the bush war back home reached me mostly through brief newscasts that did not explain what was happening in northern Uganda. The occasional letters that my parents and siblings sent were equally barren of any deeper insight about the war, who was fighting and why they were fighting. Perhaps in an effort to keep me from worrying about their safety, most of the letters barely mentioned the war. I would learn much later, when I returned to Uganda for the first time in 1988 and could not travel to my home in Pamin-Yai, that the war had moved from central Uganda to the northern part of the country. My parents, meanwhile, had left Pamin-Yai to seek internal refuge in another district, settling in Kiryandongo, a town 120 kilometres away. My mother remains there today. Of Pamin-Yai, all that's left are the river, the rock, and the bushes. And the memories and stories of what it used to be. *Things have changed.* I have changed.

One thing that had changed and that I could not quite grasp was how Acholi children were being abducted by fellow Acholi from their homes and violently forced to become child warriors. Acholi-on-Acholi violence of that magnitude and scale was new to me. Post-colonial conflicts in Uganda, though not strictly ethnic in character, often echoed ethnic tensions, pitting northerners against southerners, Luo-speaking groups including the Acholi against other groups in south and western Uganda, including the largest ethnicity, the Baganda. In 1966 Milton Obote, who hailed from the north, used the army to oust the constitutional head of state and king of Buganda, Sir Edward Mutesa II. When Obote was in turn toppled by the military coup led by Idi Amin on 25 January 1971, there was celebration among the Baganda because Amin had given Obote a taste of his own medicine. Idi Amin, although from northern Uganda, was an ethnic Kakwa, and he was particularly violent towards the Acholi and Lango throughout his eight years in power (Kasozi, 2001; Kasozi, Musisi, & Sejjengo, 1994; Ruganda, 1980). The killing on 26 February 1977 of two prominent Acholi, Anglican

Archbishop Janani Luwum and Minister for Land and Natural Resources Wilson Erenayo Oryema, had a profound impact on the Acholi, who saw it as the ultimate slap in the face (Avirgan & Honey, 1982; Kasozi, 2001).

By the end of Amin's reign in 1979, the cyclical demonizing of political rivals along ethnic and linguistic lines was firmly entrenched. When Gulu town was finally liberated from the forces of Idi Amin on 20 May 1979, for instance, I witnessed the unleashing of violence against anyone remotely associated or accused of being associated with Amin's ethnicity. As the targets of Amin's repressive policies, some Acholi felt justified in perpetrating violence against other ethnicities, especially those from Amin's home area in West Nile. As the liberation troops, consisting of Tanzanian army soldiers and Uganda exiles, pushed northward against the dismal remnants of Amin's forces, it was common to hear on the streets of Gulu and in the villages the Acholi expression *Tong oromo obibi* (the spears have finally overwhelmed the ogre). The euphoric jubilation that spilled out on the streets as Gulu residents waved *oboke olwedo* (the leaves of the *olwedo* tree are used by Acholi as a symbol of victory) and sang and danced quickly turned into a bloodletting targeting the Madi, Lugbara, and Kakwa, as well as some Nubians in Gulu and in Amin's home region of West Nile (Crisp, 1986; Ginyera-Pinycwa, 1989; Ingham, 1990; Zolberg, Suhrke, & Aguayo, 1989).

One of the most searing examples of these ethnic killings took place in a field where UNIFAT Primary School now stands, about a kilometre from Gulu town centre. As I watched, a former officer in Amin's army found hiding in the ceiling of a local hotel was dragged out by a rowdy crowd eager for his blood. The dishevelled officer was brought before a lackadaisical Tanzanian army officer who was using a small pocket knife to eat a mango picked from a nearby tree. Barely looking up at the wretched man brought before him, the Tanzanian officer, still eating his mango, gave the order for the officer's immediate execution by firing squad. As the man was lined up, and two soldiers trained their AK-47 machine guns at his head, the Tanzanian officer changed his mind with a simple wave of the hand, saying in Kiswahili *usiribu shila* (do not waste your bullets). Instead, he told the onlookers to administer mob justice. The boisterous crowd obliged, converging on the victim. Sensing his impending demise, he attempted to run away, but he barely took a few steps before someone with a machete cut off his legs. Then, as he fell to the ground, a second person delivered the coup de grâce, cutting his head clean off his shoulders. When someone lifted the severed head, the crowd cheered and moved on to look for more victims to kill. There were reports of many similar retaliatory killings on that day and the days following the collapse of Idi Amin's forces in Gulu.

Terribly unjustified and inhumane though the killing of the doomed soldier was, ethnicity seemed to offer an explanation, if simple and unsatisfying – he died because he was from a different ethnicity. But this explanation failed completely in the face of the LRM/A killings of fellow Acholi. In essence, this book is the culmination of my own attempt to come to grips with what transpired in Uganda from the mid-1980s to the present, to attempt to gain insights into this war's devastating impact on children by exploring the testimony of former LRM/A CI soldiers, both those I interviewed and those who are quoted in the literature. First, I endeavour to understand how the LRM/A as an organization mobilized, used, and, in a sense, repurposed Acholi culture to turn abducted Acholi children into soldiers. Second, as part of the culturally mediated analysis of these stories, I look at how abducted Acholi children employed culture to fashion survival skills in war. Throughout, I examine the role that culture plays in how returnees who survived the war are received in their communities and how their reintegration occurs. The underlying thread that connects the various aspects of the book is the understanding that, although the war was and remains between the Uganda People's Defence Forces (UPDF), commanded by Uganda President Yoweri Museveni, and the LRM/A leader Joseph Kony, the bulk of LRM/A combatants until recently were Acholi, the war was mostly fought in Acholiland, and most of the victims, although not all, have been Acholi. The war, in other words, was executed within the confines and context of the Acholi's cultural experiences as an ethnic group.

Finally, I attempt through this book to offer a critique of the oversimplified view of children in war, namely that children are recruited, given guns to fight, turned into killers, and subsequently victimized. Usually left out is the perspective of the child, the core evolution of the child's soul, so to speak, that occurs as the child is transformed from a child into a soldier. There is a gap between what these approaches imagine is happening to the child and what the child presumably feels.

Meeting the Storytellers

As the story-listener, I chose to hear the voices of seven CI soldiers – Can-Kwo Obato, Jola Amayo, Ringo Otigo, Miya Aparo, Payaa Mamit,

Amal Ataro, and Camconi Oneka – whose names are changed here to provide anonymity and ensure their security. The selection of these individuals was based primarily on their availability and their willingness to tell their stories to a researcher. GUSCO carried out the outreach to contact the participants, make the appointments, and ensure that they came to the venue at the scheduled time. That they were abducted at different periods allowed me to compare and contrast the experiences that they went through.

The informants were interviewed between 15 July and 24 July 2008 in Gulu, northern Uganda. The stories of two of them, Jola Amayo, thirty, and Ringo Otigo, twenty-seven, are explored in depth in chapters 4 and 5 respectively, where I focus on their experiences prior to abduction, after abduction, and when they returned home. Jola Amayo was abducted at night on 10 October 1990 as she slept with her sisters, one of whom, older than Jola, attempted to intervene by offering herself in Jola's place. The LRM/A did not release her until twelve years later, on 12 June 2002. She had left home as a child and returned home as a mother of two children. Ringo Otigo, the ninth in a family of eleven children, was abducted on the evening of 10 December 1996 as he returned from the stream with water for family use. He spent six years as a bush doctor for the LRM/A before escaping with six others on 7 December 2002.

The two were chosen for several reasons. Foremost, of the seven informants, the two provided the most detailed information about their lives prior to, during, and after their service as CI soldiers. Jola Amayo's stories are especially rich with details about her life prior to her abduction by the LRM/A, while Ringo Otigo provides more information about his life and times with the rebel army. Where one is silent on some aspects of his or her experience, the other tends to fill the void. For instance, Jola Amayo speaks at length about her combat involvement but hardly says anything about her developing sexual maturity in the bush. Almost out of the blue in the telling of her story, she talks about her son Otim. There is no preamble or introduction of Otim, just an abrupt mention of the child she had with another rebel fighter. I sensed that this is partly because, culturally, it is difficult for an Acholi woman to speak about her sexuality with a man who is not her husband (or her doctor). The other possible explanation goes back to the horrific nature of the experience that female LRM/A recruits go through in the bush as soldiers. Rather than press for an answer during these silent moments, I relied on the voice of Ringo Otigo, who was less reticent about speaking about his experience of sexuality in the bush, or rather the lack of it, and why he chose to be celibate.

Second, the two provided contrasts that went beyond gender. Ringo came from a family that had a 'name' in the community in that his late father was a doctor in Gulu Hospital. Although he grew up poor, he held to the sense that he came from a respectable family. It made him angry, he said, when someone showed a lack of respect for his widowed mother. Jola, meanwhile, grew up without any claim to social status beyond that conferred by being a member of a tight-knit family in a village in Acholiland. She was barely beginning to read and write when she was abducted by the LRM/A. Her maturing into a young woman happened in the bush as a combatant with the LRM/A.

Despite different socio-economic backgrounds, there are echoes of similarities in the experiences of Jola and Ringo as they made the transition from ordinary children to lethal child combatants. Both were stripped of their humanity at the beginning of their bush experiences, subjected to the most brutal treatment, and subsequently taught to fight for a cause they barely understood. Yet their experiences in the bush with the LRM/A were not identical.

The different standards by which the CI soldiers were treated dictated how they confronted and responded to challenges in the bush, and ultimately how they gained their freedom from the LRM/A. Even though she displayed combat bravery far superior to that of many male counterparts, and achieved the rank of second lieutenant, Jola Amayo and the other female CI soldiers were mostly under the immediate supervision of male officers. In contrast, as the son of a doctor, Ringo had received a good education and thus had the wherewithal to 'speak' with some measure and degree of self-assuredness, something that the other CI soldiers often lacked. With time in the bush, for instance, he acquired sufficient autonomy that he was allowed to conduct operations in faraway places without the direct patriarchal supervision of the top commanders. An LRM/A officer respected by those he commanded, he could make his own decisions at critical points. In essence, he became a trusted soldier whose judgment was relied on by other commanders.

When the LRM/A experiences of Jola and Ringo are examined side by side, there is a persistent sense that deep suffering seemed to dog the former over her entire time with the rebel army. She had to fight not only to be recognized as a fighter of worth within the male-oriented LRM/A structure but also to remain a nurturing mother to the children she bore in the bush. Where there were differences either in the stories told by these two or in their interpretations, the voices of the other five former CI soldiers provided additional perspectives. Payaa Mamit, for instance, was only in Grade Two when she was abducted by the LRM/A in September 1992; she attempted to escape but was recaptured, and her life was spared only by the intervention of LRM/A leader Joseph Kony. She became a mother in the bush, and when her LRM/A husband attempted to take away her child, she decided to escape from the LRM/A in September 2003.

Miya Aparo, the firstborn in a family of eleven children, was abducted at night on 13 April 1993 and spent the next eleven years as a child combatant with the LRM/A, returning home on 6 June 2002. After her homecoming, Miya Aparo tried her hand at different forms of small business. She now works as a counsellor for other former LRM/A returnees in Gulu.

Amal Ataro was the firstborn in a family of seven children. She was abducted by the LRM/A on 18 August 1994 and spent the next eleven years as one of the wives of LRM/A leader Joseph Kony, whom she said raped her when she went to live in his household in Sudan. According to her, all attempts by Sudan President Omar al-Bashir to rescue her from Kony failed because Kony repeatedly told the president that Amal was his sister. She gave birth to three children in the bush, all of whom were fatherd by Kony; the second child disappeared forever during an attack on the camp where she was then living. At the birth of the third child, she initially wanted to abandon it because 'there was no food to eat and my breast milk was dry,' but her older child insisted that she carry the baby. She, her firstborn, and the baby were rescued by the UPDF on 22 January 2005, after first being fired upon and miraculously escaping a hail of bullets that 'tore my dress to shreds.'

Can-Kwo was abducted on a rainy afternoon in May 1996 and would spend the next eleven years with the LRM/A, returning home on 20 October 2007. He was badly wounded during his time with the LRM/A when his unit was bombed by the UPDF.

Lastly, Camconi Oneka was abducted on 15 August 2001 and spent the next three years as an LRM/A child combatant. He freely admitted killing other children after being ordered to do so. Never forgetting his home life, he attempted to escape numerous times. He finally succeeded after being wounded in a shootout with the UPDF, and was rescued on 15 July 2004.

Put together, the experiences of Jola and Ringo and the other five former CI soldiers serve powerfully to illustrate how the LRM/A used

Acholi culture in recruiting, training, and retaining Acholi children in the war. Understanding this cultural link makes it clear that the almost two decades of horror visited upon children by the LRM/A were not a matter of *bahati mbaya*, the Kiswahili phrase for bad luck, but a deliberate, calculated, and focused effort to cause maximum dehumanizing violence against innocent young persons in order to control them.

The Cultural Link

When I met her for my first interview, I recognized that Miya Aparo's life before her abduction seemed to echo my own childhood in Pamin-Yai where all twenty-six of us, children of three mothers and one father, lived in a polygamous compound.[2] Miya and I shared a common Acholi heritage and spoke to each other in the Luo language. Our separate life journeys began in small rural villages, mine at Pamin-Yai village, west of Gulu town, and hers in Ajulu, in the Patiko region, northeast of Gulu town.

In my own case, I remember my childhood as an idyllic time. The children ate from the same dishes and slept together, girls in one house, boys in another; adults slept in the bigger house. While lunch and dinner were communal affairs, shared by everyone, a child could eat breakfast in any of the mothers' houses. Often, I ate breakfast in the house of my First Mother, Mama Alici, my father's senior wife. When not working or at school, we played *dini-dini* (hide and seek), spent time looking after cows, and occasionally went to hunt birds and small wildlife like *anyeri* (the edible rat) and *apwoyo* (rabbits). These were delicacies when smoked over the open-fire hearth and cooked in sim-sim (sesame) sauce, eaten with *kwon bel* (millet bread) The Acholi people believed that millet made them a hardy lot, strong and incredible runners and walkers. I was a fast runner.

Miya and I, though sharing a common herritage, were also different in many ways. She was barely able to read and write in any language, her education having been interrupted by the war, while I received a formal education and made a career as a *lapwony* (teacher). Also, I had not lived in my hometown for twenty-seven years and did not experience first-hand the war that started in 1986 and caused the death of countless people while displacing others into internal refugee camps. What notion I had of what it meant to be an Acholi was not mediated by the war and its continuing social, economic, and cultural impact. I was a stranger now, a son of the land returning to a devastated home, albeit one who was keen to explore and make sense of what had led to the ruin of what he had once loved.

Miya Aparo, on the other hand, had been in the middle of the war and had experienced its devastation. After she was abducted from her home by the LRM/A in 1993, she lived the next eleven years as an active participant in the rebel army until the day she returned home in 2002. She was one of thousands of Acholi children abducted by the LRM/A over a period of two decades and turned into soldiers. She saw the LRM/A up close, lived in camps in southern Sudan, and waged a relentless fight against the UPDF. At thirty-one, Miya was not a child any more; however, she was a survivor insofar as she was alive and working to make a living in the community.

She began her compelling story in a quiet voice, taking me back to the day she was abducted by the LRM/A at age twelve. And the stories she told me were nothing like those I heard growing up in Pamin-Yai village, not far from where we were sitting. Listening to Miya, I found myself simultaneously replaying in my head my own childhood stories and comparing them to the gritty tales she was telling me. I heard her voice but I also heard my own. *Ododo mera ni yoo* (I have a story to tell) ... So began many nightly stories told by our elders as we were growing up in Pamin-Yai, seventeen kilometres west of Gulu town. Storytelling was a part of the nightly ritual for Acholi children in those days, the way in which elders imparted life's lessons.

In the dry season, after the harvest, we sat in a circle around *wang-oyo*, a bonfire created in the centre of the compound, listening to story after story. 'I kare meno dong, Apwoyo ocito ka limo lawote, Twongweno' (Once upon a time, the Hare went to visit his dear friend the Rooster) ... That one was a favourite, always with the same sad ending where Rooster tricks Hare into believing that the dinner Hare was eating was one of Rooster's legs when in fact the trickster had hidden one leg beneath his wing. When Rooster visits Hare a few days later, eager to have the favour returned, Hare gets his mother to cut off one of his legs and cook it for dinner. After dinner, and with Hare now bleeding to death, Rooster walks away on two legs. The moral of the story: *Aporabot oneko Apwoyo* (Imitation killed the Hare) ...

In an instant, I am pulled back to the present as Miya Aparo narrates her life story:

When I was abducted, the first moment, it was around nine at night, and my life became difficult. When they came to abduct me, I was busy stone-milling. I had returned from school, fetched water from the well, and was stone-milling simsim paste. I was almost done stone-milling the paste. My mother was peeling wild yams to be eaten with the simsim paste that I had prepared ...

I thought to myself, 'How am I going to carry this entire load?' They showed me how to carry everything; I needed to throw the bag on my back, wrapping its strings across my shoulder. The large cooking utensil needed to be tied and hung around my neck, letting it rest on the bag on my back. Then I had to put the two bucketsful of simsim on top of my head. A string was tied around the spout of the jerry can of sugar, and then tied around my neck, allowing it to hang on my side. The chicken in the polythene bag – there were four chickens – were brought for me to carry. I asked again, saying, 'How am I going to carry this entire load?

We began walking and, before long, crossed the main road that ran behind our home. I fell down, my chest congested such that I could barely walk, my breathing laboured. The baggage had completely overwhelmed me, the one weight was pushing down on my chest, the other was pressing my shoulder, and meanwhile the one on my head was extremely heavy. I fell again and, this time, they came and began kicking me to get up. They hit my back with a machete, accusing me of refusing to carry the load, refusing to walk. The machete peeled some skin off my back. Someone came and said, 'Look, the load is too heavy. This is a small child who cannot carry such a heavy load.' I was crying. I was told that if I continued crying, I would be killed.

When I was growing up in Pamin-Yai, killing was not a part of our cultural experience. As with many Acholi, even the mention of killing brought fear of *cen*, the evil spirit that followed the killer and wiped out the killer's family. Everyone feared the spirits of the dead. As children, we heard the story of how my father, Alipayo Oloya, left teaching in Gulu town to become a farmer in the early 1950s. He settled in the valley called Pa Min-Yai, which translates as 'that which belongs to Yai's mother.' Flanked on one side by the Ayago River on its gentle flow towards the Nile River, and on the other side by Pamin-Yai Rock, a large outcrop that jutted defiantly out of the earth, the village was a few clusters of grass-thatched homes. The dusty narrow winding road that passed through the valley led to Gulu town to the east, Anaka centre, twenty kilometres to the west, and on towards Pakwach and Arua towns. But the road carefully skirted Pamin-Yai Rock. We children were told that the road builders did not want to incur the wrath of Min-Yai, the Mother of Yai and the spirit keeper of the rock. I never found out who Min Yai was, but many believed that she lived a long time ago in the foothills of the rock. Indeed, while playing or herding cattle, we occasionally found bits and pieces of broken pottery from long ago that lay buried there.

My parents often related the story of villagers taking bets on how long my father would last in his new home near the Pamin-Yai Rock. There were too many *jok* (vengeful spirits) around the rock, the villagers told my father. Some said the spirits came out at night, often in the shapes of beautiful women to lure away unsuspecting travellers to their demise. So strong was this belief that few dared to traverse the pathway that ran beside the rock at night. But my father lasted a week, then a month which turned into several years. When people saw that nothing happened to him and his young family, they began to settle and stay in the valley too. But often one heard the whispers, 'The children of Oloya are protected by the spirits of Pamin-Yai,' whispers that made me feel somewhat special as a child. Believing in the world of spirits was very much a part of Acholi culture. Miya Aparo was a part of that culture. So was I.

In working to gain insight into the role of culture in the LRM/A insurgency, I reflexively glimpsed continually at my own cultural upbringing in an Acholi village for context, meaning, and contrast to the narratives of the former child combatants. I discuss in more detail the duality of being a researcher as well as participant in chapter 1.

The term culture as I use it in this book is not only at the heart of the transformation of children into soldiers, but plays a crucial role in their daily struggles to make sense of the violence in which they have become a part, and, ultimately, to attempt to take some control of their lives within it. In taking the view that children do not come to war empty-minded, without some ideas and thoughts from prior enculturation about what violence and suffering mean to them, I borrow P. Alasuutari's (1995) definition of culture as 'a way of life or outlook adopted by a community or social class' (25). This definition sees culture as the knowledge, skills, attitudes, values, needs, and motivations that shape how the child adapts to the cultural milieu in which he or she lives. In this sense, culture is the aggregation of shared values in a defined system from which individuals derive not only their identities but also their orientation to the world. There is an assumption of solidarity and unity of purpose among those who subscribe to those values.

The implicit premise of the culture perspective is that the given society clearly defines its value system and proscribes how individuals may live within it. Cultural life in Pamin-Yai village was simple in that it followed the seasons, *cwii* (rainy season) and *oro* (dry season). In the hot months, we harvested the crops and prepared them for storage. One of our favourite pastimes during this time was cooking *layata abur* (pit-roasted sweet potatoes). We dug sweet potatoes from the field and built fires in small pits, heating the earth until it was red hot; then we threw in the freshly dug potatoes and covered the whole thing with a heap of fresh earth. The heated earth cooked the potatoes overnight, and in the morning we pulled out perfectly roasted and truly sweet tasting potatoes. We ate it with *odii nyim* (sesame paste).

When rain came, we worked hard in the field planting and tending to crops like maize, tobacco, cotton, and beans. This was also the time for trapping *ngwen*, the delicious flying white ants that came out after the first rains. We draped grass skirts around *bye-agoro* and *bye-aribu* (anthills). And after a downpour of rain, the worker termites opened the tiny 'eyes' on the anthills, allowing flying ants to flood the night or early morning sky with their silver wings flickering against the light. The grass skirt placed around the anthill acted as canopies to prevent the flying ants from escaping and flying away, forcing them instead into the *pony*, holes dug on the side of the anthills for just that purpose. All one needed to do then was to scoop up the fat succulent ants, eat some of them raw, and take some home to be ground into *anying* (meatballs) or dried and ground into the delicious oily *odii ngwen* (ant paste). I loved my *odii ngwen* mixed with a touch of honey and eaten with roasted *gwana* (cassava).

A strict teacher who insisted on formal school education, my father, Alipayo, forbade us from learning some parts of Acholi culture such as playing the *lukeme* (thumb piano) and attending the *laraka-raka* youth dances that were held in the dry season in neighbouring villages. The latter, also known as *myel-moko* (the 'get-stuck' dance), brought young girls, whose breasts were just beginning to peek from behind their colourful *kalega* (bras), into close proximity to young men whose voices had 'broken.' Clad in colourful beads, the young men held large half-gourds in one hand and wire beaters in the other, and formed an outer circle around the girls, singing while simultaneously beating the half-gourds in unison. A girl freely chose which young man to 'get stuck' with, usually someone she liked and wanted to get to know better. As part of the dance routine, the newly 'stuck' couple briefly left the circle of dancers to whisper sweet words into each other's ears before rejoining the circle again.

For my father, ever the schoolteacher, these were primitive distractions from the serious business of classroom learning. But, as young teenage boys, we learned to steal away from our beds in the dead of the night to join the *laraka-raka*. We eagerly joined the circle of dancers, and occasionally I was lucky and got 'stuck' with a dancer or two. We danced until night sky turned into the red of dawn. Then we rushed home before our parents discovered us missing.

While my childhood recollection of culture is filled with good memories, the LRM/A made violence and killing routine experiences for Miya Aparo and other child combatants who were manipulated to believe these were normal part of Acholi culture, which they were not. She recalled her first encounter with the LRM/A's brutality:

We walked for two days, going way up to Patongo, all the time keeping in the bush. There we came into a clay area which stuck to the bottom of the shoe such that it was impossible to walk. I was attempting to shake away some of the dirt when the sharp blade of grass went straight into my leg, burying itself between the bones. My leg went numb, paralysed, such that I could not walk.

Some of the rebels said I should be killed on the spot. One of the officers, a young man from Alero, argued that I should not be killed, I should not be killed. His name was Triga,[3] the other name Okello, called Okello Triga. He was always called by that name; perhaps it was a name he got from the bush; I didn't know. He said I should not be killed, that he be allowed to look for a bicycle to be used to carry me because my foot was so swollen. The sharp blade had entered deep into my bone, a big thing this size, the stalk of millet.

When the officer [Okello Triga] brought an old man pushing a bicycle, I was put on it and pushed for a week in the convoy. When we were close to meeting with the main rebel group led by Kony, instead of being freed to return home, the old man who had pushed me on the bicycle was simply killed. When the old man was killed, I realized that I, too, could be killed. After all the help the old man gave me, he was killed just like that? The old man had faithfully rolled me along on the bicycle, and now even his bicycle was cut into pieces. The old man, *dano adana*, a human person, was killed next to the pieces of what was his bicycle.

Dano Adana (Human Person)

What stood out for me in Miya Aparo's narrative was her use of the Acholi notion of *dano adana* to emphasize how the old man was killed next to the pieces of what was his bicycle. This was the second time I had heard a former CI soldier use the exact same phrase. The first was at the World Vision Center[4] in Gulu in March 2000. I had returned to my hometown with Christa Schadt, a Canadian film-maker planning to make a film about children who fight in wars. My role was mostly that of a translator and 'fixer' with the local contacts whom I deemed crucial to the successful making of the movie. On my home turf, I was able to negotiate details including accommodation, transportation, and meetings with the former child combatants, something that my Canadian colleague would have found difficult to do since this was her first trip to Uganda. Over several days, between 12 March and 18 March 2000, once they felt confident enough to open up to me as *latin Acholi me Canada* (the son of Acholi from Canada), as they referred to me, these ex-CI soldiers revealed themselves to be a resilient, stoic lot that never complained about what they had gone through. Though quite young, between the ages of eight and fifteen, when forced to join the LRM/A, these former fighters neither sought pity nor expressed regret for what had happened to them – life simply happened to them, and that was the way it was.[5] They were capable of – as indeed many told us in their stories of life before, during, and after the war – the most brutal acts of violence, causing deep suffering to both combatants and civilians alike.

As I listened to their stories, one eighteen-year-old who had spent six years with the LRM/A kept repeating, 'Wan dano mere calo dano adana ni ya' ('We are human persons like everyone else') (field notes, Wednesday, 15 March 2000). It later occurred to me that, by using this phrase, the former child combatant was expressing an ongoing inner struggle to reconstruct, transform, and transcend the limitations of the term 'child combatant,' as employed by his home community, which viewed him and others like him as killers, and by the international charity machine, which insisted on referring to these ex-soldiers as victims in fund-raising campaigns in Europe, the United States, and Canada (Cook, 2007; Mawson, 2004).[6] As *dano adana*, they had moved from the fringes of society to become integral participants within it. The former child combatants, in other words, saw themselves as 'normal' within the context of a society at war where violence itself had become banal.

Throughout the book, in the context of children caugh[t]
reference as *lanyut* (pointer or signpost) the Acholi cult[ure]
dano adana, universally recognized by all cultures as the
son.' In the Xhosa and Zulu cultures of South Africa, for exa[mple,]
tu (personhood) describes the essence of humanness (Battle, ___9, 1–2).
In my own case, the stories we were told as children had moral endings
that instructed us how to relate to people around us as *dano adana*, a
core identity endowed on each individual which determined how
that individual viewed him/herself and was treated by others within
the community.

My parents often taught us how we should behave by emphasizing
kit ma omyero ibed calo dano adana (how you should live like a human
person). I heard that phrase just about every day. It was part of the daily
Acholi conversation, used casually in greeting, in jest, in arguments,
and in serious discussions. 'Ah, pe dong imoto dano, an bene dano adana ya!' (Why, you don't say hello any more? I am a human person like
everyone else!) At the village stream, one often heard the shout – 'Nyee,
kong wun wukuu manok, dano adana pud tye ka lwok' (Hey, just wait
a minute, human persons are still taking a bath). Since the pathway ran
past the stream, you knew that the 'human persons' in this case were
caught in the compromising situation of taking a bath naked. If the intruders were indeed members of the opposite sex, protocol required
that they cool their heels, hidden from view, until the bathers had fin-
ished washing and put something on. Often older village women coming to collect water from the stream cheekily ignored our shouts of
warning, sending us boys dashing nude into the bushes while covering
our privates with our hands. 'Come on boys, your little things are barely dangling, there is nothing to hide,' one of the women would shout
with laughter in her voice, to which one of us would respond – 'Aac,
wan dano adana bene ya' (Whatever, but we are human persons like
everyone else!) It was our way of reasserting our humanity at that
particular moment.

Sometimes the phrase *dano adana* was used as emphasis to convey a
story of a serious incident, say an accident. 'Dano adana owane marac'
(A human person was seriously injured). These kinds of stories usually brought a collective gasp of disbelief and expression of concern.
People getting injured in accidents, such as during communal hunts
or because of a lightning strike, were such rare events that they became a big story for everyone in the village. When death occurred –
'dano adana oto tin' (a human person died today), with the word

'human' used to underscore the unexpectedness and tragic nature of the incident – there was an immediate expression of shock and grief from the audience and the news spread fast throughout the entire village. Then there was palpable urgency as the community rallied to respond to the sad story, often accompanied by the loud wailing of women converging on the deceased person's compound. But not all stories of death were treated with the same degree of sadness. The death of a child, of a young unmarried adult, or of young mothers and fathers was a bitterly sad event. Not as sad were deaths of respected elders who had reached the grand old age of *dayo* (grandmothers) and *kwaro* (grandfathers). In such cases, there was little grieving, and people generally anticipated the joyful celebration of *guru lyel*, the last funeral rites when extended families and clans gathered for the final goodbye to the dead person whose life was considered ripe and rich because of the many children and grandchildren left behind. The celebration often lasted many days, with much singing, dancing, eating, and drinking, and was usually held during the dry season. The distinctive sound of *bul-lyel* (funeral drums) wafted through the still night air, throbbing in a steady beat, itself telling the story of a life lived and ended within the Acholi life cycle of birth, childhood, youth, marriage, parenthood, old age, and death. That was the rhythm of Acholi culture as carried through time by each succeeding generation, in peace and in war, in happy times and during communal suffering, with the emphasis always being on *dano adana*.

Suffering, Agency, and Human Personhood in Child-Inducted Soldiers

Acholi poet Okot p'Bitek (1966) wrote in *Song of Lawino* that in Acholi culture the measure of a person's ability to be resourceful is based not on age but on how he or she does certain things:

> A person's age
> Is shown by what he or she does
> It depends on what he or she is,
> And what kind of person
> He or she is
> You may be a giant
> Of a man
> You may begin to grow gray hair

You may be bold
And toothless with age,
But if you are unmarried
You are nothing   (p'Bitek, 1966, 105)

p'Bitek's culturally mediated understanding of children as human persons, which is the view adopted in this book, differs somewhat from the definition used in the Cape Town Principles and Best Practices, which define a child soldier based on chronological age as:[7] 'any person under 18 years of age who is part of any kind of regular or irregular armed force or armed group in any capacity, including but not limited to cooks, porters, messengers and anyone accompanying such groups, other than family members. The definition includes girls recruited for sexual purposes and for forced marriage. It does not, therefore, only refer to a child who is carrying or has carried arms' (Legrand, 1997). Based on a rigorous international legal framework for the protection of children, the Cape Town designation of child combatants is useful in defining the problem, raising global awareness about it, and mobilizing resources in response. In legal proceedings focused on war atrocities, former child combatants could presumably, and with some justification, base their defence on the innocence of childhood. A good example of the need for such a legal defence is the incarceration and trials at Guantánamo Military Detention Center in Cuba of Omar Khaddar, the former child combatant who fought and was captured in Afghanistan by U.S. forces in 1995. The U.S. military prosecutors focused mainly on Khaddar's current chronological age while ignoring the experiences he went through as a child in combat. A big man with a big beard now, Khaddar bears no resemblance to the skinny kid he was many years ago, and his current physical appearance is exploited by military prosecutors eager to portray him as a radical hard-line jihadist who was an enemy combatant and not a child combatant.

Yet, although popular and entrenched, I argue that the term 'child soldier' is a misnomer, one that implies a development frozen in time in which the child remains a child even when he or she is now a thirty-something-year-old adult with a family. It is not useful in describing who these 'children' are, the nature of their cultural upbringing and orientation towards life, and the life skills they bring with them to war, and out of war. It is an extreme view that ignores completely the transformation that children undergo after being forcibly or voluntarily inducted into soldiering.

More so, the Cape Town definition paints a picture mostly associated with dependence, lack of fully developed decision-making skills, and inability to take care of oneself. Under such circumstances, child-inducted soldiers are often seen as helpless victims who lack personal agency and the wherewithal to control their lives amid the violence of war. With this view has often come the one-size-fits-all solution that sees former children emerging from wars as broken victims in need of repair rather than as *dano adana* who, in the act of survival, have shown incredible resourcefulness.

This stigmatized view of children who survived war has often led to further victimization. In Acholiland today, the returning former child combatants who are the focus of this book are referred to as *olum*, a derivative of the word *lum*, which I translate as 'bush'; *olum* means 'the one who belongs to the bush.' Just as the label 'child soldier' conjures up certain negative images in popular Western media – for example, in M. Ockslong et al. and E. Zwick's (2006) film *Blood Diamond*, with its half-crazed, drug-addicted, bloodthirsty child-killer wielding an AK-47 machine gun – the local label *olum* is laden with stigmatized meaning for the former child combatants, who are shunned by the community, even by close relatives. Payaa Mamit, one of my informants, talked about being rejected by her father, who claimed she was possessed by *cen*, the evil spirits of people she had killed in her time with the LRM/A. 'Perhaps my father acted that way because he heard what people were saying, that, "If your daughter has stayed for a while in the bush, stayed for these number of years, she returns with evil spirits or there is an evil spirit in her head,"' she said.

Instead, after listening to the stories of Acholi children that illuminate the specific cultural circumstances under which they became soldiers within the LRM/A, I have deliberately coined the phrase 'child-inducted soldier' or simply CI soldier. Induction in this case stakes out the point at which the child enters into the process of becoming a combatant. It is messy and bloody, often with many children losing their lives, but it is a process nonetheless in which survivors learn to live and grow. The terms defines the starting point of the tortuous journey, initiated in childhood, that takes these children into the world of organized violence, and from which, if they survive, they often emerge not as children but as young adults. It acknowledges, first and foremost, that the soldiers once were children, tender, vulnerable, open to exploitation and manipulation by the adults in their lives. Second, it acknowledges that, over time, the children in combat are transformed into combatants, in some cases hardened killers. Third, it accepts that, by the time these young combatants leave the LRM/A, or for that matter the numerous armies that use children around the world, they are often not children anymore, but young adults. In essence this description confirms that the soldiers are not, or will soon not be, children, and may have no wish to be treated as such. At the same time, the term requires and demands that post-combat legal proceedings, compensation, rehabilitation, and so forth account for the critical fact that, when they were children, they endured gross violations of their rights and traumatic combat experiences. Moreover, it affirms the former combatants as *dano adana*, a term that I suspected was their way of attempting to cast their identities as pedestrian and ordinary. Rather than perpetuate the aura of the exotic, they desired to free their humanness, caged as much by their experiences of war as by the label of *olum*, the name applied to them by others in the communities where they resettled.

To be clear, in using the term 'child-inducted soldier' to describe children who are pulled into the vortex of war, I do not imply a genteel process which respects the rights and humanity of the child, nor do I wish to deny that children suffer in war. I do, in fact, acknowledge the many factors, most of them quite violent, that attend the creation of CI soldiers. While some children are abducted or forcibly recruited, as was the case with the LRM/A, many voluntarily join the ranks of armed fighters (Brett & Specht, 2004; Cohn & Goodwin-Gill, 1994; Machel, 2001; Singer, 2006). Often, the conditions under which the children are targeted for recruitment as CI soldiers include displacement due to war, separation from family, and lack of education. Poverty is also cited as pivotal in drawing mostly poor children into the military, where access to food and shelter is better guaranteed (Brett & Specht, 2004; Singer, 2006).

That said, the notion of CI soldier challenges the dominant and widely accepted image of children as young as six wielding light but lethal automatic weapons in war zones (Klare, 1999; OXFAM, 2006; Salopek, 2002; Singh, 1995; Stohl, 2002; Stohl & Smith, 1999). Those promoting this image point to the availability of guns, such as the Chinese G3 assault rifle, the Russian-made Kalashnikov, and American M-16, that enable children to enter the fray of combat with the same degree of lethal effectiveness as adult combatants. But, while such factors are important in explaining how children are pulled into wars, this book focuses instead on the CI soldiers' inner struggles as they try to make sense of war and to take some measure of control over their lives so as to manage the unpredictability of the situation in which they find themselves.

By examining and understanding the nature of the CI soldiers' survival, I maintain, we gain deeper insights in how Acholi and non-Acholi children abducted by the LRM/A, and perhaps children in other wars around the world, are forced to become active combatants and then struggle through personal agency to find meaning within the context of violence. The term 'personal agency,' as I use it in this book, is defined as a form of self-production that fosters and utilizes cultural experiences and skills to overcome a series of traumatic life experiences in order to reassert a sense of self.

More often than not, as the stories in this book make amply clear, life is harsh for CI soldiers. By comparison, my life at Pamin-Yai seemed closer to what Okot p'Bitek described as *Lak taa miyo kinyero iwi lobo* (the whiteness of teeth makes people laugh on earth). This could be interpreted to mean enjoying a life unencumbered or uncomplicated by conflicts and dangers or unnecessary worries. There were dangers, to be sure, such as snakes and wild animals, but these were dangers that did not threaten our way of life and routines. In the village of Pamin-Yai, I was welcome in any home. I could walk at night without worrying about my safety. Indeed, many strangers passing through often came to our home for food and a place to sleep before continuing their journey at first light.

When I was growing up, I did what many children did then. I made the daily walk to Pamin-Yai Primary School, located seven kilometres away, following the circuitous route around Pamin-Yai Rock. A shortcut through the bush and across the Ayago River became impassable in the rainy season as the river flooded, forcing us to go the long way. Our trip back home at the end of the school day was leisurely; often we stopped along the way to pick delicious wild fruits such as *oceyo, olam, kano, obwolo,* and *oywelo.* Occasionally we raided a wild bee's nest for sweet honey. Somewhat less afraid of bee stings than my sisters, I often volunteered to plunge my hands into the crack of the tree trunk where the heavy honeycombs were stacked, pulled out the sweet stuff, and threw some down to my sisters, who waited anxiously on the ground. The bees always got nasty, and we fled for dear life.

As an abductee, however, Miya Aparo was not concerned with being stung by bees but with survival itself, and more often than not there was no previous experience or script from which to work. Confronted with the problem of survival, the CI soldier often had to rethink what previously seemed possible or even impossible. That was the case for Miya on the march to Sudan:

> We stayed a while; we stayed for four months before starting the journey to Sudan. Thirst was the biggest problem. When we started the journey, all the water had dried off. With so much dust, many people died of thirst, hunger, there was no cooking. If you had water with you it was because you had filled your container in Atyak. That water had to last you at least two days, a ten-litre container. When it was finished, that was it.
>
> We trudged on, some people were crying for the urine of others. You cried for urine, asking to drink urine to survive, to help you. You drank urine. This went on until we reached Sudan, then a vehicle was sent to fetch us from Pajok, taking us to Palotaka.

You drank urine. In Acholi culture, indeed in many African and world cultures, such an action would be considered a social taboo, with stringent consequences for the person undertaking it. But, in the sweltering heat of the desert wilderness, where water was scarce, one would drink any liquid, even urine, to survive. Urine became hope. Ultimately, personal agency for CI soldiers like Miya, I argue, was not about inventing a new culture in order to survive, but reinterpreting existing cultural meanings to foster new relationships within the violent world they were thrown in. *You drank urine* because that was the only liquid available under the relentless desert sun, over which you had no control.

In a similar vein, when confronted with harsh treatment at the hands of Raska Lukwiya, a relative who was an LRM/A commander, Miya Aparo was forced to rethink her prior Acholi cultural experience of what it means to be related to someone. In Acholi culture, a relative is someone you can rely upon in difficult times, someone you can trust and expect to help you out of trouble. This is understandable because, as P. Oruni (1994) points out, identity and relations between individuals are defined by *wat* (constitution). He notes, 'Every aspect of Acholi life, the rights, obligations and privileges of the individual, social service-administration, civics, politics, defence and security, is defined and exercised in accordance with provisions of Wat Constitution' (18). Under the Acholi wat constitution, the *onyu* (newly born child) is as much a part of the family as the old grandmother who can walk only with the help of a stick.

For Miya Aparo, though, the encounter with Raska Lukwiya made her think that 'a relative is the last person to help you.' She would

discover, throughout her personal struggle to survive during the period spent with the LRM/A, that she needed to constantly re-evaluate
her understanding of Acholi cultural norms in order to respond to new
experiences in the bush. She, like the other informants, told me that
survival was about making sense of the situation of war, and establishing control over their lives even as they were drawn deeper into an
unpredictable and violent environment.

Paradoxically, as detailed in the Conclusion, as war survivors who
used their cultural conditionings to overcome many odds, fight battles, and come out alive, returning CI soldiers face a culture that views
them with a mixture of awe, fear, and superstitious beliefs. Their identities as returnees assume a new dimension in the eyes of the community, which sees them as superhuman aliens rather than as children
who survived war. This is not to deny that children who serve as soldiers in wars are victimized; on the contrary, as R. Brett and I. Specht
(2004) put it, 'war comes to them' (123). But, in taking up the question
of culture as a source of identity crisis for returning CI soldiers, I acknowledge the dilemma that these children face when they return
home. It was a dilemma I could hear in the voice of Miya Aparo and in
the voices of the other CI soldiers as they told me their autobiographical stories of survival.

In the next chapter, I look at some of the conceptual and practical
challenges of conducting an ethnographic study of this nature in a frag-
ile environment of war. Central to the discussion is a consideration of
both the possibilities and limitations inherent in my position as a native
returnee trying to make some sense of the horrendous experiences of
CI soldiers, and to reconcile these with my own nostalgic memories of
a peaceful, happy childhood. Then, in chapter 2, I attempt to situate the
LRM/A war within the historical context of the Acholi myth of defence
of the homestead and ethnic politics in post-colonial Uganda. I explore
how these two factors, one generated at the local level and the other at
the national, are relevant to how Acholi children are transformed into
soldiers by the LRM/A.

In chapter 3, I consider the notion of liminal repurposing of culture as
a method of transforming and controlling CI soldiers. As I use the term
here, 'liminality' describes the intensely emotional, psychological, and
physical experiences through which abducted Acholi children are
transformed into child combatants within the repurposed culture of
violence and combat. In chapter 3 I argue that there is ample evidence
to suggest that LRM/A's skilful exploitation and subversion of Acholi

culture, and not Stockholm Syndrome, enables the rebel movement to transform, train, and control the army of children in war. This notion is further explored in chapter 4 and chapter 5, where I analyze the particular cases of Jola Amayo and Ringo Otigo respectively. In the Conclusion, I contemplate the dilemma of the returning CI soldier, who was made to give up childhood to become a combatant and whose resourcefulness (and luck perhaps) allowed him or her to survive, but whose resilient qualities are now ignored – or even rejected – by the community. Through these thematic and systematic approaches, chapter by chapter, I hope to peel back, in a small way, the fog surrounding the question that is at the heart of this book: What happens when children are forced to become soldiers?

Chapter One

Conceptual and Practical Challenges

In his book *Being There*, Daniel Bradburd (1998) extols the importance of the ethnographer being in the field of study, getting close to the subject, as he did with the Iranian Komachi pastoralists. As an Acholi returning to my own childhood backyard to inquire into a subject in which I had personal interest, I could say 'I was born and grew up there.' However, my status as a native of Gulu who has lived abroad for nearly three decades also gave me the identity of a 'halfie,' to use the term coined by L. Abu-Lughod (1986, 1993, 39), that is, one who retains some claim to insider's connection but with an outsider's education and perspective. I still chuckle at an incident in Amuru centre, thirty kilometres west of Gulu, when a little Acholi girl said to another excitedly while pointing towards me, 'Nen munu ca' (Look, there is a white man). To her, I may have the skin and the language of the Acholi native, but I also have the mannerisms of the foreigner, of *munu* (white man). 'Who are you calling a white man?' I shot back in perfect Acholi, using the idiom spoken in the villages. In any event, I was keenly aware of the tension between being too close to and keeping one's distance from the focus of one's study.

Confronted with such a dilemma, B. Sandywell (1996) describes the natural reaction to 'castigate this obsessive reflexivity as enervating narcissism, abandon self reflection altogether and either return to the fold of grounded theory, or simply follow the accelerating velocities of change in aesthetics, intellectual, moral and cultural spheres, wherever these may lead' (2). Without going to either of the extremes suggested by Sandywell, I take the view that grounded theory – that is, the formulation of theory from systematically gathered and analyzed data (Glaser & Strauss, 1980; Strauss & Corbin, 1997) – is not only not possible in an ethnographic field work conducted against the uncertain backdrop of war but perhaps not desirable given the speculative nature of the findings. As conceived, my research relied on the information provided by the CI soldiers, and for the reasons discussed below, namely the unreliability of memory and the difficulties involved in cross-checking this information for accuracy, it was necessary to provide room for speculative and tentative insights into what happens when children are transformed into soldiers.

Furthermore, in reflexivity, as pointed out by M. Hammersley and P. Atkinson (2007), researchers accept that they are shaped by their socio-historical locations, and that their work may in turn influence the climate in which political and practical decisions are made. They write: 'What this represents is a rejection of the idea that social research is, or can be, carried out in some autonomous realm that is insulated from the wider society and from the biography of the researcher, in such a way that its findings can be unaffected by social processes and personal characteristics' (15).

As a researcher, therefore, I acknowledge both the opportunities and the shortcomings inherent in my status as an Acholi doing research on Acholi CI soldiers. For one, notwithstanding the issues discussed in the previous chapter, I saw my Acholi background as a good thing because I did not have to face some of the challenges associated with language and cultural nuances that often confront field researchers. My Luo language skills were advantageous in communicating with a group of people who speak mostly Luo, and in understanding the cultural and contextual nuances of the Luo language when it came to translating the CI soldiers' testimony into English. As the Acholi proverb goes, *labul tongweno ngeyo ka pene* (the one who roasts the egg knows where the umbilical cord is located).

Perhaps more important, the initial rapport of kinship based on shared culture, of speaking to a fellow Acholi in our mother tongue, allowed the former CI soldiers to relax, speak naturally, and go deeply into details, thereby opening a window for me into the world that they experienced in combat. E. Husserl (1970) suggests that, to better understand life experiences, it is crucial to shed light into the 'life-world,' the world as it is immediately experienced. M. Merleau-Ponty (1962) further describes this life-world not as another layer of experiences that needs to be uncovered, but as what is experienced itself. He argues, 'We must not, therefore, wonder whether we really perceive a world, we must instead say: the world is what we perceive' (xviii).

Viewed through the lenses of Husserl and Merleau-Ponty, my situation as an Acholi allowed me to avoid the pitfalls of becoming wholly preoccupied with trying to decide whether what I was seeing, experiencing, or hearing was really the 'real deal.' This was critical, to paraphrase M. van Manen (1990), in uncovering and describing the structure and internal logic of the lived experience of CI soldiers' survival of war. Understanding the Acholi language rendered the experience all the more vivid. Specifically, it gave me a fuller appreciation of how abductees' sense of humanity was transformed or sustained in the midst of what former CI soldiers described as *can matek*, which I translate to mean 'intense suffering' and which is the opposite of *kwo mayot* (easy life). In Acholi, *mayot* can be translated as 'lightness,' 'easiness,' or 'goodness' of a situation. Used in association with *kwo*, which is translated as 'life,' 'living,' and 'existence,' it describes an 'easy time,' a 'good life,' a 'relaxed life.' The informants often spoke about *kwo odoko yot* (life became easy) and *onongo wabedo maber* (we lived well or we lived a good life), concepts associated with what S. Finnstrom (2008) calls *piny maber*, which he defines as 'good surroundings' (4).

Meanwhile, *matek*, defined as 'strong,' 'intense,' or 'tough,' modifies and emphasizes the noun *can* (pronounced ch-an), which can be translated to mean poverty, suffering, pain, even death. For example, 'can matek otime' (an intense suffering has occurred) usually prefaces bad news about a critical incident where a person or persons are seriously injured or killed. *Can matek* has the same import as *kabedo mading* (tight space) and is usually associated with *piny marac*, defined by Finnstrom as 'bad surroundings' (4). What Miya Aparo experienced in her journey into becoming a soldier could be described as *can matek* (intense suffering).

However, culturally, and as used by the former CI soldiers, the terms *can matek* and *kwo mayot* do not describe absolute conditions, but rather, at the very minimum, a fluidity of life experiences that range from extreme suffering to relatively less suffering, and occasional joy. In this sense, the informants did not see their life experiences as cumulative suffering over time such that the suffering of yesterday combined with the suffering of today to make one big suffering. Instead, they used these terms to suggest that their life experiences while living with the LRM/A included intense feeling of pain at specific moments in time, interspersed with moments of, relatively speaking, easy living and even the occasional joy.

For example, the period immediately following their abduction was reported by all the informants as a time of intense suffering. Later, after establishing new relations in the bush, the informants experienced suffering when a bush colleague or a bush husband or wife was killed in combat. At such moments, the informants experienced *can matek*; they were in mourning, depressed about the loss of rebel colleagues who had become like family members, and, possibly, weighed down with feelings of isolation from the rest of the LRM/A community, feelings that were particularly acute whenever death was the result of an execution ordered by rebel commanders. At the same time, amidst the violence and harsh surroundings, the informants reported happy times too, for example, when food was plentiful, when there was a prolonged period of peace, and when communal celebrations like Christmas were held. The informants reported that such times were almost akin to being 'back home,' an earlier time in their lives when they were surrounded by loving and extended families.

In any event, while being an Acholi afforded me an insider's vantage point from which to contemplate and understand how the LRM/A abductees survived the extremes of living conditions, evolving with time under violent circumstances while maintaining hope, I had to keep reminding myself that they retained distinct voices in their autobiographical recalling of what happened during war.

Autobiography and Voice

In choosing to organize in autobiographical form the information collected, I recognized, first, that Acholi oral literature, as in many African oral traditions, radiates from the teller – the person who is at the centre of the story and who, in telling the story, not only recreates what happened but assumes the various voices in a dialogic manner. Second, although the stories about war are filled with gut-wrenching, unimaginable, and terror-driven violence, their telling is now a part of the living Acholi oral literature because, as Isadore Okpewho points out in *African Oral Literature* (1992), 'an oral performance really exists where there is an audience that compels the respect of the performer and puts the performance on record (whether of memory or tape)' (57). For the children who fought in Uganda's most destructive war, the telling of war stories is a way to confirm, not only for the listeners but also for themselves, that the war indeed happened, that they were a part of it, and, most important, that they survived it. The telling of the stories validates who they are even as the stories themselves take on social and pedagogical meanings that serve to underscore not only the terror of war but its lingering consequences.

As storytellers of what the war did to them, and what they did during the war, these former CI soldiers cease to be merely passive voices floating in the void of destruction. Using their stories, they cover salient moments of their violent lives, the moments they feel are worth salvaging, worth remembering, and worth repeating. If words could be captured in bags, this is the bagful of experiences a CI soldier would hand over – here, take this bag; it is the story of my life at war in the bush.

Evidently, the emotional complexities that are in play as they tell their stories come from the depth of the CI soldiers' first-hand experience of war, where moments of silence are as eloquent as vivid descriptions. In their collective stories reside the possibility of retrieving the salient details that inform what it is like to be a child amidst cultural devastation before the onset of war, what happens during the course of the war, and how children reorient their thinking in the process of surviving war.

Naturally, there are limitations to relying on the child's own memory to collect autobiographical information. C.D. West (2004), for instance, discovered in the narratives of girl soldiers in Mozambique that memory of an event ostensibly shifts from person to person, depending on the narrator. A similar observation is made by C.P. Thompson, J.J. Skowronski, S.F. Larsen, and A.L. Betz (1996) in their study *Autobiographical Memory*, in which they write: 'Over time, it becomes more and more necessary to reconstruct the details of an event' (8). Likewise, in *The Death of Luigi Trastulli and Other Stories*, Allessandro Portelli (1991) illustrates the fluidity of memory in what is remembered and forgotten in recalling a single event. To Portelli, the death of a twenty-one-year-old Italian steelworker from Terni, killed in a clash with police in 1949, is important because 'it became the ground upon which collective memory and imagination built a cluster of tales, symbols, legends and imaginary reconstructions' (1). Different people in Terni later came to remember the single event differently, in some cases adding details that were unverifiable. V.R. Yow (2005) explains that a gap occurs between what is remembered and what actually happened because memory picks only salient points in an expansive landscape of experiences. 'The recording of a memory from the beginning preserves a partial record because we cannot take in every detail in a scene and therefore takes in only what seems significant for us' (38).

To authenticate and legitimize the author's claims to objectivity, traditional autobiography often seeks multiple sources of information, documents, archival records, and other media information. In such works as Benjamin Franklin's *Autobiography* (2007) and Winston Churchill's *Memories and Adventures* (1989), where the author's self-portraiture is the sum of critical events and personalities within a specific discipline (in politics, literature, education, philosophy, science, and so forth) at a specific historical moment that have influenced him (and that he in turn has influenced), the author relies on both memory and independent sources of information (Thompson, Skowronski, Larsen, & Betz, 1996). But this is not possible for former CI soldiers in war situations where independent records are not generally kept and personal information about the particular child may be non-existent. Some of the former CI soldiers told me that they could not remember dates of specific events such as birthdays, how long they were in the bush, and the names of people and places that were salient in their stories. For example, when recalling how he finally escaped from the LRM/A after eleven years in the bush, Can Kwo Obato mentioned that he was with five other rebel CI soldiers when he reached the decision to leave the bush. As the ranking officer at the time, he recalled sending home 'four of the young rebel soldiers, saying, "Guys, you go ahead, I will come and find you there."' But a little later, in recalling the same event, he said, 'So the three children went. I followed them later the next day ... I left my deputy in the bush, we left three of them. Four of us came back home.' Not only do the numbers not add up, just how many of the CI soldiers left the bush on the first day is not clear since the number changes from four to three.

Moreover, when CI soldiers tell their own stories (e.g. Beah, 2007; Keitesi, 2004), the venue, time, and manner of telling are often prompted and mediated by others, such as in co-authored child-soldiers' autobiographies (McDonnell & Akallo, 2007; Eggers, 2006), court testimonies provided by CI soldiers (Arts & Popovski, 2006; Dawes & Cairns, 1998; Kuper, 1997), or interviews of CI soldiers by researchers and writers (de Berry, 2004; Goodwin-Gill & Cohn, 1994; Honwana, 2006; Machel, 2001; Wessells, 2006). The CI soldier's audience, in other words, is the counsellor, the news reporter, the court, the researcher, or the co-author. As a result, the 'voice' in the autobiographical voice of the CI soldier is

often dissimilar, for example, from the voice in the valedictory autobiography *Ecce Homo* (Behold the Man) in which Friedrich Nietzsche
(1992) sees autobiography as a self-revelatory reckoning of the individual with his or her past, an acknowledgment of one's existence
which is potentially redemptive. Nietzsche, without overstating its self-
healing qualities, was suggesting that the autobiography retains for its
author what P.R. Brown (1969) in *Augustine of Hippo*, a critical look at
St Augustine's *Confessions*, describes as the 'self-portrait of a convales-
cent' (177). In this phrase, Brown underscores expressive introspection
as both restorative to the individual's conflicted inner self and revela-
tory of the new persona formed through that healing process. Jacques
Derrida (1988) adds that the personal narrative 'is not autobiographical
for the reason one commonly understands, that is, because the signa-
tory tells the story of his life or the return of his past life as life and not
death. Rather, it is because he tells himself this life and he is the narra-
tion's first, if not only, addressee and destination – within the text' (13).

For Derrida, Nietzschean autobiography is introspective in that it
aims, foremost, at illuminating the author's own mind for his or her
sake. To this self-initiated process of telling about oneself, the audience
is secondary insofar as the autobiographical voice is concerned.

As I listened to their stories of life in the bush with the LRM/A, it
became apparent to me that some of the former CI soldiers were unable
to speak, read, and write in what F. Lionnet (1989) terms 'classical
modes of expression' (2), namely English and French, and lack the resources to record their experiences of war (Machel, 1996). In short order, I became the ear that hears and the hand that records what the CI
soldier experienced. This arrangement was further complicated when
the informants told their stories in the Luo language, and left it to me to
translate into English. Being a native Luo speaker rendered the task of
translation both a blessing and a liability. I consider myself a fluent native Luo speaker; it is my mother tongue, my first language, and I like
to think that I speak it with authentic idiomatic nuances. Still, my inter-
pretive lenses have broadened because my life straddles two cultures
now, Acholi culture and Western culture, and the way I understand the
Luo language is mediated by these two world views. Or to paraphrase
Acholi poet Okot p'Bitek, reading the books of white people has 'captured my head.' I had to take as much special care as a non-Acholi
would (e.g., Finnstrom, 2008, 2003) to be non-judgmental about the
experiences of CI soldiers. For instance, when Jola Amayo, one of the
informants, spoke about the period following her father's death, she

mentioned that her family was reduced to eating 'spinach, sour leaves and okra.' To my Westernized ear, it sounded as if she was saying that her family became poor and could not afford the kinds of food that were available when her father was alive. However, in the Acholi culture, poverty is not defined by lack of money or resources alone. You are poor when you do not have anyone around you, especially extended family, and you lack the strength and energy to take care of yourself – hence the Acholi saying *lacan bedo kene* (the poor person lives alone). In fact, Jola Amayo hastened to say, *wabedo, warii* (we lived, life continued) as the family pulled together to till the land. This does not suggest poverty because the family is still viable, able to work, and depend on each other and extended kin for support.

But even as I tried very hard to be accurate in translating the stories from Luo into English, I could only 'capture' what the former CI soldiers were saying rather than translating word for word, sentence for sentence, paragraph by paragraph, everything that was said. That is not because I am a bad translator, but because the construction of spoken Luo does not translate neatly into the English language. What I write in English does not do justice to the depth of meaning and experiences as expressed in Luo.

Spoken Luo, moreover, can be treacherously ambiguous at the best of times even to a native speaker like me because it conveys many shades of meaning. Consider this single Luo sentence uttered by an informant: 'Dano omyero odong adonga.' Without context, and in direct translation from Luo to English, there are almost a half-dozen interpretations. It could mean, 'People ought to stay behind.' It could also mean, 'People should beat up Adonga.' A third translation could be, 'Human beings ought to grow up.' Even, 'Let people stay, Adonga!' My translation was: 'A person needs to grow up.' She uses the word *dano*, which, depending on the context, can be translated into the singular 'person' or the plural 'people.' I chose the former because the context of the sentence was about children recruited as CI soldiers being forced to skip childhood. The informant was reflecting on her life, and lamenting the fact that she did not go through the various natural stages of childhood.

Indeed, through interview questions, the CI soldier is prompted to tell what happened (Seidman, 2006), and in some instances to speak the unspeakable. At moments such as this, the autobiographical voice of the CI soldier holds the possibility of opening the archival record for reconstructing the events *before*, *during*, and *after* the war, and assessing their transformative impact on how the child related to others within the cultural space carved out by war, or what D.E. Jonte-Pace (2001) calls 'shadowy and fragmentary narrative,' in which case the audience is left with 'guessing at what lies underneath' (140), or even the disappointment of stark silence from a soul that has experienced too much and is unable to talk about it. As one former CI soldier told me in Gulu, 'this is really just a brief overview of what happened because there is a lot to tell. In some cases, there is so much that cannot be told. This is just a synopsis because the suffering we went through is unspeakable. If I were to tell you everything, it would take two days, and even then there would still be more left to tell.'

Notwithstanding the aforementioned limitations, the autobiographies of CI soldiers can be rich with meaning and information about their lives in war. At the very least, even when the CI soldier chooses silence, we can surmise the pain, suffering, and extreme experience that rendered the child speechless, and perhaps use our imagination to reconstruct what happened. Through fiction (e.g., Iweala, 2005), or actual events disguised as fiction (e.g., Eggers, 2006), or non-fiction (e.g., Beah, 2007), the CI soldier's narrative retains the promise of an insider's rich perspective into the underlying tension and motivation that guide the children towards making certain choices in the process of becoming CI soldiers. As M. McQuillan (2000) points out, autobiography as narrative performs the story as well as plots how the story is told. According to McQuillan, the plotting is the dynamic process that drives the audience's interaction with the narrative form.

Wrestling with the Curse of Autochthony in Post-Colonial Uganda

Being an Acholi who closely sympathized with the ordeal that the Acholi people generally and especially former CI soldiers went through, I am also keenly aware of the pitfalls of identifying too closely with the subject and thereby losing all sense of balance and objectivity. In doing field research, D. Druckman (2005) warns the ethnographer 'to reflect on and be explicit about how their own biases, life experiences, status and power, and character shape their findings and analysis' (236). In order to avoid writing a book that could be read as an apologia for the LRM/A's gross crimes against humanity, or conversely as a cover-up for what some believe is genocide in Acholi perpetrated by the government of Uganda (Otunnu, 2006, 44), I needed to confront and wrestle with the ethnocentric mindset that Arjun Appadurai (2006) calls 'autochthony.' The term describes 'primary claim to peoplehood, territory and citizenship for persons who can show that they are from their respective places, unlike others who are migrants or foreigners' (89). This often leads to explosive ethnic-based violence with many casualties (Appadurai, 1998).

But, while Appadurai's explanation of autochthony does not quite describe post-colonial Uganda when compared, for example, to the former Yugoslavia where full-fledged conflicts unfolded purely along ethnic fault lines between Serbs, Croats, Albanians, and others (Cornell and Hartmann, 1998; Vuckovic, 1997), there are strong tell-tale signs of colonial policies intensifying these conflicts. In post-colonial Uganda, after all, violence tended to play along ethnic lines at the state level as a function of political power (Hansen, 1977; Ibingira, 1973). But inter-ethnic conflict was not always a given for the numerous ethnicities that peopled what became Uganda. As the descendants of the early Luo of Tekidi,[1] for example, the Acholi experienced many clan battles, especially during the reign of Kuturia (Equatoria Province), which extended the power of the Khedive of Egypt from central Sudan through northern Uganda. The 'Kuturia'[2] reign set many Acholi clan states against others. War was rampant and those clan-states that had the best weapons and support of the Arab administrators and traders gained the upper hand over opponents. But, even in times of conflict, the clan-states adhered to the philosophy of defence of the homestead against the enemy established by earlier generations of Luo. J.M. Onyango-ku-Odongo (1976) writes: 'It should be noted, however, that in a fight between the Luo of Payira and the Luo of Puranga, or between any two Luo groups, houses were not destroyed. The warring factions would take great care never to harm women and children. No looting or taking of captives was allowed, though all these actions were permissible in wars against other ethnic groups' (161–2).

When inter-ethnic wars took place, such as the Jie-Acholi war (Lamphear, 1976; Lamphear & Webster, 1971), the Acholi did not consider the other ethnic group as mortal enemies. Instead, there were many examples of inter-ethnic cooperation, as was the case when Luo ancestors helped form the ruling Babito clans which founded the Bunyoro-Kitara Kingdom around the latter part of 1300s (Crazzolara, 1950). Several hundred years later, when the Omukama Kabalega, the king of Bunyoro-Kitara Kingdom during the colonial period, was defeated by a combined British and Buganda force in November 1894, he fled northward where he was sheltered for a while by the Acholi, whom he regarded as his kin. Interestingly, when he became dissatisfied with the growing influence of the British in Buganda, King Mwanga rebelled in July 1897 and, upon his defeat by the British army, escaped, was briefly detained by German forces, and escaped again, fleeing north to join his erstwhile enemy the Omukama Kabalega in Acholi and Lango. The pair were finally captured in 1899 and exiled to Seychelles Island. That the two kings could find refuge in Acholi was testimony to the good relations between the Acholi and the other larger ethnicities in Uganda.

The roots of modern-day ethnic tension and conflicts involving the Acholi and other ethnicities in Uganda can be traced to the inauspicious arrival of Sir Samuel Baker, the first white man in Acholi. The colonial English adventurer could barely conceal his surprise at the pleasant welcome that he was accorded by the natives, but he nonetheless stated that, as part of the colonial enterprise, his mission was to 'convert the greater portion of savages into disciplined soldiers' (Baker, 1874, 302). By the early 1900s, in what would later become known as Uganda, neat geographical and political boundaries were drawn around ethnic groups that were growing suspicious of each other, penning them within tight spheres where the expression of identity was bound to lead to further suspicion, ethnic tension, and possibly violence. Early on in the establishment of the British hegemony over Uganda, for example, Buganda was armed and used to subdue other ethnic groups to the east and to the north (Twaddle, 1985, 1993; Karugire, 1980; Kiwanuka, 1971).

The colonial policy of divide and rule had two fateful consequences in Acholiland. First, it introduced the notion that other ethnic groups were the enemies of Acholi people. An early example was the Lamogi Rebellion of 1911–12 (Adimola, 1954), when Buganda soldiers were used to suppress Acholi opposition to the new political arrangement under British colonial rule. A localized resistance that began when the British colonizers, aided by their Baganda collaborators, attempted to take away firearms that had proliferated throughout the Acholi countryside, the rebellion became an example of Acholi resistance in the face of a bigger foe. The move to disarm the Acholi was part of a larger colonial effort to make them more amenable to the establishment of British authority over the rest of Uganda, an effort that also included recruitment into the army, where they constituted the bulk of the troops, and forced participation in the growing of cash crops. Unhappy with the proposed action by a colonizing power, the people of Lamogi resisted the disarmament program, taking off to the Guruguru Hill where they held out for several weeks until they were finally disarmed.

Although the British saw the squashing of the Lamogi Rebellion as an unqualified success, the narrative played out differently among the Acholi (Adimola, 1954). Instead of feeling defeated, the Acholi viewed the rebellion as a badge of honour, an emblem of courage in the face of the oppressor. It also came to symbolize what many Acholi people felt in their heart, namely, that no outsiders could humiliate them without a fight. Furthermore, in the Lamogi Rebellion, the Acholi's ethnocultural identity as defenders of the homestead came of age in modern Uganda political history. The British, through their agents from Buganda, were the invaders who had to be repelled by whatever means possible, and, although the rebellion had foundered, there was a feeling that the Lamogi had not surrendered.

Divide-and-rule policy also stoked inter-ethnic rivalry by nurturing the Acholi's ethnocultural pride in their perception of themselves as courageous warriors. J.R.P. Postlethwaite (1947), the first colonial administrator in Acholi (1912–17), recalled in his memoir that the Acholi 'took to soldiering like ducks to water' (71). Over time, from the 1920s to the 1950s, the Acholi's military bravery, courage, and fierceness became first mythologized and then institutionalized through a policy that saw massive recruitment of Acholi into the security services in colonial and post-colonial Uganda (Mazrui, 1975; Mazrui, 1977; Parsons, 2003).

The large presence of Acholi in the security forces was perceived differently depending on one's vantage point. From the perspective of the population in central and southern Uganda, it seemed that all the shortcomings of the military were attributable to the Acholi. Meanwhile, among the Acholi, their strong presence in the army gave them the impression of strength in numbers. In the post-colonial milieu, the Acholi and other ethnicities in Uganda were set on a collision course in which brute military force, rather than the age-old art of ethnic diplomacy and traditional methods emphasizing caution and prudence in decisions about whether to pursue war and peace, was seen as essential for ethnic survival.

The Politics of Otherness in Post-Colonial Uganda

After Uganda's independence in October 1962, using their ethnocultural affinities as a springboard, various state actors demonized other

ethnicities as the source of Uganda's problems. That is to say, the politics of 'otherness' as a by-product of the colonial policy of divide and
rule were used to intensify ethnic resentment between groups classified
by the colonials as 'bantus'[3] and those labelled 'nilotics'[4] or northerners. Early contact with Europeans promoted literacy in the south earlier than elsewhere in Uganda, and as a result southerners came to see
themselves as superior to unsophisticated, illiterate, and 'militaristic
northerners' (Jorgensen, 1981; Sathyamurthy, 1986). For their part, as
one of the northern ethnicities, the Acholi viewed the southerners as
luloka (*laloka*, sing.), *those from across the river or lake or valley* who formed
the distinct other. Embedded in the concept of *loka* was contrasting
group self-identity, which, for the Acholi, was succinctly expressed as
wan (us) or expansively as *wan luleb* (we of the same tongue). Implicit in
the notion of *luloka* was the untrustworthy, unprincipled, and dangerous other. For political mobilization and in determining who should
get what, the *wan luleb* felt marginalized by those from *loka* whom they
perceived as controlling much of the economy. The polarizing impact
of culture and language further sharpened these ethnic self-interests
in opposition to the interests of others. In fact, viewed through the internal lenses of each ethnic group, all other ethnicities are *luloka, from
the other side of the river*, with the valley in between filled with mutual
ignorance.

In 1966 a political power struggle became a crisis. Then Prime
Minister Milton Obote, an ethnic Lango closely allied with the Acholi
through the Luo language and culture, abrogated the constitution,
which allowed for the sharing of power with Kabaka of Buganda as
head of state. Obote swiftly used the military to oust Kabaka from his
palace at Lubiri on the night of 24 May 1966. Artillery shelling of the
palace set it on fire; Kabaka Mutesa, meanwhile, fled into exile in
Britain. Ethnic Baganda felt strongly that Milton Obote had betrayed
their king.

The 1966 constitutional crisis, also known as the Buganda Crisis, became a seminal event in the history of Uganda, with reverberations felt
decades later. In the narrative of post-Idi Amin Uganda in the 1980s,
with four political parties contesting the election, ethnicity mattered.
Former president Obote led the Uganda People's Congress (UPC); Paul
Kawanga Ssemogerere, a Muganda from the south, led the Democratic
Party (DP); Yoweri Museveni, a Munyankole from the west, led the
new Uganda Patriotic Movement (UPM); and Mayanja Nkangi, a
Muganda from the south, led the monarchist Conservative Party (CP).

All these leaders tended to play on ethnic fears of the other. In May 1980, for example, the politics of ethnic mobilization were in full gear, as demonstrated at a political rally I attended at Pece Stadium in Gulu (Oloya, 2005). The main attraction was the legendary commander of the Uganda National Liberation Army (UNLA), Major-General David Oyite-Ojok. Though supposedly neutral as the commander of a national army that boasted a rank and file drawn from all ethnicities across Uganda, Oyite-Ojok, an ethnic Lango, was campaigning on behalf of former president Obote, who had returned from exile in time for national elections slated for 10 December 1980. Speaking in Luo, Oyite-Ojok warned, 'Wan kom pe odok ii tim odoco. Ka owubolo kwir arac, ci wubino tingo matafali me yubo Lubiri' (We will never go back into exile again. If you cast your votes carelessly, you will be forced to carry bricks for rebuilding the Lubiri).[5] The mostly Acholi crowd roared back in appreciation.

Speaking on the eve of the first national election in almost two decades, Oyite-Ojok was reminding his audience that the contest was a choice not just between Uganda's four political parties but also between the ethnicities of the leaders who led those parties. In his logic, voting for a party led by the wrong ethnicity, in this case, either the DP or CP, both led by Baganda, invited the potential for retaliation over the events of 1966. After all, at that point in post-Amin politics, barely a year after Amin was ousted from power, the leadership of Uganda had changed hands twice in bloodless coups. Professor Yusufu Lule, a Muganda intellectual, installed in April 1979 as the interim president in Amin's wake, was himself ousted from power two months later, on 20 June 1979. Lule's successor, Godfrey Lukongwa Binaisa, also a Muganda, fared little better, lasting eleven months until he, too, was removed from power on 11 May 1980. For Oyite-Ojok, whichever ethnicity won the December 1980 elections would decide who got what, when, and how. That was the game as he saw and played it.

Moreover, Oyite-Ojok was also tapping into the Acholi sense of alienation from the rest of Uganda since independence from colonial Britain. On 10 December 1980, several months after Oyite-Ojok made his statement in Pece Stadium, Milton Obote returned to power. However, Yoweri Museveni, who was a member of the powerful four-man provisional leadership, accused Obote of stealing the election (Avirgan & Honey, 1982; Clodfelter, 2002). Even as the newly elected Obote consolidated his power, Museveni retreated to the bush to form the Popular Resistance Army (PRA), later to become the National

Resistance Movement/Army (NRM/A). The narrative adopted by the NRM/A in its insurgency against the ruling government was that of a populist uprising striving for a more democratic Uganda (Ngoga, 1998). Yet, in the ears of non-northerners, the NRM/A war was about not only the restoration of democratic ideals but also the overthrow of the northern hegemony that had begun with Milton Obote at the inception of nationhood in 1962, carried through the dictatorial years of Idi Amin, and resumed in full force with the return of Obote to power in 1980, inaugurating an era that became known as Obote II (Keitesi, 2004). To gain popular support in central, southern, and western Uganda, the NRM/A used propaganda to demonize northerners generally and the Acholi in particular as the enemies of a stable Uganda (Behrend, 1999; Nyeko & Lucima, 2002; Otunnu, 2002). In the south-versus-north politics of the day, the very survival of southerners was deemed to be at stake, depending on whether the NRM/A won or lost the war (Kutesa, 2006; Keitesi, 2004).

The Obote government's bloody counter-insurgency campaigns against the NRM/A in Luwero in south-central Uganda, presided over by Major-General Oyite Ojok until his untimely death at the end of 1983 and later by two Acholi generals, Tito Lutwa Okello and Bazilio Olara-Okello, led to the genocidal killings of thousands of innocent Baganda. The atrocities committed against civilians in Luwero were mostly blamed on the Luo, especially Acholi soldiers in the UNLA (Behrend, 1998, Gersony, 1997; Mutibwa, 1992), although others finger Museveni's NRM/A (Witzsche, 2003). This view of events would later have a dramatic impact on the Acholi population, which believed that the NRM/A had come to avenge the Luwero killings (Behrend, 1998). The gruesomely orchestrated counter-offensive by Obote and subsequently by General Okello notwithstanding, the NRM/A expanded the resistance front to the west, at the same time slowly marching towards the capital city of Kampala. In January 1986 the NRM/A, comprised partly of CI soldiers known as *kadogos* (the little ones), overran Kampala. Yoweri Museveni, a westerner, and regarded by Acholi as a *laloka* (from across the river), came to power.

Yet, in line with Appadurai's notion of autochthony in which ethnicity is the perpetual stake in the belly of nationalism as a unifying ideal, where each ethnicity blames the others for conflict while ignoring its own role, it is common in Uganda's post-independence political discourse to hear the aggressor described as the Acholi, the Baganda, the Banyankole, the Banya-Kigezi, the Teso, the Madi, the Lugbara, the

Karimojong, and so forth. The simplistic, often repeated argument that Acholi society is warlike, for example, is used to explain the long record of the LRM/A rebels in abducting mostly Acholi children to be trained as CI soldiers (Cheney, 2007). This argument is based on the view of the Acholi as a 'military ethnocracy' (Mazrui, 1975; Doom & Vlassenroot, 1999) or a 'militarized ethnicity' (Mazrui, 1976, 250). E. de Temmerman (2001) puts it more bluntly when she writes, 'The people of [the] northern region (the Acholi and Langi) were made into the country's military elite' (vii). The supposed belligerency of the Acholi, their characteristic martial attitudes and natural inclination towards violence, has been used to explain the role of the Acholi in the violent post-colonial history of Uganda (Gutteridge, 1969, 13; Ogunbanjo, 2002, 5).

The undertone of the same argument is discernible in the description of the war in Acholi since Yoweri Museveni came into power in 1986 as ethnic cleansing of the Acholi by vengeful southerners (Dolan, 2009, 153). But, when violence in post-colonial Uganda is viewed through the lenses of Appadurai's autochthony, it cannot be attributed to the character of any particular ethnic group, or even deemed to be perpetrated along purely ethnic lines. Rather, a complex picture emerges in which Uganda's numerous post-independence conflicts and violence tend to hint at ethnicity but not always be strictly based on it.

Indeed, as this book unfolds, I will suggest that in northern Uganda, where the war served different purposes for different entities including the government of Uganda, the LRM/A committed crimes against humanity not in defence of the Acholi people or Acholi interests, seen to be threatened by Museveni's NRM/A, but against the Acholi themselves. It is my contention that the LRM/A is an opportunistic and predatory self-styled rebel movement that keenly exploited the chaos following the entry of the NRM/A in Acholi, and employed mass killings against the Acholi and other ethnic groups in northern Uganda to attempt to carve out a territory under its control with the leader Joseph Kony as the overlord. In the next chapter, I distinguish between the war led by Alice Auma Lakwena, which I characterize as an ill-fated, confused, poorly equipped, and spontaneous grassroots uprising to defend the Acholi against NRM/A incusions, and the destructive war waged by Joseph Kony's army of mostly CI soldiers for control of Acholiland.

Chapter Two

Gwooko Dog Paco
(Defending the Homestead),
Cultural Devastation, and the LRM/A

As a little child growing up in Pamin-Yai, I acquired an education about moral issues and social responsibilities through *ododo*, folktales that were taught around *wang-oyo*, the evening bonfire. Some of my favourite stories were about Obibi, the human-eating ogre. In the gathering twilight, trees took on forms of giants, and the cacophonous screeching of night birds sounded like the laughter of devilish creatures up to no good. I imagined that Obibi was waiting in the blackness of the night to gobble me up.

Luckily for me, as illustrated in the collection of Acholi folktales by Alexander Mwa Odonga (1999) under the title *Ododo pa Acoli. Vol. 1*, the same happy outcome was expected in every Obibi story whether it was about *obibi lawange acel*, the One-Eyed Ogre, or the most terrible of them all, *obibi lawange apar*, the Ten-Eyed Ogre. The monster is always slain by the warriors. In one such story, a village maiden named Akello, her mother, Min Akello, and the rest of the family are living through a particularly bitter famine that had ravaged the land. Facing certain starvation, Akello and Min Akello discover that Obibi has plenty of food in his large well-tended garden. Akello and her mother resolve to steal some of that food. The theft goes on for a time until, one day, the thieving duo are caught red-handed by Obibi, who takes them as prisoners. The following day, Obibi demands that Min Akello cook Akello for dinner. But, while Obibi is away during the day, a leper whose acquaintance the pair had made prior to their captivity suggests that Min Akello instead cook an animal skin. Upon returning home that evening, Obibi sits down to a meal he believes is Akello. He grumbles that the meat is tougher than previous human meat he has eaten, but, still believing this was Akello, he eats the skin for dinner. Akello, meanwhile, escapes back to her village.

The next day, Obibi demands that Min Akello cook herself for dinner. As before, she conspires with the leper by preparing the skin of an animal for Obibi's dinner. But as Obibi, grumbling, eats the tough meat, Min Akello, who is hidden inside a granary, makes some noise, thereby alerting the monster to her presence. Obibi at once realizes the trickery and begins chasing Min Akello as she escapes back to her home. While running, Min Akello begins to sing. The wind carries her voice to the village, alerting the community of the impending danger. Young warriors in the community rally with spears. On the outskirts of the village, the warriors meet and slay Obibi. They then cut off one of Obibi's toes and use it to beat a drum whose magical qualities allow all the victims hitherto devoured by the evil Obibi to return back to life. The village is saved.

Gwooko Dog Paco as an Acholi Ethnocultural Identity

The *ododo*, like the one about Obibi and Akello's family, resonate among the Acholi today because the stories illustrate and express a central part of the Acholi ethnocultural identity as *lu-gwok dog paco*, which, translated word for word, means *lu* (those), *gwok* (defend), *dog* (mouth), *paco* (homestead), or 'those who defend the mouth of the homestead' or engage in the act of *gwooko dog paco* (defending the homestead). Implicit in the concept of *gwooko dog paco* is the Acholi belief in communal responsibility whereby the people rally to defend the homestead when the *oduru* (alarm) is raised to signal an attack under way. This belief, with its emphasis on self-preservation, is not unique to the Acholi but rather can be found among any identifiable group with shared identity and cultural traits, not only in Uganda but in the African continent as a whole and indeed throughout the world.

The ethnocultural attitude of a particular group is shaped by its historical experiences, and in time that attitude determines the manner in which the group views and portrays itself in a multi-ethnic community. It establishes 'the extent to which an individual or group is committed to both endorsing and practicing a set of values, beliefs and behaviors which are associated with a particular ethnocultural tradition' (Marsella, 1990, 14). Thus, for the Acholi as for many African ethnicities, defending the home against threats that include but are not limited to wild animals, invasion by cattle rustlers, and inter-clan and ethnic warfare is an integral part of who they are as individuals and as a collective. In every Acholi household, the menfolk keep at least several *tong* (spears) for the protection of the family and, at a moment's notice, when the *oduru* is made, every able body adult, usually men, can be relied upon to respond to the general threat facing the community because everyone subscribes to the notion of *gwooko dog paco*.

The Acholi's particular concept of *gwooko dog paco* is rooted in the pre-colonial metamorphosis from fragmented Luo chiefdoms into present-day Acholi ethnicity. The collectivization of Luo chiefdoms into larger polities was born of the necessity for survival. According to R. Atkinson (1989), 'being part of a larger group provided at least potentially greater security in times of danger or disaster. Other benefits included larger groupings of closely associated village lineages with which to hunt, go on trading expeditions, or exchange women' (15). But, unlike such empire builders as Shaka[1] in southern Africa, Sundiata Keita of Mali,[2] or, closer to home, Mtesa I,[3] the king of Buganda to the south of what became Uganda, the Luo did not keep a standing army for imperial purposes. Rather, faced with a common threat with potential to destroy the community, young men were mobilized. At such times, a defensive war was not only permissible but a matter of duty: every able-bodied youth was expected to *dyeere* (sacrifice) himself to fight the enemy in defence of the homestead.

To their sometimes allies and enemies, the Langi and the Alur, these predecessors of present-day Acholi were known as *'Ogangi or Lo-gang*, which was probably derived from Acholi word "gang," meaning "home" or village' (Ocitti, 1973, 8). As used, the description meant the 'ones who stay home,' likely a derogatory reference to the fact that, being mostly agriculturalists, the Luo rarely ventured beyond their ancestral homesteads. It could also mean that the Luo invested the defence of the homestead with *lapir*, a moral determinant of just wars that safeguarded against quixotic or opportunistic military adventurism. As explained by Acholi diplomat and former United Nations undersecretary for children and war Olara Otunnu, *lapir* is an unwritten Luo rule of engagement in times of conflict that was grounded in the notion of the just war, which required a 'deep and well-founded grievance against the other side.'[4]

The formalities of *lapir* required that the chief and a council of elders discuss whether or not to wage a war. Indeed, contrary to H. Behrend's (1999) assertion that Acholi distinguished between *lweny lapir*, when 'warriors set out to take women, cattle etc.,' and *lweny culo kwo*, 'war as a retaliatory measure after an attack by an enemy' (39), a war was fought as a matter of necessity when all else had failed, and mostly as a pre-emptive or defensive act. The principles of *lapir*, in other words, did not authorize unsanctioned aggression against enemies for any reason, but they did sanction a pre-emptive strike against an enemy about to attack, defending the homestead during attack by the enemy, and engaging in hot pursuit while the attacking enemy retreated. *Lapir* did not permit the use of children and women in war, although there were occasional instances when the leader of a war party was a woman (Onyango-ku-Odongo, 1976).

The principles of *lapir* also required pre-colonial Luo states, when faced with a formidable opponent, to prefer diplomacy or temporary retreat, fighting only when absolutely necessary. Onyango-ku-Odongo (1976) recounts the story of Rwot Chua Omal, a successful Luo king who faced invasion from a neighbouring ethnic group in the mid-1600s. When the Tekidi settlement was attacked and ransacked, he ordered the community to build a defensive sanctuary in the mountains. Later, when a fearsome warrior tribe known as the Galla attacked the Luo settlement, Rwot Omal and his subjects strategically retreated to the mountain-top refuge. Unknown to the Galla invaders, the Luo had hauled huge stones to the top of the mountain and carefully positioned them at the mouths of the few paths leading to the hideouts. As the Galla warriors attacked, the Luo defenders rolled down the big stones, which crushed to death many of the invaders.

Thus, when Yoweri Museveni fought his way into power in January 1986, the Acholi had to choose between defending their traditional borders from the incoming NRM/A, which lacked the professional and national character that its successor, the UPDF, now has, or simply allowing the newly minted government free passage into the heart of Acholiland. The latter option seemed the least favourable to the Acholi, since the NRM/A's ascension to power demonstrated that, in post-colonial Uganda, the mobilization, utilization, and legitimatization of non-state violence – including ethnic violence as state violence – was not only possible but necessary to establish ethnic hegemony. By ethnic hegemony, I mean the establishment of a particular ethnic character or dominant ideology over competing ethnicities or ideologies, usually by coercive force. M.S. McDougal and W.M. Reisman (1981) argue that, historically, international law involved a covenant among state elites which specified that only they had the right to regulate the use of coercive power. Private practitioners of coercion were tolerated if they sold their services to state elites by working as mercenaries.

For the Acholi, there also were other considerations. As discussed earlier, the Acholi viewed the NRM/A as *luloka*, foreigners who were about to breach the very boundary of the Acholi's ethnocultural identity as defenders of the homestead. This fear was rooted in the colonial project that classified and highlighted cultural differences rather than similarities, thereby fragmenting Uganda's indigenous people into 'bantu,' 'nilotes,' 'hamitics,' and so forth (Oliver, 1986). The NRM/A consisted mostly of fighters from south-central and western Uganda who were perceived as the enemies of the Acholi, and, consequently, they met with intolerance, suspicion, and outright hostility. This made the war different from Sierra Leone's deadly civil war (1991–8), which pitted the Revolutionary United Front (RUF) against the Sierra Leone army in a struggle for control of diamond fields (see Abdullah, 2004; Richards, 1996; Rosen, 2005, 81–5) and the sale of 'blood diamonds' (Roberts, 2003, 218), or Liberia's war (1989–97), fought between the rebel National Patriotic Front of Liberia (NPFL) and the Armed Forces of Liberia (AFL) over control of the country's rich mineral fields and timber resources (see Adebajo, 2002; Sayndee, 2008). In the case of northern Uganda, notwithstanding continuing Acholi suspicion that the Museveni government wanted to take away their land, the war was not over resources but over dominating, and not being dominated by, other ethnicities.

As Robert Gersony (1997) aptly observes, 'many Acholi shared a collective identity as proud and able professional soldiers in the Colonial and post-Independence uniformed services. This included the long-held view that Acholis do not surrender, especially in their home areas, and to some degree that "only Acholis should rule in Acholi"' (15). This attitude would harden over the next several months as the successful NRM/A, with growing ruthlessness, extended and established control over the Acholi region.

The Cultural Devastation of Acholi

At first, as the NRM/A took control of the entire Acholi area in February and March 1986, there appeared to be no persecution of the Acholi population by the victorious NRM/A soldiers. Reporting to the U.S. government, Gersony (1997) noted that the NRM/A 'conducted itself in an exemplary and restrained manner in the first few months' (14). But this was only temporary, according to C. Keitesi (2004), a former CI soldier who served with the NRM/A in northern Uganda. In her autobiography, Keitesi notes that the Acholi had good reason to be afraid of the new army. Recalling her first few months in northern Uganda as part of the advancing NRM/A, she writes: 'Many Acholi people were considered rebels, and even if some of us knew that they were not, we still looked at them as one. The hate we had for Obote, the former Uganda president, never changed, and the Acholi seemed to be paying the price. Drago's second-in-command spoke Kinyankole, and he took everything personal. To him every Acholi was a rebel, and they deserved nothing but death. Every time we captured an Acholi, we had to kill them, and Drago hated this' (204).

In time, the Acholi began believing that the era of the NRM/A was worse than Idi Amin's eight-year dictatorship (Finnstrom, 2008). When interviewed by Human Rights Watch (1997), Paulino Nyeko, my former principal at Sir Samuel Baker Secondary School in Gulu, painted a grim picture of NRM/A violence:

> National Resistance Army soldiers would do all they could to make things difficult here (in Gulu and Kitgum). They would defecate in water supplies, and in the mouth of slaughtered animals. They would tie people's hands behind their backs so tightly that people would be left paralyzed. They went into villages and took guns by force. They looted Acholi cattle and did nothing to prevent [cattle raiders from Karamajong district] from stealing the rest. Over three million heads of cattle were soon lost, and it made the people embittered. (Human Rights Watch, 1997, 63–4)

Meanwhile, reports of civilian deaths began to surface in the months after the NRM/A established control in the two Acholi districts of Gulu and Kitgum. A pattern of brutal extrajudicial killings was set by the NRA's 35th Battalion, stationed in the Namukora area in Kitgum (Gersony, 1997). In one incident, on 16 August 1986, NRM/A soldiers burned down over 100 homes and arrested 44 men and one woman in villages around Namukora. The unarmed detainees were placed on the back of a truck while armed NRM/A soldiers followed in a pickup truck commandeered from the Catholic mission nearby. A short time later, all the men and woman were shot dead. According to the NRM/A, the prisoners had attempted to escape. But Amnesty International (AI) reports on Uganda for 1990, 1991, 1992, and 1999 detail many similar killings by the NRM/A. For example, on 18 August

1986, the 13th NRM/A battalion, based at Akilok, killed eighteen un-armed civilians, some of whom had been burnt alive in their homes; and on 20 September 1986 the 7th NRM/A battalion, located at Oryang, in the Labongo region, killed twenty-two unarmed civilians. The intensification of atrocities against unarmed and defenceless Acholi civilians went far beyond what the government designated eu-phemistically as 'mopping operations' or 'pacification of the north.'

The NRM/A killing of civilians became more frequent over the next several months, with reports implicating other battalions. A July 2001 report by Isis-Women's International Cross Cultural Exchange (Isis-WICCE) quoted an Acholi informant who referred to 'killing of civil-ians some of whom were buried in latrines and mass graves or burnt alive in their grass-thatched huts as in Pabo, Opidi, Anaka, Ongako, Pagoro sub-counties; and suffocating prisoners in pits dug in the ground as in Burcoro and Palenga sub-counties' (24). The Bur Coro in-cident gained notoriety as much for the fact that innocent civilians were killed as for the manner in which they were killed. Though the actual number of victims is disputed, with some reports putting the figure at 'scores' (Adyanga, 2006; Onyango-Obbo, 1997), another at three (Dolan, 2000, 2), and still another at 'hundreds' (Curtus, 2005), what is certain is that many civilians were rounded up by NRM/A soldiers in a place called Bur Coro. The unarmed civilians were forced into a large pit dug into the earth. The top of the pit was then covered with soil and grass, which was then set on fire. In another version, pepper was set on fire and the bitter smoke piped into the covered pit (Onyango-Obbo, 1997). Victims screaming with terror slowly suffocated from smoke and heat. Such sadistic and, for the Acholi, humiliating deaths became ever more common, confirming Acholi suspicion that the NRM/A was bent on revenging the killings in Luwero which had been attributed to Acholi soldiers serving in Obote's UNLA.

Some elements within the NRM/A, meanwhile, further victimized the civilian population through rape. As an act of intimidation, rape has a long and well-documented historical association with war (see Brownmiller, 1975; Chang, 1997; Nikolić-Ristanović, 2000; Sanders, 1980). This violent physical act has far-reaching psychological conse-quences not only for the victims but also for those who witness it. In the context of war, rape is directed at 'all women who belong to other men' (Brownmiller, 1994, 81). Rape, usually of a woman, is a severe cultural taboo among the Acholi, and the perpetrator is treated with severe sanctions (Liu Institute for Global Issues and the Gulu Justice Forum,

2006). But in northern Uganda, rape became a way for the rogue groups within the NRM/A to show how powerless the Acholi men were in protecting themselves and their womenfolk. In the early months of its conquest of Acholiland, some soldiers within the NRM/A began to rape both men and women, which to the Acholi would have amounted to excruciating cultural and psychological abuse. Representative of the numerous reports of rape emanating from all over Acholiland in the period from 1986 to 1988 was the testimony of a victim named Sabina, as reported by O. Bennett, J. Bexley and K. Warnock (1995): 'The [worst thing about] the NRA soldiers was having forced sex with women one after the other. Men and women were collected during what they called a "screening exercise to flush" out the rebels from the community. The men and women were then put in separate groups. Then in the evening, the NRA soldiers started fucking the women in the compound. One woman could be fucked by up to six men; and this went on for three days' (99).

The rape of a man in front of other men and family had no cultural description or name among the Acholi because of its outrageous and alien nature. To describe the brutality of rape orchestrated by the NRM/A on Acholi men in villages in places like Alero, Amuru, and Guruguru, the Acholi developed the phrase *tek gungu* (as soon as one kneels one is raped from behind) (Dolan, 2002, 74; Dolan, 2009; Finnstrom, 2003). The phrase could also be translated as 'the pain of kneeling' or 'the difficulty with kneeling' and interpreted to mean that the simple act of *gungu* (kneeling) is associated with immediate severe pain. In any case, it telegraphed the cultural humiliation and degradation that Acholi men, culturally seen as the protectors of their families, were now subjected to by the NRM/A. Some men were reported to have committed suicide after such rapes (Bennett, Bexley, & Warnock, 1995).

The increase of HIV/AIDS, likely because of the deteriorating conditions of war, was viewed as suspicious by the Acholi, with some accusing the regime of Yoweri Museveni of deliberately sending HIV/AIDS-afflicted soldiers to infect the population with the deadly virus as part of an extermination program (Finnstrom, 2008). This notion of an HIV/AIDS pogrom was given further credence when various reports indicated that the rate of HIV/AIDS infection in Acholi was higher than elsewhere in Uganda (Fabiani et al., 2007; Muleme, 2004; Spiegel & Harroff-Tavel, 2006).

The war's greatest impact, however, resulted from the widespread looting of foodstuff, especially livestock, by NRM/A soldiers, Karimojong raiders, local militia groups, and others. Livestock had always been an integral part of Acholi culture, used to determine wealth, social status, and personal worth. So important was livestock to the Acholi that money earned from wages was translated into what the Acholi called *lim ma kwo* (living wealth) (Girling, 1960; Finnstrom, 2008). A person could be very rich with money saved in the bank, but if he did not have *lim makwo* he was considered poor. The wealthy household possessed several head of cattle, which served as a 'store of wealth' (Leggett, 2001, 28) for hard times such as drought, for paying school fees, for daily sustenance, and for ploughing the field in the rainy season. But, most important, cattle were used for meeting the Acholi customary obligation of paying dowry.

The centrality of livestock in Acholi culture was idealized by Acholi poet Okot p'Bitek in *Song of Lawino*. The protagonist Lawino reminds her estranged husband about her worth in dowry before he married her, saying:

> And my brothers called me Nya-Dyang
> For my breasts shook
> And beckoned the cattle
> And they sang silently:
> Father prepare the kraal
> Father prepare the kraal
> The cattle are coming   (44)

During the first year of NRM/A's entry into Acholiland, there were an estimated 300,000 to 1,000,000 heads of cattle. Gersony (1997) observes that 'the area possessed large herds of cattle, goats, sheep and other livestock and the potential for almost 100 percent on-farm employment' (18). Within a very short time, as I. Leggett (2001) puts it, 'the productive base of the Acholi rural economy was removed wholesale' (28). Leggett blames the Karimojong cattle rustlers for the unprecedented loss of livestock. Gersony, for his part, spreads the blame evenly among owners who pre-emptively liquidated part of their herd, provided livestock to the anti-NRM/A Uganda People's Democratic Army (UPDA), or lost cattle to NRM/A, while also noting the role of diseases like rinderpest and pneumonia. The Acholi, however, were very clear about who was responsible for the devastation of the livestock herd. Reports emanating from the villages indicted the NRM/A soldiers as the primary looters of livestock and other property from Acholi villages in 1986 and 1987 (Dolan, 2000). Later, in 1987 and 1988, Karimojong warriors from northeastern Uganda appeared to take advantage of the insecurity in Acholiland and began rustling cattle in large numbers (Dolan, 2000).

Without exaggeration, the cultural devastation arising from the decimation of the livestock was felt immediately and for a long time afterwards in Acholiland. According to C. Dolan (2000), 'the toll on the economic and social fabric had already begun to be felt. Dowries began to be given in the form of cash rather than cattle due to the extensive rustling of 87/88' (10). Dolan also recorded stories of suicides due to the loss of cattle: one respondent reported that such loss of property pushed a close family member to take his own life, stating, 'My brother drowned himself after NRA took 100 cattle.' The incredible devastation suffered by the Acholi was summed up by Acholi Bishop Macleod Baker Ochola II of Kitgum Diocese when he said, 'Amin's terror affected the military, the civil servants, but it did not really affect ordinary people. That's the difference with this government – our cattle, granaries and houses. The cattle rustling of the Karimojong was the first step in a process that has left the Acholi people deep in the pit of poverty' (as quoted in Leggett, 2001, 29).

In deciding whether or not to fight back, the Acholi faced the same dilemma that other ethnicities in central and western Uganda had previously confronted in the face of the extreme violence perpetrated the by the Uganda National Liberation Army during the regimes of Milton Obote and General Tito Lutwa Okello. The first resistance against the NRM/A was a haphazard grass-roots defence of the homestead that spanned many ethnicities, with an illiterate Acholi woman leading the fight. The second insurgency targeted the Acholi as much as other ethnicities in its ruthless quest for power and control in northern Uganda. The latter insurgency became known to the world as the Lord's Resistance Army.

The Rise of the Holy Spirit Movement

From an Acholi perspective, the arrival of the NRM/A could be likened, metaphorically speaking, to Obibi penetrating the defence erected around the village by the young warriors and then entering the village itself. The only question worth considering at the time, given the Acholi tradition of *gwooko dog paco*, was whether the brave warriors should fight such a powerful foe or simply give up to avoid further casualties. Following the defeat of the Tito Okello government in January 1986, the Acholi saw the prevailing wind of change in apocalyptic terms, as signifying nothing less than their impending extinction. In the initial phases of the NRM/A invasion of Acholiland, uprisings against the unfolding calamity were restricted to the former members of the Uganda National Liberation Army. When these failed, the Uganda People's Democratic Army, a resistance force, was founded in May 1986 in Juba, southern Sudan. It was comprised mainly of former professional soldiers loyal to Bazilio Okello, who conducted a classical guerrilla war against the NRM/A. Despite some limited successes, the UPDA collapsed owing to indiscipline and low morale among the troops (Behrend, 1999).

The instinctual response for self-preservation, I contend, was a critical factor for the grass-roots uprising led by Alice Auma Abongowat Lakwena that began in August 1986. Although disguised with all sorts of magic and claims to superhuman powers, Auma's Holy Spirit Movement (HSM) adhered to the principles of *gwooko dog paco*, which include assessing the likelihood of success of war, the justness of the war, and the human cost of declaring war. The HSM was based loosely on biblical references to the oppressed Israelites, who were simultaneously the victims of malevolence and the beneficiaries of God's unwavering support. An Acholi spirit healer and barely literate market vendor, Alice Abongowat Auma portrayed herself as the spirit medium for this Christian movement. She said that she was sent to rescue the Acholi from their own sinful excesses as well as from oppression and certain annihilation at the hands of the invaders (Behrend, 1999). Auma also claimed that she was possessed by various spirits, the leading one being *Lakwena* (the messenger), the spirit of an Italian captain who died at Murchison Falls in northern Uganda in the First or Second World War (Behrend, 1999). Lakwena suffused her movement with mystical qualities. The various spirits that possessed her at different times conducted the war, she said, and her soldiers were asked to obey every single command, however bizarre.

Contrary to the argument that the Acholi responded to Lakwena because of her message that 'they should repent their sins' and because they wanted 'to put an end to the bloodshed in Acholi' (Behrend, 1999, 31), I would suggest that, in the absence of an alternative political leadership and credible defensive response to their humiliating defeat and subsequent cultural devastation following the incursion by the NRM/A, the Acholi were desperate to find a rallying point. Lakwena raised that alarm, and many responded to the call.

Although interpreted by some as 'most bizarre' (Woodward, 1991, 181), and dismissively described as 'a combination of myth, superstition and voodoo to enchant the population to rally to its cause' (Nantulya, 2001, 88), the HSM uprising in northern and eastern Uganda was a populist phenomenon in the original Acholi sense of *gwooko dog paco*. Lakwena was able to mobilize a sizable army that at its apex numbered several thousand recruits, many of them hastily trained civilian volunteers. HSM soldiers smeared their bodies with shea-butter oil, believing it made them impervious to bullets. Indeed, the HSM strategy of singing while fighting strengthens the argument that the uprising was initially conceived as *gwooko dog paco*. In traditional Acholi battles, soldiers often sang war songs as they faced the enemy (p'Bitek, 1974). Singing provided the warriors with courage to keep moving forward. In one of the early battles against the better-organized and well-armed NRM/A soldiers, the HSM sang hymns as it advanced.[5] This behaviour, which, Behrend points out, 'contradicted all military principles' (1999, 57), might have been prompted by a fear of engendering more violence.

Despite some victories in the few months that it existed, the HSM was defeated by the NRM/A in October 1987, whereupon its volunteer recruits went back to their villages. After the failure of the HSM, the desperate and disparate responses to the threat facing the Acholi no longer followed established cultural norms, including the protection of children from harm. In conditions of severe stress, A. Honwana (2006) points out, disoriented individuals continue to perform what amount to culturally empty gestures denuded of the significance they once held before the disintegration of the vibrant culture. The absence of an overarching moral umbrella in times of war provides the opportunity for 'anything goes' because of the uncertainty over what is normal or abnormal, real and unreal, acceptable and unacceptable. Indeed, I contend, the demise of the HSM saw the beginning of a war which was cleverly disguised as *gwooko dog paco* but which in fact targeted those it purported to protect. The new phase in the war involved the forcible recruitment of children to be trained into soldiers. It was the beginning of one of the most heinous crimes against humanity perpetrated in modern times.

Joseph Kony and the Lord's Resistance Movement/Army

In his book *Radical Hope: Ethics in the Face of Cultural Devastation*, Jonathan Lear (2006) recounts the story of the native Crow Nation in the mid-nineteenth-century United States to explore the question of how a self-sufficient culture might respond when facing cultural devastation. Through the eyes of the last Crow chief, Plenty Coup, Lear traces events before 1850, a period that saw growing encroachment on Crow territory by white settlers:

> Happiness consisted in living that life to the full. This was an active and unfettered pursuit of a nomadic hunting life in which their family life and social rituals could prosper. Because the tribe was threatened by other tribes, they developed a warrior culture to defend their way of life. The martial values – bravery in battle, the development of the appropriate character in young men, and the support of the warriors by all the tribe – were important constituents of happiness as understood by the Crow. (55)

By the turn of the century, the self-sufficient culture of the Crow was a mere shadow of its former self. The Fort Laramie Treaty of 1851, and subsequent treaties with the U.S. government, ceded ever larger parts of the Crow's traditional hunting ground. Lear highlights a statement attributed to Chief Plenty Coup: 'But when the buffalo went away the hearts of my people fell to the ground, and they could not lift them up again. After this nothing happened' (2). *After this nothing happened.* To be sure, the Crow nation continued to exist on the reservations long after this date, but the very sinew that stitched them together as a people, that defined their way of life and, consequently, their very identity, had been broken. History, as the Crow knew it, had stopped once they resettled on the reservations. For Chief Plenty Coups, whatever happened after that could not be added to the autobiographical voices of the Crow because the Crow were no longer the nation they once were. As Lear points out, the Crow could have continued to fight the white settlers as other natives did, but Chief Plenty Coup saw his people's hopes for survival as resting not on their ability to wage war with the whites but on their absorbing the whites' knowledge to fashion a new existence separate and apart from the nomadic lifestyle the Crow had once known. This entailed thinking outside what the Crow were traditionally good at, fighting the Sioux and hunting buffalo, and reaching for something they had little knowledge of, diplomacy and peacemaking.

Following the defeat of the HSM, the Acholi, like the Crow, needed to come to terms with the NRM/A as the new power in the land and, for the most part, they did (Lamwaka, 2002). However, Joseph Kony, who fashioned his rebel movement along the same spiritual idea as the

HSM, and initially on the premise of defending the Acholi, quickly demonstrated startlingly different strategies. The LRM/A in fact was less concerned with the survival of Acholi than with the creation of a huge area under its direct control. In the pursuit of this goal, the LRM/A made the Acholi, and indeed many other ethnic groups including the Lango and Teso, the target of its bloody campaign.

Virtually unknown before 1988, Joseph Kony was born in the early 1960s in a small village of Odek, about thirty-five kilometres east of Gulu town. His father, Luigi Abol, was a peasant farmer who also doubled as a Catholic catechist, and his mother was a homemaker. Kony had an unremarkable childhood, though he excelled at the Acholi *laraka-raka* (Nyakairu, 2008). He dropped out of school after sitting for Primary Leaving Certificate Examinations in 1981 (it is not known whether he passed).

Uganda's economy in the 1970s and early 1980s provides further context for the dilemma that Kony's contemporaries faced while growing up in rural Acholi. One of the recurring themes in the war in northern Uganda is the position of dispossessed Acholi youth who, feeling disconnected from the promises of the post-colonial era (Finnstrom, 2008), live lives of idleness. This is nothing new. For many of us who grew up in Acholi villages in the shadow of Gulu town in the 1970s, the most difficult aspect of our lives was not the persistent concern about the systematic killing of thousands of Ugandans, and especially the Acholi, by Idi Amin (Melady & Melady, 1977; Okuku, 2002), but the scarcity of goods in the shops, the absence of services, and the lack of job opportunities for school leavers. It was near impossible to get simple household items such as salt, soap, sugar, and medicine. Amin's declaration of economic independence in 1972 saw many Asian traders and shopowners deported to Britain and Canada (Kuepper, Lackey, & Swinerton, 1975). Asians had performed the crucial role of linking peasants and the commercial industry, buying farmers' produce such as cotton and tobacco for commercial sale and, in return, supplying the essentials needed by the peasants. Once the Asians were eliminated, their role was taken over by local businessmen, a few of whom became known as *mafuta mingi*, translated as 'those who have a lot of fat [in their stomach].' Many of the businesses, though, did not have the commercial connections and know-how to run shops. Consequently, long queues formed in front of shops as customers responded to rumours that an essential item was about to go on sale. Shops were otherwise mostly bare, with proprietors spending the day sitting around and doing little or no business.

When I travelled into Gulu town as a boy and young man, the *mafuta mingi* left me with a feeling of awe, even envy. They seemed to have it all – shiny new cars, beautiful families, and the good life. Children of the new rich went to the best schools in town and always looked smart in school uniforms and shiny black shoes. For the majority of Acholi rural children our age, in contrast, the day began with the family ritual of *bayo lagot*, literally, 'throwing the hoe' to till the field for cotton, maize, or another crop. Later, those lucky enough to be enrolled as students rushed home to wash themselves and eat *angica*, the cold leftover food from the previous evening, before dashing barefoot to the village school. It would be a lucky day if one had some food for lunch or some pocket money to buy a ripe banana or a stick of sugar cane to chew to deaden the sharp pangs of hunger.

To supplement family incomes, which came mostly from selling crops, our mothers, like most village women in rural Acholi, sold *kongo arege*, an illicit locally brewed gin. Often, most of the money went towards paying school fees, buying school uniforms, and paying for medicine. Gulu Hospital, the main government hospital, was located in town. Though patients were treated free of charge at the hospital, there were usually long line-ups and no drugs available. The better-equipped hospital was Lacor Missionary Hospital, located six kilometres west of Gulu town on Juba road. It was run by Canadian-born doctor, Lucille Teasdale, and her Italian husband, Dr Piero Corti.

Getting to town along the winding dirt road was quicker by automobiles, but cars were a rare sight in the villages. Some people had bicycles with carriers attached at the back which were used to carry heavy loads and passengers. Most people, though, used what the village wags referred to as *bac pa Ladeny*, 'Ladeny's bus,' a reference to walking on foot. Sick villagers suffering life-threatening medical emergencies were often placed on the small carriages on the backs of bicycles and slowly pushed to the hospital. Many patients often died en route. It was not unusual to see bundled-up corpses on the backs of bicycles being rolled back to the villages for burial.

The same bleak conditions persisted in the post-Amin era of the early 1980s under the second regime of Milton Obote, which failed to produce any significant changes to the political and economic fortunes of northern Uganda generally and rural Acholiland in particular. Kampala remained the centre of business and politics, and the trickle-down benefits for the rural districts were meagre. Corruption ensured that the basic infrastructure that had helped develop the Acholi economy in the

1960s, such as cotton ginneries and tobacco cooperatives, was never revived following the economic collapse of the Amin years. Poverty among youth of a certain age remained rampant as peasant farmers stopped producing for the export market, focusing instead on food crops that gave immediate financial returns (Kasekende & Atingi-Ego, 2008). Disillusionment became a part of the reality of those youth who had celebrated the fall of Idi Amin, seen as an oppressor of the Acholi, and had hoped for more under Obote's second regime. There was nothing to do, and being educated did not guarantee a paying job.

When war broke out in 1979 as Idi Amin was pushed out of power, and again in the early months of the NRM/A invasion of Acholiland, the resulting breakdown of law and order created chaos for everyone; villagers and town people, rich and poor, faced the same uncertain future. And, although there is no hard evidence to suggest that this was the scenario that unfolded for Joseph Kony after the demise of the Holy Spirit Movement, it is conceivable that, with little or no prospect of finding steady employment in the skilled trades or in the service industry, a young man with a similar background to Kony's might have seen opportunity in joining the insurgency, not to protect the homestead but for personal advancement.

This is not to argue that Kony was motivated by a desire to fight for the economic equality and dignity of all people, including the Acholi. It is meant only to provide a possible context for understanding how some Acholi youth of Joseph Kony's generation, with very little formal education, might have taken up arms and then behaved so appallingly in the war that ensued.

Economic context, certainly, does not explain how a young Acholi with Kony's background could rise to become such a prolific, and vicious, killer. For that, we need to examine the cultural devastation of Acholi at the time and the perfect cover it provided for a psychopathic mass murderer like Kony to build an elaborate army of terror that was large enough to commit transnational genocide.

The Evolution of the LRM/A

At least initially, after the collapse of the HSM, Kony seemed to be encouraged by some Acholi elders to keep up the fight against the NRM/A (Finnstrom, 2008). Following the NRM/A's successful invasion of Acholiland in early 1986, remnants of the UNLA had crossed over to Sudan where it reconstituted itself as the Uganda People's Democratic

Army. One version of events suggests that Kony joined the local UPDA forces to fight the NRM/A in 1986. Another version has Kony joining Lakwena's HSM, and himself becoming a spirit medium, or *lakwena*, possessed by several spirits, the dominant one named after a former army officer in Idi Amin's regime called Juma Oris (Allen, 1991; Behrend, 1999; Dolan, 2009, 80). The most likely scenario is that, in the initial resistance against the NRM/A, the various groups united and disbanded when it suited their immediate goals. Kony likely associated himself with several groups at once while building his army into a viable force. What is clear is that, by the time HSM had fought to within a hundred kilometres of Uganda's capital of Kampala before being defeated by the NRM/A, Kony had established a small largely ineffectual insurgent army which was fashioned as an offshoot of Lakwena's HSM in Gulu district and which, for a short time, strategically appropriated the HSM name. The disintegration of Lakwena's HSM provided Kony's movement with much needed personnel when some of her supporters joined him. The insurgency then underwent a name change, calling itself the United Holy Salvation Army (UHSA) to reflect the absorption of the new group. But the movement was still mostly concerned with creating a moral dimension for the war against the NRM/A. Like its predecessor the HSM, the UHSA claimed to want to clean the Acholi people of the sins of which they were guilty (Behrend, 1999). This meant waging a holy war mostly against the superstitious faith healers known as *ajwaka*, and those deemed unholy (Behrend, 1999).

Likely in tune with the desperate social conditions of the Acholi people, and also with the paradigmatic appeal of salvation as a mobilizing ideology, Kony insinuated himself as the leader of the new resistance. By invoking the Lord's name, and claiming to be fighting to restore the Ten Commandments, Kony positioned his movement to grow at the expense of the widely popular Alice Lakwena. The religious context was a means by which Kony could stake the purity of his *lapir*, the moral claim to wage a war. Like Auma's Lakwena, Kony spoke of being sent 'to destroy evil forces in the world' (Behrend, 1999, 179). However, in the much discussed 1993–4 peace talks, Kony is also recorded on video saying that 'land is wrested by spear,' implying that war was a necessary weapon for forcefully asserting ownership over resources.

Furthermore, Kony exploited the Acholi's antipathy towards those in the south and west to recruit for the insurgency. According to informants who spoke to me in Gulu, Kony channelled a high moral calling to fight off what he described dismissively as 'Yoweri's army.'

Notwithstanding that the Yoweri in question was the de facto president of Uganda, the founder of the LRM/A contemptuously saw him as an usurper of power, a carrier of *opoko*, the gourd used by cattle herders from western Uganda.[6] In other words, rooting out the invaders, restoring the Lord's commandments, and freeing the Acholi people from tyranny was a noble duty. Initially at least, a religious orientation provided Kony's insurgency with the legitimacy it needed to continue to use violence in a space where violence was condemned. It also allowed Kony to distinguish his insurgency from other agents of violence, notably the NRM/A and the UPDA, both of which were accused of atrocities (Behrend, 1999).

The secularization of the UHSA began in early 1987 when, using force and persuasion, Kony began incorporating elements of the UPDA. In February 1987 he peacefully co-opted a UPDA unit commanded by Okello Okeno, persuading some officers to join him while taking those who refused prisoner (Behrend, 1999, 179–80). The biggest boost to the UHSA came in May 1988. The UPDA signed a peace accord with the NRM/A, marking the end of resistance by a force consisting mainly of professional soldiers. However, a breakaway group of thirty-nine soldiers, led by former UPDA commander Odong Latek, refused to surrender because of suspicion of NRM/A trickery, choosing instead to join Kony's UHSA. The nomenclature arising from this alliance, the Uganda People's Democratic Christian Army (UPDCA), reflected both the fluidity and the conflicted duality that characterized the early prototypes of the LRM/A. By claiming a democratic goal, Kony seemed to acknowledge the need to broaden the political and military coalition to fight the NRM/A. At the same time, he persisted in retaining the religious dimension that had marked Lakwena's HSM.

The creation of the UPDCA as an insurgent force using conventional guerrilla strategies of hit-and-run transformed what was mostly an insignificant uprising with religious overtones into a rebel movement that focused on recruiting, training, and deploying its army against the battle-tested NRM/A. It also marked the escalation into a complex transnational insurgency war that would later straddle Uganda and Sudan at the beginning, and move into the Democratic Republic of Congo (DRC) and the Central African Republic (CAR) at a later stage. The key reason for the metamorphosis of the insurgency into a rebel movement that was finally recognized as a threat in northern Uganda seemed to be Kony's ability to network and make deals with other forces. His group succeeded in linking up with some former Amin soldiers who operated under the West Nile Battle Front (WNBF), led by the aforementioned Juma Oris. Some time between 1991 and 1992, the UPDCA became the Lord's Resistance Army.

Given the superior force deployed by the NRM/A in consolidating its hold over Acholiland, one could speculate that the choice of name was a deliberate attempt at one-upmanship in which the 'Lord' in the Lord's Resistance Army was arguably more fearsome and omnipotent than the 'National' in the National Resistance Army. In any case, it betrayed the persistent appeal of religion as a mask for the war that Kony wanted to fight. More important, it also showed that Kony would do anything in order to come across as a credible opposition to Yoweri Museveni, even though his rebels early on were less focused on defending the Acholi people against an attacking army than on achieving power.

Children into Soldiers: The New War

At the height of the insurgency between 1996 and 2006, Joseph Kony's LRM/A used thousands of child-inducted soldiers on the front lines in southern Sudan and northern Uganda. By then, the LRM/A had become a formidable killing machine that wiped out entire villages, as happened on the night of 20 April 1995, when it murdered in cold blood over 240 people in Atiak on a single day (Justice and Reconciliation Project, 2007). This was followed by the Mucwini Massacre in the early morning of 24 July 2002, when fifty-six women, men, and children were murdered (Justice and Reconciliation Project, 2008), and the Barlonyo Massacre on 21 February 2004, in which over 300 civilians were murdered (Justice and Reconciliation Project, 2009). It should be pointed out, that prior to these well-publicized mass murders and throughout the period, the LRM/A killed and maimed thousands of civilians in northern and eastern Uganda, and in southern Sudan, usually in small numbers. Culturally, these mass murders and the forcible displacement of over 400,000 Acholi into camps left the population shell-shocked (Human Rights Watch, 2003a, 2005). Internationally, the killings led to the indictment of five senior LRM/A commanders, including Joseph Kony, by the International Criminal Court (ICC) for war crimes and crimes against humanity (ICC, 2002; Lee, 1999).

One of the earliest known forced recruitments of children occurred in April 1988 when the LRM/A attacked Sacred Heart Secondary School just west of Gulu town in northern Uganda, taking a number of students (Behrend, 1999; Human Rights Watch, 2003a, 2003b). But it was in mid-1991 that Kony intensified the abduction of children from the Acholi countryside (Human Right Watch, 1997). The LRM/A may have adopted the use of child combatants from the NRM/A, which, after all, had relied on the *kadogos*, 'the little ones,' as combatants in the five-year guerrilla war that toppled the Okello government in January 1986. The exploits of the *kadogos* were freely admitted by President Museveni (Museveni, 1997). Given the LRM/A's ethnocultural chauvinism, which denigrated the efficacy of the enemy while emphasizing its own abilities, it is not far-fetched to consider the possibility that Kony saw Acholi children as better fighters than Museveni's *kadogos*.

Whatever its rationale for abducting children, the LRM/A seemed to recognize very early on the necessity of using an army of children to sustain its war effort. The period of eager adult Acholi volunteers willing to fight the NRM/A had ended with the defeat of Alice Lakwena's HSM. The Acholi were also tired of a war that had caused misery to many yet did not bring commensurate gain to the beleaguered communities (Gersony, 1997). The LRM/A's decision to forcibly recruit children for combat would have come out of the realization that adults could not always be relied upon to remain disciplined, loyal, and highly motivated. Children, by contrast, could be trained to do as told. Can Kwo, one of the former child combatants I spoke to in the summer of 2008, believed that the LRM/A abducted children out of necessity, for keeping the insurgency alive. Speaking in Luo, he noted:

> So Kony is strong because he abducted children, and completely made them forget their home experiences. As an adult, you could not forget your home experience. Perhaps you were abducted when you already had a wife or you were abducted just when you were ready to elope with a girl or you were abducted when you were dancing and already knew how sweet life was. But we who were abducted as children knew nothing. All we knew was that combat is a good thing. As a young child you are treated according to your size, given some small reward that fits your thinking and size to entice you. For an adult given a big reward, he or she is immediately aware that you are trying to bribe him or her.

However it came about, the LRM/A decision to abduct children was rendered possible by the extreme culture devastation in which the Acholi were living at the time. Cultural as well as formal institutional safeguards that forbid abduction of children and that would have normally protected children from harm were non-existent owing to the violence that permeated every facet of communal Acholi life. Acholi elders, whose voices could have provided a moral counterweight to the LRM/A's decision to use children in combat, were themselves struggling for survival as the war intensified and destroyed social and cultural life. What would have been unthinkable in the Acholi community prior to the 1986 war was now a reality.

As my informants saw it, families were no longer able to protect their children from either the NRM/A or the LRM/A. By the mid-1990s, child abduction had become an entrenched LRM/A modus operandi that set it apart from many previous insurgencies in sub-Sahara Africa. The vastly unprotected countryside in eastern and northern Uganda and the ineffectual response by the UPDF made it easy for the LRM/A to abduct children from their homes, schools, and public spaces. The forced internment of Acholi population into camps beginning in October 1988, ostensibly to deny reinforcements and food resources to the LRM/A, served to create centralized depots where the LRM/A could now snatch many children at once (Dolan, 2009). According to UNICEF, by 1999 as many as 20,000 children had been abducted by the LRM/A and turned into CI soldiers. The most infamous abduction, which took on an international dimension, occurred on 10 October 1996 at St Mary's College for Girls at Aboke, near Lira town in northern Uganda. Under the cover of darkness, the LRM/A abducted 139 girls that night, of whom 109 were later freed upon the personal intervention of the deputy headmistress of the college, Sister Rachele Fassera (Cook, 2007; de Temmerman, 2001).

The abduction of the Aboke students exposed to the international media the role that Sudan had played all along in nurturing the LRM/A. In addition to providing bases from which the LRM/A could launch its attacks on northern Uganda, the government of Sudan gave the movement arms, money, and legitimacy, thereby lifting it from its relative obscurity to international attention. In doing so, Sudan was retaliating against Uganda for the support it had given the Sudanese People's Liberation Movement/Army (SPLM/A), which was attempting to carve out an independent state in the south of the country. In return, one might speculate, the LRM/A may have promised its help to the government of Sudan in its fight against the SPLM/A. Whatever the nature of the arrangement between the government of Sudan and the LRM/A, the latter never fought a sustained war with the 'Dinka,' as it called the SPLM/A. Instead, the occasional exchanges of fire between the two rebel armies appeared incidental, mostly a result of rivalry over sources of drinking water. According to the testimonies of the former child combatants interviewed for this study, the LRM/A occasionally retaliated against what it saw as SPLM/A transgressions around the water wells. Miya Aparo recalled the nature of the resulting skirmishes, which occasionally flared into a full-fledged battle:

> We returned and stayed, instead of fighting against the Dinka. Mostly because Dinka came to get water, there was no water! You would go dig the spot where water had already dried up. There was mostly sand. You would dig deep into the sand and discover water below the sand. The Dinka would then come to collect the same water. They would wait until Kony's soldiers were not at the water well, and would come and collect water … One day, they shot an [LRM/A] officer, hitting and breaking his thigh. An order was given that everyone should move in on the intruders and push them all the way to their defence [lines]. They began chasing the intruders from the water well, [and] along the way you would find some of them with their intestines pulled outside. We went all the way to their defence. We found many women and children. Most of their soldiers had fled, and many had died. Many children and women died once we started firing on their defence.

Interestingly, in his first public appearance in 1994, which was widely reported, Kony did not address the presence of children in the ranks of LRM/A combatants, instead focusing his bitterness on Acholi elders whom he accused of being turncoats who supported Museveni's NRM/A. Those he considered to be state collaborators, a category that may have involved whole villages, would be punished, he said: 'If you picked up an arrow against us and we ended cutting up the hand you used, who is to blame? You report us with your mouth; we cut off your lips. Who is to blame? It is you. The Bible says that if your hand, eyes or mouth is at fault, it should be cut off' (Schadt, 2001).

It is possible that the virulent war on the Acholi was the result of the subsequent falling out between Kony and Acholi elders (see Finnstrom, 2008, 212–13). But even such bitterness cannot explain the ferociously indiscriminate atrocities, which fit the description of war crimes (Dormann, 2003), that Kony subsequently carried out against his own people and others. If anything, despite the many and often contradictory statements the LRM/A leader made to justify his war, such as fighting to restore the Ten Commandments, toppling Yoweri

Museveni, protecting the Acholi people, ridding Acholi society of witchcraft, and so on, the evidence points to a man obsessed with complete control over the population, and willing to use every brutality known to humanity to achieve that goal. In targeting for violent punishment those it termed betrayers, the LRM/A appeared to reflect the maxim: Either you are with us or you are with the enemy. The difference in this case was that the enemy was everyone outside the LRM/A.

In other words, from the anonymity of village life in rural Acholi, Kony was now thrust into the limelight where he commanded attention by the sheer notoriety of the gruesome murders, maiming, and other atrocities that were daily committed by the LRM/A. Through it all, as we see in the next chapter, the LRM/A ruthlessly, if cleverly, subverted Acholi culture in the creation, manipulation, and control of an army of child abductees, who formed the bulk of its forces as it waged a campaign of terror against the population in northern Uganda, southern Sudan, the Democratic Republic of Congo, and the Central Africa Republic.

Chapter Three

Culture, Identity, and Control in the LRM/A

Regarding the small groups [of LRM/A], if they operate independently, what keeps them from escaping and who would be in charge of each small group, i.e. the ones killing civilians on their own?

(e-mail message, 23 February 2009)

The above question was posed to me by an Acholi living in the diaspora. She was baffled by a news report blaming the LRM/A for the massacre of an estimated 620 villagers in the Democratic Republic of Congo between 24 December 2008 and 13 January 2009 (Human Rights Watch, 2009). She wondered how it was that leaderless groups of so-called child combatants could cause so much suffering and destruction. Such killings were never part of Acholi culture, she concluded.

For my correspondent as for many of us, it is perhaps unthinkable that children can be raised to be CI soldiers. Our desire to protect and care for children sometimes interferes with our ability to listen to stories of a complex process of indoctrination in violence and killing. In wanting to know how and why children become violently transformed for unthinkable ends, we can be too quick to assume moralistic stances rather than see education and culture as processes used by figures of authority in various positions of care, trust, and learning to manipulate the young for their own objectives. While the formation of CI soldiers is my particular focus, education and culture may be exploited for other dehumanizing purposes.

Studies give many psychological and social explanations for why and how children become CI soldiers (Boothby, Crawford, & Halperin, 2006; Coalition to Stop the Use of CI soldiers, 2001, 2004, 2008; Machel, 1996;

Raundalen & Dyregrov, 1991; Wessells, 1997). In this chapter I offer a cultural analysis using testimonies of CI soldiers to trace how Acholi children are taken at a young age and trained through the repurposing of culture and education to serve in war. I argue that Acholi culture has become the means by which abducted children are manipulated, controlled, and exploited in the LRM/A's war against the government of Uganda and civilians. The LRM/A achieves its goal of transforming children into combatants through a series of cultural conditionings that over time force children to live with dual identities, one in which they retain their sense of belonging and identity within Acholi culture, and the other in which they serve the violent agenda of the rebel organization.

The LRM/A's exploitation of CI soldiers is an extreme but not unique object lesson in how adults can use and abuse education and culture to entrap children into fighting wars not of their choosing. For example, J. Schafer (2004) notes that, in the post-colonial civil war that occurred in Mozambique from 1975 to 1992, patriarchal father-child imagery was manipulated by the various armed forces to engender compliance and cohesion among the young recruits, who viewed their commanders as father figures. In their cultural understanding of father-son relationships, where fathers are seen as representing absolute authority, the Mozambique child combatants could never contemplate disobeying their fathers' orders, however absurd or ridiculous these might be. Schafer observes: 'During the war, the young recruits clung defiantly to practices and beliefs which maintained their links with home and family' (91). But the extensive exploitation of children's prior cultural experiences in the context of war, I would argue, has been refined and expanded by the LRM/A to an unprecedented scale. Rather than rely solely on the threat of punishment or even the fear of death to control abducted children in the theatre of war, the LRM/A exploits various elements of Acholi culture that allow the abductees to bond with their abductors and to fit within the 'family structure' provided by the organization.

On the issue of who is in control, the LRM/A or the abducted children, several popular positions have emerged. While acknowledging the important contributions of these positions in advancing understanding of the dynamics that surround child-inducted soldiers, I have chosen to examine religious fundamentalism and the concept of Stockholm Syndrome to illuminate the transformation of children in the LRM/A insurgency.

Religious Indoctrination and LRM/A Control of Child Combatants

The mythologizing of the LRM/A as a Christian fundamentalist organization, I argue, is grounded in the historical reality and the utterances of its leaders at its inception in 1987. At the time, the fledgling insurgent movement that would become the LRM/A fervently sought to cast itself as a worthy successor to the defeated Holy Spirit Movement of Alice Lakwena by highlighting its religious credentials, which it continued to do until at least 1994.[1] Perhaps unwittingly, the overarching claim of LRM/A religious fundamentalism was given further credence by the efforts of international human-rights organizations to draw attention to the plight of children abducted by the group. Amnesty International, for example, in a report titled *Breaking God's Commands: The Destruction of Childhood by the Lord's Resistance Army*, documented cases of 'institutionalized physical and psychological violence, including killings, rape and other forms of torture' for children as young as ten (Amnesty International, 1997, 10). One fourteen-year-old girl, named only as 'B.,' told how she was abducted in February 1997; beaten 'terribly,' she watched as the LRM/A 'killed my mother' (Amnesty International, 1997, 10). Despite the echo of organized religion in the title of the publication, the many former LRM/A abductees quoted in the report, all of whom described the horrific violence to which they were subjected by the organization, barely mentioned religious indoctrination or control based on religion. Yet that did not seem to matter. The LRM/A's attempt to portray itself as a crusading Christian organization was seized on in the West to illustrate the threat of domestic terror.

In the era of the Global War on Terror, media and researchers alike have constructed a widely accepted narrative that views the LRM/A as a transnational Christian fundamentalist rebel movement operating across several borders in Uganda, southern Sudan, the DRC, and the CAR. Brian Beary defines fundamentalism as 'the literal translation of holy texts and rejection of modernism' (Beary, 2010, 107) and describes the LRM/A as 'Christian fundamentalist' (Beary, 2010, 109). This interpretation argues that religious fanaticism, as a method of both indoctrination and control, explains the longevity of the LRM/A as a rebel movement and its tenacious hold on child combatants. Furthermore, R. Petraitis (2003) claims that kidnapped children 'are forcefully indoctrinated into the LRM/A's grand vision of an Acholi nation based on

the Ten Commandments – savage beatings are meted out to all nonbe-
lievers' (para. 3). In a similar vein, G.N. Smith (2008) writes, 'As far as
I can figure, there is no coherent ideological component in their fight,
but rather a combination of Christian fundamentalism and opposition
to Museveni's government' (19).

In attempting to link the LRM/A to the fight against global terrorism,
P. Hough (2008) draws a parallel between the LRM/A and the U.S.-
based Ku Klux Khan:

> Christian fundamentalism has long been blended with crude racism in
> US white supremacist groups such as Aryan nations and the Ku Klux
> Khan. In recent years the most prolific overtly Christian violent non-state
> actor has been the Lord's Resistance Army (LRM/A). The LRM/A, who
> are largely based in southern Sudan, have been conducting a civil
> insurgency against the government of Uganda since the late 1980s aimed
> at the establishment of a theocratic state governed by the Bible's Ten
> Commandments. (Hough, 2008, 70)

Hough's claim that the LRM/A is an organization that uses religious
fundamentalism as a method for indoctrinating and exercising control
over child abductees is rejected elsewhere as a media creation (Finnstrom,
2008, 123–4) or simply as unsupported by evidence (Finnstrom, 2008,
108–12; Rice, 2006) or by the LRM/A itself. Writing on the subject for
United Nations High Commission for Refugees (UNHCR), G. Prunier
(1996) asserts that 'this bizarre blend does not seem to coincide with any
sort of Christian fundamentalism, any more than does another of his
[Kony's] stated objectives, namely to transfer the Central Bank of Uganda
to Gulu, in Northern Uganda, so that "the people will become rich"'
(para. 5).

In fact, at the well-publicized Kacokke Madit, a conference of Acholi
in London in 1997, the LRM/A distanced itself from any claim to fundamentalism. LRM/A spokesperson James Obita dismissed outright the
idea that the LRM/A is a religiously fundamentalist organization, saying: 'Propaganda by the Museveni regime and the media that the LRM/A
is a group of Christian fundamentalists with bizarre beliefs whose aim is
to topple the Museveni regime and replace it with governance based on
the Bible's Ten Commandments are [sic] despicable and must be rejected
with all the contempt it deserves' (Obita, 1997, section, 3.4).

As supported by testimony by my informants which I discuss
later in this chapter, the experience of LRM/A child abductees was

characterized by a mix of physical violence, exploitation of Acholi cultural rituals such as *wiiro moo yaa* (anointing with shea-butter oil), and rigorous physical regimes that included marching for hundreds of kilometres with little or no food. But, at the same time, the LRM/A occasionally referred to the Ten Commandments to reinforce its organizational rules. For example, Can Kwo Obato recalled edicts such as 'Do not commit adultery, don't smoke, don't drink.' But he admitted that these rules, especially the one that said 'Do not kill anybody for any reason,' 'was not simply a rule for the LRM/A only but was part of Acholi tradition.' Other former child combatants referred to religion as a source of personal strength rather than as an instrument of control perpetrated through indoctrination. To endure her life as an abductee with the LRM/A, Jola Amayo told how she used to recall her parents' teachings that 'everyone is created by God, God created all as equal.' Meanwhile, on the day he deserted the LRM/A for good, Ringo Otigo prayed to his ancestors to guide him back home safely. In sum, none of the stories told by my informants corroborate the claim that religious indoctrination was a method for controlling LRM/A child abductees.

The Context of Stockholm Syndrome

The phenomenon of Stockholm Syndrome is named after a 1973 Swedish incident in which four bank employees were taken hostage by an escaped convict, and held for five and a half days in a bank vault (Fitzpatrick, 2009). In time, the hostages reportedly developed an attachment to the hostage takers, going as far as asking authorities to treat them with leniency (Burgess & Regehr, 2010, 43).

The concept of Stockholm Syndrome has been tremendously influential over the last three decades in offering explanations for the complex motivations that propel hostages to bond with their captors instead of being repelled by them. Stockholm Syndrome has been used to explain the battered-spouse syndrome in which the victim stays in the relationship and even shields the abuser from prosecution (Dutton & Painter, 1981; Ehrlich, 1989), the concentration-camp victims who idolize the guards who badly mistreat them (Bettelheim, 1943; Eisner, 1980), cult members who faithfully follow the leader regardless of potential harm to themselves (Mills, 1979), and many unrelated abductions where the victims later act in a manner that appears to benefit their abductors. The most famous of these abductions, familiar to North Americans but by no means the complete list worldwide, include the cases of Patricia Hearst,[2] Elizabeth Smart,[3] Shawn Hornbeck,[4] and Jaycee Lee Dugard.[5]

More recently, notwithstanding its Eurocentric roots, attempts have been made to use elements of Stockholm Syndrome to explain the experiences of child combatants in the civil conflicts in Liberia (Wessells, 2006, 66), Sierra Leone (Richards, 2002; Denov & Maclure, 2006, 79; Junger, 2000), and Uganda (Barry, 2006). The parallel drawn between Western hostages and their captors, on the one hand, and child combatants and their commanders, on the other, hinges on the observation that despite the mistreatment they suffer and the harsh conditions of war, child combatants are loyal to their abductors to the exclusion of all other considerations including their own safety and well-being (Richards, 2002). K. Peters and P. Richards (1998a, 1998b) describe Sierra Leonean child combatants who fought in the 1991 civil conflict as 'heedless of danger' (1998b, 183) in following the orders of commanders. Similar bonding was observed between child combatants and their commanders in the Liberian civil conflict, prompting M.G. Wessells (2006) to speculate that this may 'reflect a psychological process called Stockholm Syndrome, wherein captives identify with their captors.' Wessells further notes:

> That their captors, who could kill them, spare their lives, creates a strong sense of gratitude in the captives. Isolated from the outside world, they come to see their captors as good people or even as saviours, forging bonds of identification with them. A similar process may affect child soldiers who recognise that the armed group could kill them at any moment but who see particular commanders as having saved them. The resulting gratitude can create a strong sense of loyalty and obedience to the commanders. (66)

However, to understand why Stockholm Syndrome has limited usefulness in explaining the relationships between Acholi child abductees and their LRM/A commanders, it is imperative to examine the original context of the syndrome and subsequent interpretations of it. The original incident began on the morning of 23 August, 1973, when a desperate convict named Jan-Erik Olsson attempted to rob Sveriges Kreditbankens in Norrmalmstorg, Stockholm. During the incident, which lasted almost six days, Olsson held four bank employees as hostages. They were Elizabeth Oldgren, twenty-one; Kristin Enmark, twenty-three; Sven Safstrom, twenty-five; and Brigitta Lundblad, thirty-one.[6] At the demand of the hostage taker, a second convict, Clark Olofsson, was later rushed to the scene to help with the negotiations. As the ordeal dragged on, Kristin Enmark, one of the hostages, told police negotiators that she felt safe with Olsson but worried that police might escalate the situation, a comment she repeated on the second day of the drama when she spoke by phone with Swedish Prime Minister Olaf Palme (Buzacott, 1991, 41). Enmark chided the prime minister for not conceding to the demands of the robbers.[7] After almost 131 hours of drama which was broadcasted live on Swedish television, the crisis ended when police drilled a hole through the flat above the bank vault and piped in noxious but non-lethal gas. The two suspects surrendered almost immediately and, as they were being led away, Enmark, who was on a stretcher, reportedly smiled and called out to Olsson, saying, 'We'll see each other again.'[8] Her behaviour was interpreted by criminologist Nils Bejerot, who had been helping police with negotiations as well as providing psychological context to the drama on live television, as a survival mechanism that the hostage deploys in order to appease the hostage taker (Bejerot, 1974). He coined the term Stockholm Syndrome to describe the behaviour.

In its original usage, therefore, Stockholm Syndrome is a condition defined by positive feelings that develop between the perpetrator and hostage or victim in hostage-like circumstances where the stakes are either life or death – for the hostage (Lynn & Rhue, 1994; Strentz, 1980; Symonds, 1975). In explaining this contradictory behaviour, D.L.R. Graham, E. Rawlings, and N. Rimini (1988) propose that, for Stockholm Syndrome to be present, the condition must be attended by: (a) a perceived threat to survival and the belief the captor will carry out the threat; (b) the abductee's perception of some small act of kindness from the abductor within the context of terror; (c) isolation from perspectives other than that of the abductor; and (d) a perceived inability to escape. Furthermore, M.J. Schabracq (2007) suggests that victims stay with their abductors not because they have bonded with them but because 'by adopting this mindset they can better predict what the captors are up to' (66). F.M. Ochberg and D.A. Soskis (1982) believe that the positive rapprochement between the abductee and the abductor is established slowly, but is set by the third day. The strength of the bond between the two is dependent on the intensity of the experience, its duration, the dependence of the abductee on the abductor for survival, and the psychological distance between the abductee and the authorities.

But, in attempting to link Stockholm Syndrome to LRM/A abductees, D. Barry (2006) claims that control over child combatants is exerted
through 'apocalyptic spiritualism,' which gives rebel leader Joseph
Kony 'Stockholm Syndrome powers over the young boys he has abducted into his army' (Barry, blog, 2006). The claim of apocalyptic spiritualism suggests that Joseph Kony and the LRM/A has, for example,
end-of-world tendencies similar to those of Jim Jones and the Peoples
Temple in Guyana, where members committed mass suicides by drinking poisoned cola in November 1978 (Chidester, 2003; Klineman, Butler,
& Conn, 1980), and David Koresh and the Branch Davidian sect in
Waco, Texas, whose members perished in a huge fire on 19 April 1993
rather than submit to arrest by U.S. federal officials (Bromley & Silver,
1995; Hall, 1995; Hall, 2002).

This explanation, like many others attempting to apply Stockholm
Syndrome to explain the relationships between child combatants and
their commanders in various civil conflicts in Africa generally and
specifically in northern Uganda, is of limited usefulness at best. First
of all, Stockholm Syndrome was originally conceived to explain hostage situations mostly in confined spaces such as a house, an airplane,
or a train. In this scenario, both the hostage and captor understand
that the conditions in which they find themselves will last until a resolution occurs and, on the basis of this assessment, mutually develop
the ground rules under which to operate to avoid escalating the crisis.
This may explain why Kristin Enmark, the sympathetic hostage in the
Stockholm crisis, was upset with the authorities, whom she perceived
as attempting to escalate the situation by violating the rules that had
been established between the hostages and the captors. Her vantage
point as a hostage placed within the same room as the captors gave
her the advantage of being able to 'read' the captors, and, on these
grounds, she reached the conclusion that the captors would not be
dangerous so long as they were not provoked. Swedish authorities
thought otherwise.

Second, as happened in the original Stockholm crisis, the drama
generally plays out within several hours to a few days, enough time
for Stockholm Syndrome to develop. Throughout the ordeal, the in-
terplay between the abductee and the abductor is underwritten by
fear. The bond that forms between the abductor who holds the power
of life and death and the unfortunate abductee is symbiotically driven
to benefit both the abductee and the abductor in some way. We could
surmise that the abductee needs to survive until he or she can escape

or be rescued, while the abductor's goal is to achieve his or her demand or satisfy certain needs.

The same, however, cannot be said of the LRM/A abductees who have undergone transformation into CI soldiers. For one thing, these children traverse and operate in vast geographical areas of forests and jungles spanning several countries, which offer far more opportunities for escape. Also, the LRM/A abductees are kept for much longer periods, from several months to more than a decade. On average, my informants spent five years with the LRM/A, far longer than the hostages in Western countries whose behaviour in captivity has been explained using the concept of Stockholm Syndrome. Further limiting Stockholm Syndrome as a viable explanation for abductees' contradictory behaviour is the 8 per cent rule proposed by Federal Bureau of Investigation psychologist D. Fuselier (1999). According to Fuselier, only 8 per cent of hostages develop the condition described as Stockholm Syndrome. Fuselier adds that 'those occasions where the Stockholm syndrome actually occurs remain the exception to the rule' (Fuselier, 1999, 22). If we apply Fuselier's 8 per cent rule, we cannot explain the thousands of child combatants who operate under the command of the LRM/A, bonding with their commanders, following orders during battles and raids, carrying out extremely dangerous cross-border assignments, and returning to the main base camp wherever it is established.

I learned, for example, from several of my informants that desertion often came about because the circumstances changed or because of new factors that made it imperative for the child combatant to leave. In one case, a child combatant who had become a mother deserted the LRM/A when the father of her child threatened to take the child away from her. She explained that she walked away because, had she remained within the LRM/A, she and her children could have been killed, thereby wiping out her family lineage. The reason for leaving the rebel organization, in other words, did not arise from a desire to quit working for the LRM/A or even from a need for self-protection from the LRM/A. Rather, her motivation came from an Acholi cultural context in which being childless is considered one of the worst possible calamities that can befall a healthy woman of childbearing age (Ocitti, 1973, 27–8; p'Bitek, 1966, 105). Her action is understandable when viewed in the cultural context of fear of becoming childless, itself further evidence of cultural retention despite her being conditioned to work for the LRM/A.

Ringo Otigo decided to return home after his team ran out of food while in northern Uganda and he himself was unsuccessful in rejoining the main LRM/A in Sudan. A similar circumstance forced another group led by Can Kwo Obato to return home after trying unsuccessfully to cross a big river in order to join the main LRM/A in the Democratic Republic of Congo. In all these cases, the decision to desert the LRM/A was not arrived at because of a sudden opportunity to escape, as the Stockholm Syndrome would require us to assume; instead, leaving the LRM/A evolved out of unforeseen factors that enabled the CI soldiers to break out of what I. Martin-Baro refers to as the 'stigmatized identity' (Martin-Baro, 1994, 132) that the LRM/A had forced them to accept.

The CI soldier's personal escape from a stigmatized identity, in which he or she is forced to perform certain tasks, including rape and pillage, and to adopt the persona of a killer in a culture that abhors killing, I suggest, is possible because the LRM/A manipulates the children to make these actions appear normal through liminal repurposing of Acholi culture. But, as I explain in greater detail below, because the child combatants also retain their original, desired identity, which was formed within the cultural freedom of their villages prior to their abduction, the possibility always exists that this identity may re-emerge when circumstances change.

Towards a Theory of Liminal Repurposing of Acholi Culture

As I develop the idea here, *repurposing of culture* presumes a deliberate manipulation of culture from its intended use in order to achieve another end. This subversion of culture exploits well-understood cultural norms, turning them inside out, reinterpreting them, and eroding established meanings while giving new meanings that serve the intended purpose. Implicitly, the concept of repurposing culture acknowledges that children's initial world view is formed within the family, community, and shared culture in which they live. Their understanding of the world is received through the community that sanctions, promotes, and prohibits certain activities (Harkness & Super, 1991; Nsamenang, 1992; Weisner, 1984). Shared culture, defined as 'a set of common understanding manifest in act and artifact' (Bohannan, 1995, 47), contributes to how individuals bond within a defined cultural space. Culture, anthropologist Clifford Geertz reminds us, should be viewed as a set of 'control mechanisms' that is malleable enough to assume different patterns (Geertz, 1973, 45–6). To Geertz, culture is a process by which humans make meaning of who they are as persons and the world around them. In this sense, culture is seen as the genesis of agency, which I define as the ability to mobilize cultural resources in the pursuit of personal production and action in the actualization of who the child imagines himself or herself to be.

Viewed thus, culture is interactive in allowing the individual to adjust continually his or her sense of self, individuality, and identity on the basis of the prevailing social conditions and environment, and in relation to those around him or her. This process of identity formation is possible because culture, as A. Swidler (1986) argues, 'consists of such symbolic vehicle of meanings, including beliefs, ritual practices, art forms, and ceremonies, as well as informal cultural practices such as language, gossips, stories, and rituals of daily life' (273). For Swidler, culture furnishes the child with the 'tool kit of resources' from which the individual can 'construct strategies of action' (273). Culture, moreover, provides the child with the ingredients for defining the specificity of his/her identity within a community. For instance, Miya Aparo, being the oldest girl in the family, assumed many of the household responsibilities at a very early age: 'You would return from school, often there was no water in the house, and you needed to grind millet on the milling stone because there were not as many milling machines as there are today. We all had to pitch in to mill the millet.'

In the context of the LRM/A war, abducted children still performed many of the familiar cultural activities they grew up with, like grinding millet, collecting water, and eating communally. The difference was that they were also now trained to fight in a vicious war in which many were killed, wounded, and traumatized. This 'normal abnormality' is made possible through the process in which the LRM/A forces child abductees to undergo the rebranding of the mind, a retooling of previously held cultural ideas, and introduction into a new thought process within the repurposed cultural space.

In developing the concept of liminality to describe the transformation of child abductees into child combatants, I borrow from Victor Turner's *The Ritual Process* (1995) in which he describes living with and observing the Ndembu tribe of Zambia perform various rituals. Turner, who builds on the idea of transformation of the individual first proposed by Arnold Van Gennep in *Rites of Passage* (1960), likens these rituals to rites of passage for individuals within Ndembu society. To illustrate his notion of liminality, Turner describes installation rites of the Kanongesha of the Ndembu during which the chief-elect 'dies from his commoner state' (100). On the eve of his ascension to the new leadership role, the chief-elect goes through the rite of *Kumukindyila*, 'which means literally to "speak evil or insulting words against him"' (100). First he must be reduced to nothing before being elevated to the chieftaincy. The chief-elect is then subjected to insults, taunts, and humiliation from his would-be subjects. Turner explains what happens next: 'After this harangue, any person who considers that he has been wronged by the chief-elect in the past is entitled to revile him and most fully express his resentment, going into as much detail as he desires. The chief-elect during all of this, has to sit silently with downcast head, the "pattern of all patience" and humility ... Many informants have told me that "a chief is just like a slave (*ndung'u*) on the night before he succeeds"' (Turner, 1995, 101).

The predicament of the freshly abducted Acholi child, I hasten to point out, is far removed from that of the Ndembu chief-elect in that, through the liminal process of transformation, the child abductee is emotionally, psychologically, and physically reduced to nothing. Any similarity between the two cases is limited to the fact that both involve transitional phases from one status to another; through culturally sanctioned rituals, the chief-elect is transformed into a chief, and through the harshest possible torture and pain, the child abductee is transformed into a child combatant. In either instance, there is a foreboding that life can never be the same again. The chief-elect can never again be the commoner that he was before his initiation, while the child abductee is transformed through liminal processes into a child combatant operating within the repurposed culture.

More fundamentally, Turner seems to suggest that, through the transformative process of liminality, the initiates gain new perspectives about the world around them. In the new *communitas*, hierarchy, class, and social standing are dissolved to allow initiates to coexist by drawing on their common humanity and values as well as good fellowship. As posited here, however, liminality is an intense process of transformation through which child abductees are subjected to physical and psychological coercion, torture, and extreme violence, which forces them to rethink their prior cultural understanding of how to be and relate as human persons, and to accept a new reality where violence is the currency of everyday existence. Violence against the abductees at this time may be interpreted as deliberate attempts by the LRM/A to create, through intense pain, tabula rasa, near-blank young minds, such that, at least in the short term, previous memories are overcome by the terror of the present. It is at these moments of utter cruelty, of the dehumanizing liminal process induced by extreme violence, that child abductees are forced to do whatever is necessary to survive, including killing other children and committing other terrible acts which over time become routine to them.

But taking on alternative identities as combatants and killers, I argue, does not mean that abductees reject the identities that had been formed before abduction by the LRM/A. Rather, I maintain that, as products of the violent, liminal process, child abductees develop alternative stigmatized identities which allow them to fit and work within the LRM/A culture of violence while retaining the desirable identities that were cultivated early in childhood. They become a tight-knit army of killers who perpetrate unimaginable acts of violence and cruelty on their victims, yes, but they also retain knowledge of who they were before they were abducted. By retaining and seeking to reclaim these pre-LRM/A identities, as we see later in the book, returning CI soldiers experience deep pain when their families and society view them not as innocent child abductees but as rebels.

As a young mother in the LRM/A camp, Miya Aparo retained the same sense of responsibility to others that she had when growing up in the village, but this time it was in the context of the battlefield: 'Out there if you cooked today, then you had food, if not then you had nothing. When you found food, you had to carry it to help you feed the children we had. I had a child, and needed to look for food, he also needed something to eat, you also needed something to eat, all the other people you had around you wanted something to eat. You had to search for food.' Having gone through the liminal culture transformation from child to child combatant, Miya, like many other abductees, still saw herself as part of a community in which she had a defined role as a provider. Simultaneously, she also adapted to the new role of combatant where she could perpetrate certain violent acts including killing. She could in an instant, so to speak, slip on her combat identity to prepare for battle. Behaviour that had been taboo prior to her abduction was now part of her daily existence, and did not hold the same moral import it once had in the familiar cultural space of her village prior to the war.

Of course, the LRM/A had an established military structure, with administrative chain of command, training regime, and war strategies, similar to that of other modern guerrilla armies. According to information offered by my informants, at the top of the structure are four spirits – Divo, Silindi, Markey, and Juma Oris – to whom Joseph Kony answers and who provide him with intelligence about the future. Kony is also assisted by senior officers with various roles and functions, including vice-chairman, head of the political wing, head of military intelligence, and chief of operations. Under these senior officers are various officers who control the brigades and the battalions (also see Dolan, 2009, 300). Information is often relayed by radio between field commanders and headquarters.

Based on the information provided by my informants, as well as other sources (notably Dolan [2009] and Behrend]1999]), I have identified eight phases in the liminal culture process that Acholi children undergo in their transformation into bona fide LRM/A child combatants. These phases are not mutually exclusive or sequential; they tend to overlap, following different steps depending on the circumstances, and taking an indeterminate length of time to complete. Some abductees report a very short phase before they emerged as child combatants, while others claim to have experienced a longer transformational period. Moreover, gender differentiation is observed in some of the stages, where girls are slotted to become wives while boys are pushed towards combat. Generally speaking, bearing in mind the variables outlined above, the eight phases in the liminal culture process of becoming child combatants are: 1) *mak* (abduction); 2) *wot ii lum* (going into the bush); 3) *lwoko wii cibilan* (washing the civilian mind); 4) *neko dano* (killing a person); 5) *wiiro kom ki moo yaa* (anointing the body with shea-butter oil); 6) *donyo ii gang* (entering the residential homestead); 7) *pwonyo mony* (military training); and 8) *cito ii tic* (going to work). The relevance of each phase in the process of transforming Acholi children into child combatants is outlined and discussed in detail below.

The Eight Phases in the Liminal Transformation of Children into Soldiers

Mak (*Abduction*)

All the informants recalled in precise detail what they were doing, the time of day, and the circumstances at the time of *mak*. Ringo Otigo was returning from the stream where he went to collect water for evening use when he was abducted. Jola Amayo and her sisters were already in bed when the door to their house was kicked open by rebel soldiers. Amal Ataro was returning from school when she was selected for abduction. Payaa Mamit was engaged in the mundane task of pounding

dry cassava when the LRM/A rebels entered her compound one evening in September 1992: 'In the evening, around seven thirty, while
pounding some cassava, I heard the dog bark. A soldier emerged from
the darkness. I was busy pounding the cassava, and was covered all
over in white cassava dust. He said, "Sit down, sit down, and do not
run!" Within moments, three others emerged. Then the whole place became dark and, as it turned out, they had surrounded the home.'

Although abductions of children also occur during the day (see
Dolan, 2009, 79), night provides the strategic cover of darkness for the
LRM/A rebels to escape back into the forest without engaging the
UPDF air and ground forces (Dolan, 2009, 79). The choice of night
abduction by the LRM/A, I would argue, is also significant from an
Acholi cultural viewpoint, mainly because of what darkness means to
the child abductees. As in other African cultures (for example, Igbo culture in Achebe, 1958, 7), in the Acholi culture, all bad things including
illness, deaths, and witchcraft happen at night. Acholi poet Okot p'Bitek
(1966) points out, 'No one moves at midnight / Except wizards covered
in ashes / Dancing stark naked' (88). The night mostly belongs to people with evil intentions known as *lujogi* (sing. *Lajok*; also *latal*), who
practise witchcraft and ply their trade at night. According to J.P. Ocitti
(1973), *latal* is 'someone who practised black magic by dancing around
people's houses for evil purposes' (16).

Often the abductees have no clue who the abductors are and where
they are being taken. For an Acholi child, therefore, being taken away
from family at night by unknown persons is psychologically disarming
and as terrifying an ordeal as the prospect of death itself. The darkness,
as it were, offers a curtain that cuts the bond between the child and his
or her family. To Payaa, 'The whole place became dark,' which could
very well be a description of the mood that engulfed her home as it
became apparent that she was about to be taken away by the rebels.

In any event, at daybreak, when sunlight finally reveals the faces of
the abductors, the child is surrounded by strangers, or at the very least
is in new, unfamiliar surroundings with no idea of what the future
portends. Occasionally, there are familiar faces, as was the case for
Can Kwo Obato when he was abducted in May 1996 from his village
in Pageya, Gweng-Diya region. He recognized a former village friend
who had been abducted two years earlier and was now an LRM/A
child combatant. Can Kwo pleaded with the rebel named Obwolo
to let him go, but the rebel refused, citing the danger surrounding such
a release:

Obwolo said, 'Is that you Can Kwo?'

I replied, 'It is me.' He took me aside and I said, 'Man, Obwolo, release me so I can return home.'

Obwolo said, 'Look, I am not going to release you because even if I let you go, they are going to find you, arrest you and kill you. In such event, it would appear as if I caused your death.'

Can Kwo, like other abductees abruptly and unexpectedly snatched from their families, was quickly learning the game of survival by distinguishing himself, creating a personal identity in the eyes of his LRM/A abductors. It was a crucial step in surviving the next phase, that of *wot ii lum*.

Wot ii Lum *(Going into the Bush)*

For the abductees, every passing day of survival in the bush brought the realization that their situation with the LRM/A was likely permanent. For Payaa Mamit, her moment of clarity concerning her new identity as *olum* (rebel) in the bush came on the second day after abduction: 'I had hoped that I would be freed, but that never happened. After two days in captivity, I realized that there was not much I could do. I said to myself, I used to hear that Holy abducts people, and here I am trying to escape and am captured again, I truly am now in the bush. From that moment, I accepted that I was in the bush.'

Payaa's apparent surrender to the new situation after only two days in the bush was likely because of what *lum* means to the Acholi. According to the *Lwo-English Dictionary*, *lum* means 'grass' (Odonga, 2005, 142). However, *lum* can also mean 'bush,' a mysterious place where people do not go without good reason, or for a prolonged period of time. In Acholi cosmology, as in many African cultures, the dual character of the bush is characterized by the bounty it yields for human sustenance and the dangers it harbours for the unsuspecting. It is a place where wild animals and *gemo* (evil spirits) live. It is a place that promises both the sweetness of *kic ogo*, wild honey collected from the hollow of large trees, and the sting of *nyig kic* (bees). 'Whatever happens in the bush remains in the bush' is a popular Acholi saying. It means that what happens in the seclusion of the bush should not be brought home since this may bring bad luck or evil spirits.

Furthermore, in relation to the bush, the Acholi distinguish between *paco* (ancestral home) and *ot* (residential home). The ancestral home is where one's ancestors are buried and where the *abila* (ancestral shrine) is located. When an Acholi leaves the ancestral home to settle elsewhere, say, in Kampala or abroad, he is said to have a residential home in the bush. However well built, the residential home is seen as a temporary place of abode because every Acholi expects to return to the ancestral home where, eventually, he or she will one day be laid to rest.

Payaa, like the other informants in this study, was keenly aware that the very act of *wot ii lum* in the company of the LRM/A forced the abductees to assume new identities in the eyes of the civil population that made them indistinguishable from those who had voluntarily gone into the bush to join the rebels. The length of time the abductee spent in the bush was irrelevant since any form of association with the LRM/A, however brief, was considered abhorrent. In this way, LRM/A abductees become *olum* upon abduction, a stigmatized identity that makes it difficult for them to escape back to their villages where they risk arrest or even death. Indeed, abductees killed by the UPDF were deemed rebels, while those lucky enough to be rescued were paraded as abductees saved from the LRM/A rebels.

Moreover, fully aware of what *wot ii lum* means to the Acholi, the LRM/A exploited this phase to construct the image of a potent, viable, and deadly insurgent not to be trifled with. Some of the boy child combatants wear *wic anginya* (dreadlocks), which are unfamiliar to the Acholi.[9] Girl combatants, who would in their normal lives in the villages wear beautifully plaited hair, instead let their hair grow unkempt. The sight of young boys in dreadlocks and girls with unkempt hair would have instructed newly abducted children that they were about to enter a new environment that had its own rules and way of looking at things. Ironically, albeit against their will, abductees became guilty by association for coming into contact with the fearsome rebels.

Finally, *wot ii lum* involves the most perilous and arduous physical exertion of walking for long stretches at a time. My informants often referred to *can matek* (intense suffering) or *piny marac* (bad surroundings) to describe their experiences during this time. Over several weeks, even months, children weighed down by looted items are marched relentlessly, often without water and food. Children perish at this stage, often too weak to take another step forward. Those too weak to walk are either abandoned or, more commonly, clubbed to death with *lokile* (small axe) (Dolan, 2009). One participant described his intense suffering this way: 'The pattern became, walk, spend the night, walk, and spend the night. We started again in the morning and bathed at two in the afternoon once we reached a big body of water. One day, we walked the entire day, no food, no cooking. On the second day we finally found water at two in the afternoon. We sat down. The permission was given for people to go bathe, and start cooking.'

The LRM/A, in effect, used *wot ii lum* as a military strategy and element of control. Lacking motorized transportation, the LRM/A made walking a part of the long war, often covering as much as eighty kilometres or more in one day (Dolan, 2009). It served to toughen up the abductees and make them more knowledgeable about bush craft, teaching them to read signs on the trails that less trained eyes might ignore. According to Ringo Otigo, who witnessed the abduction of the Aboke girls, the commanders spent many days moving back and forth over many kilometres. 'We turned around and came back. After returning, we turned around and walked back to the mouth of the river that very same day.'

Ringo Otigo goes on to say that 'it appeared that they wanted to confuse the students before taking them to Sudan. They planned to move back and forth so that the students could not remember the direction being taken.' Wọt *ii lum*, then, also served another purpose, that of confusing the abductees, in effect initiating the brainwashing phase. This was what the LRM/A referred to as *lwooko wii cibilan*.

Lwoko wii Cibilan (*Washing the Civilian Mind*)

In the *lwoko wii cibilan* phase, the LRM/A uses extreme physical exertion and beating to transform timid village children into toughened LRM/A recruits. It is akin to what communist China of the 1950s referred to as *hsi nao* – washing the brain –which aimed to reform those seen as anti-revolution into fervent supporters of communist ideology (Hunter, 1951; Hunter, 1956; Lifton, 1961; Schein, 1961). According to K. Taylor (2006), 'brainwashing aims to achieve behavioural change, but behaviour is secondary: its main goal is to change the thoughts of its victims to fit its preferred ideology' (97). In the case of the LRM/A, washing the civilian mind meant extreme physical torture of abductees. Both Jola Amayo and Ringo Otigo, whose stories are detailed later in the book, were subjected to serious corporal punishment that nearly took their lives. Camconi Oneka recalled how, over several days, the LRM/A had threatened to kill him as a fresh abductee, each time sparing his life. Finally, when they reached the destination under Kilak Hill, he was summoned to appear before the rebels:

> They said they needed to exorcise the *cen*, evil spirit in me. They ordered me to lie down, and they caned me one hundred and fifty times. Then I got up. They asked me when I was abducted, and I told them that I was abducted on such and such a day. They then asked where I was abducted from, and I told them, 'I was abducted from Camp Coo-pe.' Then they asked, 'Who abducted you?' and I told them that I did not know. They said, 'How could a big person like you be abducted just like that?' They told me that I should lie down again, and they hit me on the back seven times with the machete. The skin on my back peeled off.

As part of the torture, the LRM/A constantly reminded the abductees that they could be dealt with 'as if you are not Acholi.' The implication and the intended message to the abductees was that the Acholi, as an ethnic entity defined by a common culture and language, look out for each other. Presumably, when one was being treated as an Acholi, one did not suffer the dehumanizing indignities meted out to those considered 'not Acholi.' In essence, the LRM/A linked torture directly to identity formation of the child combatant, distinguishing those deemed to be Acholi from those who were not. Following orders and doing as one was told qualified an abductee as an Acholi and ensured no pain, whereas working against the wishes of the LRM/A brought excruciating pain. As Can Kwo recalled, abductees quickly understood what they needed to do as Acholi in order to survive:

> On certain days, beating was administered to all when a recruit escaped. To get rid of any further thought of escape, in the rebels' way of thinking, we needed to be called on, be given thorough beating before being given stern warnings. The warning given to you was very simple: Should anyone attempt to escape, the sentence is death. Or should one of you escape, you will all be killed. With that, you start thinking that your fellow recruit should not escape before you do. If my fellow abductees are about to escape, I need to spy on them so that I don't die. That was the politics that we began to consider, to think about, forcing us to keep an eye on each other.

But, as we see in the *neko dano* phase, the LRM/A made killing a necessary process in the transformation of the child abductee into a child combatant.

Neko Dano *(Killing a Person)*

Neko dano was the LRM/A's most crucial phase in transforming children into combatants. Abductees were forced to participate in killing or to witness a fellow abductee being killed (Cook, 2007; de Temmerman, 2001; McDonnell & Akallo, 2007). Ocitti (1973) points out that death is universally feared by the Acholi, and every attempt is made to carry out the proper rituals to pacify the spirit of the dead. The Acholi believe that *cen* (the evil spirit of the dead), whether killed in war or in a domestic dispute, returns to haunt the perpetrator and extended family. So serious is the issue of killing that special purifications are required to rid the perpetrator of the impending *cen*.[10] Ocitti writes: 'The Acholi respected dead bodies for fear that their spirits might become vengeance ghosts if neglected. By following certain rites in burial, the "living dead" were believed to feel respected and would therefore refrain from making trouble with the living' (23).

Furthermore, in the Acholi culture as in other African traditional cultures which abhor violence generally and forbid killing specifically, a person who kills another is said to have *kwa cwiny* (red heartedness) or *col cwiny* (dark heartedness), either of which denotes anger, extreme narcissism, and evil, qualities considered by the Acholi as anti-family and anti-community. p'Bitek (1966) writes of the Acholi attitude towards someone regarded or known to be a killer:

> A woman with a black heart
> Who kills people with poison
> Is called Akwir or Anek   (p'Bitek, 1966, 130)

But, according to my informants, not every abducted child was forced to kill someone, though all abductees would have witnessed the killing of someone within the first few weeks of living with the LRM/A. The LRM/A, it seemed, exploited the Acholi fear of death and killing in three different ways. First, the killings of civilians could be interpreted as a multipurpose military strategy which aimed, foremost, to ensure that the whereabouts of the rebels remained a secret. This seemed to be the case when, as recounted in the Introduction, Miya Aparo encountered killing for the first time after abduction. She had developed a serious leg swelling that made it impossible for her to walk. The rebel commanders had haggled over whether they should kill her since she could no longer walk. Instead, a rebel named Okello Triga commandeered an old man to push a bicycle with Miya placed on the carrier. To Miya's horror, when the services of the old man were no longer needed, the rebels killed him.

Second, making abductees watch and participate in killing served as powerful reminders of the fate that could befall those who disobeyed orders or attempted to escape. Death served as a deterrent to would-be escapees, making it clear that they would meet a similar fate should they attempt to run away.

Third, killing was deliberately trivialized, it was casual, without any apparent reason, and it was final. But it also trained the children not to be afraid of killing, inuring them to the sight of blood. The killing of the old man would have brought home to Miya Aparo the Acholi saying of *wot ki too* (walking with death), the idea that death strikes at any time, and one must always be mindful to do everything one can to stay alive. The ordinariness, some would say the banality, of the violent circumstance of the old man's death, combined with the cultural fear associated with death, would have been a strong psychological barrier against any thought of escape or not following LRM/A orders. Camconi Oneka was forced to kill two men in the second week of his captivity. He had participated in an LRM/A raid on a community centre where many civilians were abducted. As they marched back to the rebels' base at the foot of Kilak Hill, his handlers asked him to kill two of the captured civilian men:

> At first I hesitated, trying to bide my time, hoping I would not have to kill the men. The rebels told me that should I continue wasting time, I would be killed in the place of the condemned men. Given the level of threat, guns pointing at me, I decided there was no point in dying. I decided to kill the men; I killed them with a club. I clubbed them to death. Then the rebels told me to lick the blood of the dead men – it was the kind of threat which made me hate the bush completely. I licked the blood. Then they told me to scoop the blood in my cupped hands and take it to them. I did that, and they told me to take it back. I returned it to the ground.

At a deeper cultural level, ordering children to participate in killing accustomed them to the terrifying notion of being *luneko* (sing. *laneko*), killers who must forever bear the collective guilt that arises from the act of killing. It was a significant severing of the moral bridge that connected the child who grew up in the familiar culture of the village, where life is respected, to his or her new identity as a combatant, for whom killing is part of the job description.

Aware of Acholi's deep antipathy to death, the LRM/A forced the children to kill other children, thereby making them confront their own Acholi cultural upbringing in which heavy sanctions and taboos were associated with killing and the very notion of death was too difficult to countenance let alone something that one could personally bring about. In essence, the abductees were forced to choose between two equally repulsing options, suffering instant death for disobeying orders or taking an innocent life, an act that is strictly forbidden in Acholi culture and so, if committed, would result in them losing their cultural sense of being human persons. By opting to participate in killing, the abductees secured their survival, but in the process they were pushed to relinquish the notion of *leng cwiny* (clean heartedness or purity of heart), a cardinal virtue in Acholi culture and a requirement for retaining membership in the community from which they were abducted and to which they hoped to return one day. In fact, Acholi civil society regards returning child combatants as killers who, although they may have been forced to commit killings to avoid being killed themselves, need to be purified with the appropriate traditional cleansing ceremonies in which the returnees set things right with the spirits of those they killed (Liu Institute for Global Issues, Gulu District NGO Forum, & Ker Kwaro Acholi, 2005, 39–43).

Wiiro Kom *(Anointing with Shea Butter)*

In the *wiiro kom* phase, LRM/A abductees are made to undergo an elaborate ritual involving the use of a mixture of *moo yaa* (shea-butter oil) and water; the latter must be either collected rain water or water taken from a stream early in the morning before anyone else has touched it. Some of the informants were told that the mixture is a *camoflast* (camouflage) which protects the rebel soldiers from enemy bullets. Although the practice of anointing the body before battle has historical precedence in Acholi culture (Dolan, 2009), there is no evidence that the LRM/A, unlike Lakwena's HSM (Behrend, 1998), believed in its efficacy in protecting its army in a very specific way, say, from bullets. Instead, I would argue that the *wiiro kom* ritual was carefully orchestrated to convey a different meaning to the abductees. *Moo yaa* is traditionally used by the Acholi as a rare food delicacy, eaten with *dek ngor*, the thickened sauce of split cowpeas, and *kwon bel* (millet bread). It is also used at the installation of a new *rwot* (chief). Equally inescapable is the parallel to the Christian rite of baptism in which the body is anointed with holy water, signifying entry into a new community of believers. Well aware that the abductees understand perfectly the concept and the context of *moo yaa* in Acholi culture, namely its use only on the most auspicious of occasions, the LRM/A applied it to the abductees chest area as a sign of admission into the rebel movement. In this case, *wiiro kom* ritual became a form of identity card, a signifier that the recruit had crossed the threshold into the fold of the LRM/A.

The purification ceremony itself takes place in the 'Yards,' an open-air space, and is presided over by a 'controller yard.'[11] The space may also be used as a gathering spot for spirit possession and for open-air addresses by LRM/A commanders. As one informant described the ceremony:

> Once we got to the main camp, arrangements were made to have all the new abductees brought to the yard to be anointed with Lakwena's oil so that we become the army of Lakwena. If you are not anointed, you are not allowed to eat with those who have been anointed.
>
> During the purification ceremony, you took off your clothes, remaining bare-chested, and a gun is handed to you, before you step forward to be anointed. There were lines of people singing. The controller yard took some water, oil and a rock, and walked toward you, and circled you three times, placed the stone in the oil, then poured water on top, and then put the mixture on your body. The stone was placed on a string around your neck. Once that was done, you passed.

However, not all cases of anointing abductees take place in elaborate ceremonies. Often, junior LRM/A soldiers administer the *moo yaa* to abductees in the field. Camconi Oneka and Can Kwo were anointed without ceremony. For Can Kwo, undergoing the *wiiro kom* ritual marked his entry into the bush as a rebel combatant: 'The putting of *moo yaa* on my chest made me realize that, okay, what I am about to do is different from what I normally do. Furthermore, I discovered that the way I was spoken to was not to teach me. Instead, your existence was now shaped by forceful demands and beating for no reason. Those are my first experiences.'

Payaa Mamit, accused of 'speaking with the Devil,' was made to 'raise my arms so that if my body was possessed by evil spirit, it would be chased away.' Although nothing happened even with a prolonged prayer session, 'they sprinkled water on me, and put some shea-butter on my chest and my back.' In the case of Jola Amayo, who had just suffered a serious snakebite, the anointing served a dual purpose. It marked her as one chosen to become an LRM/A abductee, and also served as an antidote to the snake poison in her swollen leg:

> They came and found me lying outside beside the house. 'What is wrong with this child?' they asked.
> 'The child, yesterday, was bitten by a snake.'
> One of them said, 'Mother, God will help this child, she will recover.'
> They had with them shea-butter oil mixed with red substance obtained from the stream. Once they place the mixture on you, you would be abducted as a matter of course. One of them said, 'The child's leg will heal within three days.' The man then came and rubbed the oily mixture on my leg. 'We will come back to check on how the child is doing, tomorrow we will return to check on her.' The following day, they returned and checked on me.

The *wiiro kom* ritual also bestowed privileges that came with membership in the LRM/A. The abductees could now undergo military training, eat communally with the general LRM/A population, go to the battlefront, get married, and, generally, be better treated than those who had just been abducted and had not undergone the purification process.

Purification also heightens the gender differences for further control of abductees. Based on traditional Acholi belief that *kwe coo* (purifying the male) is different from *kwee mon* (purifying the female), the controller yard circles boys three times while girls are circled four times. As well, during their menstrual cycles, LRM/A regulations forbid females from participating in any communal life including fetching water, cooking food, or touching anything that a man might later touch. There is a similarity between this practice and the edict in the Book of Leviticus (15: 19–22) restricting the activities of any woman experiencing a discharge: 'And if a woman have an issue and her issue in her flesh be blood, she shall be put apart seven days: and whosoever toucheth her shall be unclean until the even.' Such gendered restrictions on girl abductees served to remind them that they are still expected to serve and remain subservient to the commands of men. At the same time, restrictions on female abductees also reminded the boy abductees of their role

Joseph Kony with young 'wives,' Jabuleini (Jabelein), southern Sudan, 1997. The two girls immediately flanking him were abducted from St Mary's Secondary School in Aboke on 9 October 1996.

Bare-chested Joseph Kony in his *otogo* (male house), Juba, southern Sudan, 1998.

Betty Ayero (Apaco), an abductee pregnant with Kony's child, Juba, southern Sudan, 1998. It is not known what happened to her.

Kony's sons by his wife Fatuma, Juba, 1998 – both died in a wild bush fire in 2000.

Lieutenant-Colonel Paul Okodi, personal secretary to Joseph Kony, welcoming Kony (in gray short-sleeved suit), Jabuleini (Jabelein), southern Sudan, 1998. Seated in white shirt is Brigadier Banya.

Kony's son (by his wife Paska), Nisitu, southern Sudan, 1998.

Kony's personal bodyguard Lieutenant Ogila with one of Kony's sons, Nisitu, 1998.

Lieutenant-Colonel Paul Okodi, with 'wives' Grace, Abu, and Ajok in Aru, southern Sudan, 1997. Okodi was reported killed by a Uganda army helicopter gunship on 5 January 2004 at Lacek-Ocot in northern Uganda.

Christmas Day, 2000, LRM/A soldiers in camp at Lubangatek, southern Sudan.

Kony's young 'wives' (left to right) Catherine, Doreen (deceased), and Paska Apaco (deceased) in Jabuleini (Jabelein), southern Sudan, 1997.

LRM/A deputy commander Vincent Otti, working camera, Aru, southern Sudan, 1997. Indicted by the ICC in The Hague on 8 July 2005, he was reported executed on Kony's orders on 2 October 2007.

LRM/A senior officers after meal in Jabuleini (Jabelein), 2000. Clockwise, starting with the heavy-set man seated beside the young unidentified LRM/A soldier drinking from cup, are: Sururu Abdalla, Owor Lakati, Sisto Oringa, Mickman Oryang Opuk, Patrick Lumumba, Ceasar Acellam, Livingstone Opiro, and Onen Kamdulu.

as young men (*bulu*), appealing to their sense of masculinity as protectors and fighters who must step forward bravely into battle. Moreover, gender restrictions enabled the LRM/A to maintain in the abductees' residential home in the bush the same paternalistic structure found in Acholi ancestral homes. It allowed abductees to feel at home away from home.

The *wiiro kom* ritual is also instructive during this period of transformation in that it allows child combatants to see themselves, not as 'victims' within a violent society, but rather as participants in a new cultural landscape replete with violence and uncertainty, in which they can no longer insist on life as it once was. After purification, they are forced to look at the LRM/A as their new family. They can now take the step of *donyo ii gang* (entering the residential homestead).

Wiiro kom ritual also acts as a form of control over abductees, and eventually over the child combatants as they move into the field. After the purification rituals are completed, according to my informants, abductees are told that escape is futile because the magical qualities of the *moo yaa* would ensure that would-be escapees falter in their resolve, turn around, and return back to the rebel camp to a certain death. Moreover, as a symbolic crossing over from civilian life to a soldier's life, the ritual comes with many responsibilities in the form of *cik* (prohibitions). Smoking, unsanctioned sex (only a most senior commander, usually Kony himself, decides when a girl or boy is ready for living together), alcohol, and other vices are strictly prohibited. So is the eating of pork, honey, certain fruits, and eggs (also see Dolan, 2009, 81). Speaking to a *dako ot* (married wife) is strictly forbidden. *Tuku kwele*, playing of a sexual nature or touching between a boy and a girl, is also not allowed. While these sanctions are part of the Acholi culture and belief system (for example, an adulterous person dies at the battlefront or alcohol indulgence attracts enemy bullets), they can also be found in other modern armies where professional standards forbid fraternization between the sexes in order to ensure discipline and self-control within the ranks.[12]

My informants stated that the penalty for breaking an interdiction after being purified with *moo yaa* was severe, usually taking the form of corporal punishment. As well, abductees were made to believe that a bigger misfortune awaited them in the future, say, during combat. Even after Can Kwo Obato had left the LRM/A behind, he still believed that breaking the rules against casual sex brought bad luck: 'As soon as you have had casual sex, and do not confess, you will get hit by a bullet.

However, if you confess, you must be beaten to clear away your sin. If you are not beaten, you die. I saw that with my own eyes, many died because of it.'

Donyo ii Gang (*Entering a Homestead*)

Donyo ii gang is a critical phase in the liminal repurposing of Acholi culture in order to control abductees and ensure that they remain active combatants for a long time. With this in mind, over the last twenty years of the war, the LRM/A has painstakingly recreated Acholi villages in various camps, including those in Aruu, Owiny ki Bul, Jabelein, Palotaka, Nisitu, and Garamba forest. The homes in the villages are modelled after those found in an Acholi ancestral homestead. *Ot lum atota*, a circular-shaped home with grass-thatched roof, is built along the edges of a clean-swept circular compound. The roof of each house in the compound is carefully thatched with *lum raa*, elephant grass of varying lengths that form ridges running around the building. A low doorway is constructed facing the open space of the compound, and a functional door made of wood, corrugated iron, or combination of wood and grass is put in place.

The *jokon* (female house) doubles as the cooking place as well as the sleeping place for little children and women. Meanwhile, *ot otogo* (male house), used by the patrilineal head of the household, is set slightly apart from the circle of *jokon*. Boy recruits stay in their own *otogo*, which may not be as elaborately built as the *otogo* where the head of the homestead lives, and is usually set farther away from the main compound. The open space in the middle of the yard is *dyekal*, which serves as a communal space for all members whose homes face it. Often, there is a spot in the middle of the space with burned-out remains of logs and ashes – this is the *wang-oyo* (the place of the log fire), which traditionally is used by the Acholi as a gathering spot in the evening.

Each homestead has several *deero*, small round buildings on raised stilts used as granaries for storing dried foodstuff harvested from the fields. Traditional Acholi food items such as *bel* (millet), *nyim* (sesame) *lapena* (peas), *kabir* (sorghum), *pul* (groundnuts), and *layata mutere* (dried sweet potato peels) are stored in the granaries. Following Acholi cultural requirements, only the owner of a *deero* has the right to open and remove food from it. Anyone caught opening a *deero* belonging to a neighbour has committed theft, and is severely punished. In time of plentiful harvest, food is stored in the granary. Miya Aparo recalled such a period: 'Our harvest, we had thirteen granaries full of food and a big enclosed hut filled with sorghum and dried sweet potato peels.'

In time, it is not unusual for the abductees to feel some sense of belonging and kinship to the members of household to which they have been assigned, often referring to the head of the household as *baba* (father) and the most senior wife in the house as *mami* or *mama* (mother).[13] Ringo Otigo was sent to live with the LRM/A bush doctor who had shown kindness to him during the march to Sudan. Payaa Mamit recalled her life in the home of Vincent Otti, the LRM/A's second-in-command:

> At first, I was placed in the hands of Otti Vincent, who, at the time, was not yet Kony's deputy. I stayed in the care of Otti like his own daughter. He did not want anyone to send me to do anything. When I became a young girl of a certain age, the men coming off the convoy would attempt to woo me. I would tell Otti immediately and he would tell them to leave me alone.
>
> Otti Vincent never mistreated me. He would teach us, telling us to relax ... Among the girls he cared for, we lived in his home as part of our duty as soldiers in position. He had his wives. Two of us were living with one of his wives. When he added other wives to his household, we had already left.
>
> His wife took care of us. She gave us everything we needed to eat. But sometimes, she was not there. When there was soap, she told us to take it and go wash our bodies. 'Take this oil and put on your body,' she would say. She gave us clothes, khakis to wear.

It was within the recreated residential homestead that LRM/A girl abductees learned to become not only soldiers but also homemakers. Girls who were purified were now given away to officers and commanders as wives. Girls who had not begun their menstrual cycles were given to officers who looked after them as daughters. Miya Aparo recalled this arrangement: 'The time came – when I was abducted I had not yet had my period, I was too young – in 1997 when I began having my period. In the bush, when you were young, and had not yet had your period, you were not given away to a man. As soon as you began having period, you were given away to a man. I was given to man, became pregnant, and shortly after gave birth.'

Meanwhile, when it became known that Amal Ataro had begun having her menstrual cycle, LRM/A leader Joseph Kony asked her to become one of his wives. This, Amal said, caused her many sleepless nights because she had grown to regard Kony as a father figure. She resisted at first, doing everything she could in order to avoid going to bed with him, but the LRM/A leader told her bluntly that 'whatever you do, you are going to be my wife.' She asked him how she could be his wife when all along he had called her 'my daughter.' She reminded the LRM/A leader that, in Acholi culture, a father does not sleep with his daughter. Kony reportedly replied, 'I only did that [call her his daughter] because I could see that you were always thinking about your parents and I wanted to take their place.' Amal then told Kony to kill her instead, and he simply replied, 'You try to provoke me and see what will happen.' In the end, after enduring a serious beating, Amal finally went to bed with Kony, and he brutally raped her. She conceived a child that very night.

At one level, one could interpret the horrific rape of Amal by Joseph Kony, whom the young girl looked up to as a father figure, as having nothing to do with cultural repurposing. Where is culture in such a cowardly crime perpetrated against a defenceless young girl by a war criminal? But a deeper look at the same act suggests its real motive. In fact, confining the analysis to the criminality of the heinous act by the LRM/A leader misses the deeper cultural context in which the act is buried. Fully aware that Amal regards him as a father figure, and that the young girl understands that incest and rape are taboos in the Acholi culture, Kony deliberately targets this cultural belief itself. He rapes Amal not because he wants the young victim to rethink the cultural knowledge she possesses, thereby somehow leading her to conclude that incest and rape are acceptable in the Acholi culture. Rather, the rape is committed precisely to undermine the foundation of Amal's cultural understanding of the meaning of life itself. In this case, the message to Amal is simply that nothing else matters, certainly not the cultural taboos around which she previously constructed her identity. Nothing else matters except total allegiance to the LRM/A, and doing the rebels' bidding.

Indeed, inside the LRM/A camp, young male abductees were often forced to become *wegi ot* (fathers of the house) to demonstrate their masculinity by providing for their newfound families. As *won ot*, a young man was expected to speak with authority over matters pertaining to his household. He could not be seen to be weak in the eyes of the other abductees since he was the head of the household. He must be courageous, brave, and enthusiastic, even in battle. Meanwhile, as *min ot* (mother of the house), a young female abductee was expected to serve her husband and bear his children.[14] In the community of the LRM/A, she was expected to perform all the duties of a wife, cooking, taking care of the house, and, when needed, carrying a gun to defend the homestead.

Perhaps as testimony to the degree to which the LRM/A attempted to integrate the abductees into family structures, the death of the household head was occasion for deep sorrow. The repercussions were felt throughout the household as the family was broken up and widows redistributed to other officers. Such eventualities, according to the female child combatants, were often the harshest moment of *kwo matek* (difficult life). Miya Aparo recalled having such an experience when the young man she was living with was accused of trying to escape and was executed by Kony: 'When the men were killed by firing squad, we entered a difficult period. Already saddled with children, you were labelled the "wife of a rebel" – meaning the condemned men were planning to defect to government forces. There were painful beatings; everything was taken away from us. We had cultivated many fields, and had a good harvest. We were farming, making charcoal which was taken by vehicle and sold in Juba. We had enough money to care for us.'

By contrast, returning from military operations often provided occasion for celebration. At those times, families were reunited and looted provisions were distributed to everyone.

Pwonyo Mony *(Military Training)*

The *pwonyo mony* phase usually comes after the *wiiro kom* ritual in which the kidnapped child is inducted into the LRM/A. The training lasts from a few weeks to several months. It mainly consists of using light weaponry, learning the different parts of a machine-gun, how to disassemble and assemble a weapon, and how to lay ambush. Abductees slated for the medical corps as *dakta* (doctor) or as *nac* (nursing assistant) were not expected to fight in battles, but they were required to carry their weapons at all times during combat.

Most child abductees learn on the job, walking in the convoys alongside more experienced LRM/A combatants, picking up the skills needed to lay an ambush, form a defensive line, make a safe retreat in the face of withering enemy fire, and, in general, think like soldiers. Soon after his abduction, Camconi Oneka was forced to accompany LRM/A soldiers into battle. In shootouts, his handler steadied the muzzle of the machine-gun on the boy's bared shoulder while he fired at the enemy.

'The skin peeled off my shoulders because of the heat from the gun barrel,' he reported. Can Kwo, for his part, recalled the occasion when he began to think of himself as a soldier: 'I know when I began thinking that I am now a soldier ...We were being trained on marching and how to take apart and assemble a rifle ... I realized at the time that the business of being a soldier had begun, and this was what I was brought for.'

Learning to survive in combat, where child abductees depended on more experienced fighters for survival, further fostered and reinforced their sense of belonging and solidarity within the rebel organization. Over time, there was a melting of residual suspicion and fear as the child abductees began to feel as part of the LRM/A family.

Cito ii Tic *(Going to Work)*

The *cito ii tic* phase concludes the journey to becoming a child combatant. By this time, the child abductees would have been forced to do the bidding of their abductors, kill a person or watch a killing, undergo purification rituals, and become part of an LRM/A household in a home away from home. Effectively, he or she has left the familiar cultural perspective in which the life of another person is sacrosanct, and has entered one in which the life of another is not worth a moment's consideration. As Ringo Otigo put it, 'in a way, I gave myself to do what they wanted done so that I could preserve my life.'

Gradually, my informants viewed being chosen for *cito ii tic* as a privilege that promised rewards, since items looted during an operation were often kept by those who did the looting. When he was offered the hand of a widow, Ringo Otigo declined to take her. 'I told them, at the moment, I am not in a position to care for this woman, and do not have any clothes that she can wear; to take her, I need to go on expeditions as others do.' Meanwhile, having become a young mother with a child, Miya Aparo was forbidden from going into battle any more. She told me, 'There, once you had a child, going on operations to loot food was no longer an option. Those without children went. The rest of you worked the fields in the headquarters.'

In any case, over time, the LRM/A used the phase of *cito ii tic* to build solidarity among abductees by sending them on military operations where they further bonded as comrades-in-arms. In this phase, abductors and abductees become friends, family to each other, trusted and relied upon as protection against attacks. The camaraderie enables the child to begin to see the world as a matter of 'us' against 'them.'

Noticeably, at the start of their captivity, the informants used the word *adwi* (rebel) to describe the LRM/A while government troops were called simply *mony* (soldiers) or *mony pa gabumente* (government soldiers). However, as time progressed, abductees referred to the LRM/A as *mony* (soldiers) while the UPDF troops became *lumerok* (the enemies) or even *adwi* (rebels). Furthermore, when informants spoke of LRM/A casualties, they used the word *dano* (people), as in *dano dong oto ma pe wace* (many people died beyond words). But, when referring to UPDF casualties, they used *joni* (those people), as in *waneko joni madwong* (we killed a lot of those people). The linguistic change denotes the feeling of transformation as they went from being abductees who viewed the LRM/A rebels as the enemy to insiders who identified with the rebels, whom they now considered as family. In this way, as examined in more detail in the next two chapters, the LRM/A achieved control of abductees in all their actions and behaviour as soldiers.

In conclusion, the LRM/A's brutal exploitation of Acholi culture as a war resource succeeded precisely because the abductees were forced to accept new stigmatized identities without giving up the original, desired identities that they had earlier formed in their own villages. In chapters 4 and 5, Jola Amayo and Ringo Otigo provide detailed personal stories of how as abductees they learned to reconstruct new identities in order to manage the violent environment of war (Martin-Baro, 1996; Ressler, Boothby, & Steinbock, 1988) without letting go of their earlier identities.

Chapter Four

The Jola Amayo Stories

Jola Amayo is a thirty-three-year-old Acholi mother of three children, aged two, six, and twelve. She was twelve years old when she was abducted by the LRM/A, and she subsequently spent twelve years as a CI soldier in northern Uganda and southern Sudan. Although Jola Amayo attended three different schools, she had barely completed Grade Three when she was abducted. She blames a combination of bad luck (her father passed away) and the worsening security situation due to war for 'growing up like that with no proper education.'

She agreed to provide details of her time with the LRM/A after she was asked to do so by the director of GUSCO, Robert Okeny. We met at the GUSCO offices on 21 July 2008, at 10:03 a.m. in the morning. The sun was just above the trees, casting what the Acholi call *lak nyango*, the soft mid-morning glow that precedes the intense heat of midday.

In the room that served as a library, I arranged two wooden chairs by the window that overlooked the road leading to Gulu town centre. I could see children in school uniforms walking along the dusty road, noisy motorcycle taxis known as *boda-boda* rattling by, women with babies tied on their backs and loads on their heads walking to the market, and the occasional car raising yellow dust. Inside the room, it was already getting humid and warm. I had my back to the window, facing Jola Amayo, who sat quietly, waiting to be spoken to.

What Jola Amayo lacked in formal education, she made up in common sense. In telling her story, she was alert, matter-of-fact, and incredibly gifted in remembering details of events that happened to her prior to, during, and after her life as a CI soldier. It was just as well that she is a natural storyteller because I spent just six hours with her, during which she narrated as much as she remembered or cared to remember.

The Cultural Context of an Acholi Child
prior to Abduction by the LRM/A

Jola Amayo was born on 20 November 1978 in the village of Ot Ngic, Omoro County, northeast of Gulu town in northern Uganda. Her birth was just five months shy of the end of the dictatorial reign of Idi Amin Dada in 1979. The fourth in a family of seven children, she had two sisters and four brothers. Her parents were peasant farmers who eked out a living by planting cotton, simsim, cassava, and beans. Most of the money from the produce paid the poll tax and school fees, while the rest went towards buying clothes and other household necessities. She remembered those days well, especially her close relationship with her parents, who taught her about personal integrity, morality, and Acholi tradition:

> My father loved and used to teach me things, saying, 'One day when I am no longer here, protect your name among other girls, especially when you marry in another clan, show respect to your in-laws. I do not want your hands to steal. You are still young, but stealing is not for a young girl or a young boy, instead work hard with your own hands. If you work hard with your hands – work does not kill – you will have an easier life among others.' He used to teach us, saying, 'If you are born poor, you learn by sitting beside the food granary, away from everyone else' – that was a teaching he used to teach us. He displayed his love for us through his teachings. In the evening around the log fire, he would tell us folktales. As we separated the simsim seed from the pods, he posed riddles, told folktales, teaching us at the same time.
>
> If he was not teaching us through stories, he would teach us Acholi traditional dance. He used to drink some beer, and when he returned in the evening, he would teach us how to dance Acholi dances, and other ancestral customs. He would say, 'When our fathers were still alive, they used to teach us in this manner, telling us, "You must live this way, never look down on anyone, when you see a leper, a crippled leper, when he comes to your home, and asks for water, give him water. Even when you come across someone who crawls on all fours, don't despise him, you must help him. When you meet a blind person on the pathway, do not despise her, you must help her."' Those are some of the teachings he taught us among many other excellent ones.

The closeness of family and extended family also taught Jola early on the importance of interdependence for support and to resolve disputes.

As a girl growing in an Acholi village where the 'good daughter' was judged by her ability to cook and care for her family and extended kin, she could depend on her mother and grandmother to teach her important skills:

> When we were little, our mother cooked for us because we were too young. When a lot of food needed to be made, my mother would do the cooking; but when it was everyday cooking, my mother would say, 'Peel the cassava, put it in the cooking place, and prepare peas in a pot and put it to cook. When the peas are ready, try roasting the simsim, should you burn it, that's your problem to take care of. If it is not burnt, put the simsim in the mortar and pound it and if that's not enough, prepare it anyway.' And if the simsim was prepared well we would pound it in the mortar, and if not, we would rush to grandmother's house, she would be home, she would then grind it into smooth paste. When simsim was ready, she would come, cook, and we would eat.
>
> When I visited my grandmother, she would teach us, saying, 'When we are cooking later today, stay close to the cooking place, and do not ignore cooking because cooking is life. If you are lazy, you will not eat, you will sleep with hunger. If told to do something, you run away, that's not a child who can be taught anything, a child who will never listen to her mother.' My grandmother taught us a lot of good things, including how to play such games as dini-dini.[1] As well, she taught us that when caring for twins, there should be a ritual ceremony to bless the twins and you. She showed us everything, this thing is done this way, that one is done the other way, grandmother taught us all.

Jola and her siblings attended a local school where her view of life was slowly formed, including the idea that good things happen to good people, and bad things to bad people. Jola's conception of good and bad was tested and reinforced at home, and by subsequent events that happened to her. As she put it, 'Mother used to teach us, saying, "If you despise others you meet with accidents later in life."' She therefore worked hard at being a good daughter, friend, and neighbour. She had a best friend with whom she spent a lot of her spare time. They took time helping each other's mother: 'Whenever we visited her house, we helped, and she came to our house, she helped me, she helped fetch water and grind the millet flour. When we went to her house we also fetched water, we ground millet into flour. That's how we helped each other out.'

But as Jola grew older she started to believe that simply being good did not guarantee the good life. There were always other forces at work and not all of them necessarily positive for her or her friends. Her superstitious upbringing slowly oriented Jola to believe in *yir* (sorcery), which, according to Ocitti (1973, 15), is the 'misuse of spiritual powers' to harm someone for reasons known to the sorcerer. In the case of Jola, these evil powers seemed to dog her wherever she went. First, the roof of her schoolhouse collapsed, killing two children outright. Jola escaped with some minor injuries, and moved to a new school. Then her best friend fell victim to a spell cast by a village witch. According to Jola, the witch was a neighbour with a disability who asked the two girls to help her dig cassava. After the girls had completed the chore and brought back the cassava, the witch cooked some food, summoned the girls to eat, and somehow cast a spell on Jola's friend, who started complaining about pain in her leg. Jola remembers the occasion:

We played a while, but [my friend] insisted that the pain was creeping up her leg to the thigh. I said, 'Let's go home.' My mother looked at it and said, 'This one, I think you stepped on a bewitched spot. The girl stepped on a bewitched spot and will have to undergo traditional rituals.' I ran to her house and called her mother. Her mother came and said, 'Once something like this happens, we need to look at Acholi traditional cure.' Her mother went to a diviner where she learned that the woman we helped had placed a spell, and my friend had stepped on it. The spell was meant to kill my friend, but she was not going to die. They started treating her with Acholi traditional treatment, but she was paralysed in one leg; to this day she is crippled.

The woman, meanwhile, was asked to find the antidote to her spell so that my friend would be cured. Unfortunately, her son, her eldest son, got drunk one day, returned home and hit her in the ribs, killing her instantly. Meanwhile, the girl has been crippled to this day. This was not a case of an illness that came accidentally but rather because the woman had a dark heart and people were afraid of her.

Jola claimed that, before the woman witch was murdered by her son, she cast a spell on her and then 'my father called on her with aggression in his voice, forcing her to bring the antidote to the spell, otherwise my arm would have been crippled as well.' These early superstitious beliefs, not atypical among Acholi, led Jola to sum up her philosophy of life this way: 'I was very young at the time, perhaps about seven or eight years old. I still had a childish attitude. But at the time there were many witches in the village, and if you were regarded as a talented child, you could be hurt. If you wanted to stay talented you needed to appear somewhat dumb. If you are an idiot there is no use for you, you live like a crazy person.'

Jola Amayo's seemingly contradictory ideas as a child growing up in an Acholi village mirrored the society's own contradictions. A child should be sharp, responsible, full of life, and, in the case of Jola, able to care for her family at a young age. At the same time, being seen as responsible could bring the envy of neighbours. Children were expected to respect their elders, meaning anybody older than them, responding to every call and request. But they were cautioned to be wary of *yir*, the casting of an evil spell by those who wish ill. It would seem that, for every piece of advice to children, there was a counter-saying that seemed to suggest the exact opposite. For instance, as children, we often heard the saying, *ka lwok pe doko ka twoo* (the place of bathing does not become the place for sunning oneself) – one must not spend too much time in one place lest one is overtaken by misfortune or bad luck. However, we also knew the saying, *rucu rucu omiyo kom lalur gwa* (being in a hurry left the hyena with a rough spotted coat). Jola was immersed in a culture that exalted and rewarded children for personal thrift, initiative, and the ability to take care of things without adult supervision. The child who was independently able to manage and take care of a family was said to have *kwiri*, the keenest ability to do things right. The person without *kwiri* was called *obange* (dull, lazy, and even confused). For fear of being harmed by jealous village neighbours, Jola Amayo had to adopt two seemingly conflicting personas: one was both sharp and responsible, and the other was mellow, understated, and even stupid.

The rebel movement was particularly adept at exploiting superstitious beliefs to further control the children in its custody. From the moment of initiation as a recruit into the ranks of the LRM/A, a child was made to believe that breaking one of the many LRM/A edicts, including those against stealing, pre-marital sex, drinking alcohol, and smoking cigarettes, would result in serious personal misfortune, even death. Furthermore, as Jola would later find out, the LRM/A based itself on the spirit world, whereby the supreme commander, Joseph Kony, listened to the voices of four spirits who directed what he should do, and when to do it. The fact that she believed in the spirit world made Jola Amayo, like many Acholi children who grow in villages where such 'religious beliefs and practices governed their everyday life' (Ocitti, 1973, 15), an excellent candidate for recruitment into the LRM/A. As one informant recalled:

> What I should tell you is that when I was abducted as a child, I found the LRM/A had many edicts. Do not commit adultery, don't smoke, don't drink – that is what I found in the bush. Indeed, there are certain unclean acts committed at home that are forbidden when people are going hunting, such as there should be no sex. When going hunting and there is no disagreement within the hunting party, then the sharp blade of the grass will not cut anyone. Translated to our experience in the bush, it is not the blade of grass but the gun, whereby somebody could get seriously injured, sometimes ending in death. These were the rules that saved my life because I followed them.

Jola Amayo was an attractive target for the LRM/A for another reason. She took on responsibilities that showed intelligence and presence of mind, qualities that the LRM/A valued in abducted children. When her father died, leaving her mother to care for the seven of them, Jola recalled her mother saying, 'Let us work the field.' She took on bigger adult roles in the family, occasionally leading to bitter disputes with her older sister:

> My sister was a difficult person. She would send me to dig cassava in the field, bring it back, peel it, and prepare the ingredients for beer making. At the time I was too young to do much. But I had to go dig the cassava, bring it home, peel it, cook it, crush it, and then prepare the beer. On the appointed day for making the beer, she would order me to make the beer, yet I had little knowledge about what needed to be done. She picked a stick and beat me between the fingers, tearing the skin, sending me running to Grandmother's house.

The need not to feel orphaned carried into Jola's school life where she formed strong bonds with her teachers, all of whom she remembered by name at the time of telling her story almost eighteen years later. The teachers, in turn, took on the role of extended kin, encouraging as well as disciplining Jola. She recalled: 'One teacher I remember so well who used to like me was called Adong – Lapwony Adong has passed away, her home was in Min-Jaa. As well, we had another teacher called Ojul, he is still alive to this moment, and teaching in Adak. Another teacher was called Lukwiya, who also taught in Adak. Both Lukwiya and Lapwony Adong are dead, they are no more.'

For Jola, there was always an explanation for why people act the way they do. The stern teacher was harsh because he had heart disease. The witch who bewitched her was simply jealous of her. She was taught to respect everyone, especially her elders, but she had to be careful not to become a victim of vengeful neighbours. She learned to be a good sister and daughter, but she felt taken advantage of by an older sister who bossed her around, and a manipulative aunt who revelled in taunting the family for its hard luck. She was taught to believe that being good guaranteed a happy life, but her school building collapsed on her, her father died, and her best friend was bewitched. If she believed that bad things can happen to good people, she kept that thought mostly to herself. Yes, evil existed out there, but one was okay so long as one kept his or her part of the bargain. Her preoccupation was to play the good sister, good daughter, good student, and good neighbour, and not to ask why the world was the way it was.

Although she did not know it at the time, Jola was being moulded for the uncertainty of life, getting prepared for the unexpected even while coping with the expected. After all, in her village, life could throw a curve ball at you, and you had better be ready to stare it down. It was not fatalism, but just a simple explanation for why certain events occur.

Prelude to Abduction: Learning to Look the LRM/A in the Face

In 1990, when Joseph Kony's brand of the HSM insurgency transformed itself into LRM/A, Jola Amayo was eleven years old. It was a dangerous time in Jola's village because of the possibility of becoming caught in the crossfire between the rebel forces and the NRM/A. The rebels were wary of villagers, whom they suspected of collaborating with government forces. At the same time, the NRM/A seemed to believe that anyone in the villages was likely a rebel sympathizer or even a full-fledged rebel member. As Jola remembers it, there was general confusion as to which of the two forces could be trusted: 'Sometimes you would hear that, "Ah, these people [rebels] are in a nearby village," you sit tight. When they appeared, you needed fleet feet to escape. What's more, if you ran carelessly into the forest, sometimes you could run into the rebel army. And if you ran carelessly without knowing you might get killed by government forces. People had to dodge between the armies, this way and that.'

Jola Amayo demonstrated early on that she could depend on herself in the absence of her family. On one occasion, she spent the night alone in the bush after she became separated from her family while fleeing from the rebels. This event allowed Jola to gain confidence in her own abilities: 'The next day, as daylight flooded the morning, I climbed a tall tree and spied the direction of home. I climbed down, began walking all the way home. My mother cooked food, we ate. Shortly, another report came that the rebels were nearby, we fled again. When we ran, we stayed there a while. That same day, we received news of the death of a relative. My mother left for the funeral; we remained home alone.'

The tumultuous period just before Jola Amayo was abducted by the LRM/A is instructive of her budding personal agency, that inner wherewithal that enabled her to make choices when confronted with life's crises, what R. Frie (2003) refers to as 'increased self understanding to engage the world in new ways' (18). It was a period of self-discovery that continued through abduction and life in the bush as a child combatant. When she ran to hide from the LRM/A, got lost, and spent the night in the bush, Jola Amayo coolly climbed a tree the next morning to reorient herself to find the way home. Through the ordeal, she discovered the capacity to stay calm in the face of a harrowing experience. In her own mind, she demonstrated the ability not to panic when in a tight jam.

One night, when the rebels were rumoured to be in the neighbourhood of her village, Jola's uncle led her and members of her family to a hideout in the forest. Heavy rainfall, however, drove them back home. As they walked in a single file through the bush, Jola was bitten by a snake. Her leg soon swollen, Jola needed immediate medical attention, which her mother provided: 'My mother ran back, and began cutting herbal antidote for snake poison; as well there was a rubber medication which is placed directly over the snakebite spot. I was given the herbal medication, I drank it, and immediately began vomiting, and meanwhile, the rubbery patch was placed on the snakebite spot. In the morning, I was carried back home. We had just arrived, and barely sat down when the rebels appeared.'

After the snake incident, the rebels finally showed up. Jola controlled her fear to face them, answered them back, and discovered that the rebels were only human. Until then, descriptions of the rebels had come to her mostly through what is known in Acholi villages as *radio kabir*,[2] rumours and news tidbits that are not always reliable. Jola's mother's exchange with the rebels was polite:

They came and found me lying outside beside the house. 'What is wrong with this child,' they asked.

'The child, yesterday, was bitten by a snake.'

One of them said, 'Mother, God will help this child, she will recover.'

They had with them shea-butter oil mixed with red substance obtained from the stream. Once they place the mixture on you, you would be abducted as a matter of course. One of them said, 'The child's leg will heal within three days.'

The LRM/A rebels returned numerous times to check on Jola's condition. Gradually, Jola lost her fear of them. Later on, when she was well enough to walk to the well to fetch water, she ignored news of two rebels' approach, choosing instead to go to the well one more time, saying to herself, 'Well, if they are in Aum village there is enough time to quickly go fetch more water.' While she contemplated hiding like all the other children, she was not in a panic to do so, and consequently the rebels found her at home. She knew to sit down immediately, a submissive gesture intended to show she was not a threat. In the exchange that followed, Jola Amayo showed she could think fast:

They said, 'Little girl, how are things?'

I said, 'All is well.'

'What about your mother?' they asked.

I said, 'My mother is in the garden.'

He said, 'Show us the way.'

'Aa, I don't know this area.'

'You don't know this area, where do you live?' he asked.

I said, 'My home is in Lukwii, I have just come to visit grandmother.'

'Well, since you have come to see your grandmother, get up and show us the way.'

One of the rebels said, 'Let the girl stay. The other day we came and found the girl here, her leg is not well. Her leg is not capable of walking yet, leave her.' They left me.

Abducted: A Night of Burglary, Bullets, and a Baby

Jola Amayo was abducted by the LRM/A on 10 October 1990. She was one of the first waves of children abducted in the early days when the rebel movement was making the transition from a force reliant on adult volunteers to one increasingly dependent on kidnapped children. The abduction happened one night when Jola was sleeping in her house. Jola's mother had gone away to attend yet another funeral, and had returned in the middle of the night without waking her children. When the two rebels came, the usually alert family dog, named Pe Neko Gini Bituc, did not bark, and the family became aware of the danger lurking in the darkness of the night only when the rebels shouted orders to open the door. Jola's older sister tried to shield her younger sibling, while trying to engage the rebels. She answered most of the questions, until the rebels demanded that the family hand over the family radio. In the exchange that ensued, Jola showed that she was not afraid of the rebels, despite their threats:

> They spotted a machete that was stored in the ceiling and pulled it down. They demanded that we give them the radio. We said, 'There is no radio.' By this time one had stepped on my foot and woken me up.
> He asked me, 'Girl, where is the radio?' I said, 'There is no radio.'
> 'There is a radio in this home; it is in a suitcase.'
> We did have a big radio which we had hidden under the bed. He said, 'There is a radio in this house; it should be produced immediately.'
> I said, 'There is no radio in this home.' He said, 'We were directed to this home, this home belongs to – '
> 'Yes, that is the right name but the owner of the home is not here.'
> One of the rebels said, 'You are very lippy, get up.' I stayed in bed, and one of them came and stepped on my foot, saying, 'Get up.' I straightened and sat up.

The rebels, nonetheless, accepted the story that there was no radio in the house, but chose to walk away with Jola in tow. Up to this point, Jola's abduction was both typical and atypical of other abductions. It was typical in that Jola was abducted at night, a time favoured by the LRM/A for taking children away from their homes because darkness afforded cover from possible reprisal by government troops on patrol. It was atypical in that Jola's previous contact with the rebels allowed her to 'understand' how to speak and relate to them. This insider's vantage point was both an advantage and a disadvantage. It was an advantage because she did not fear the rebels, unlike other children who were coming into contact with them for the first time. This maximized her ability to contend with whatever might happen. But, at the same time, Jola's confidence in her ability to handle the rebels was risky, even dangerous, as events later showed. Certainly, the most striking part of her story on the night of her abduction was Jola's inner strength, as reflected in her budding new voice. One of the abductors chides her for being 'lippy,' but that does not stop her from responding to her tormentors. When the rebels threaten Jola with instant death for refusing to show them the path to other homes with radios, she dares them to kill her. What is most interesting is the calm and collected manner of her response in the face of imminent death:

> One said, 'You are kidding, this very moment we are going to give you a thorough beating if you won't show us the way. Tell us where we can find a radio.' There was a man named Nyeko who had a radio; he had just bought it after selling some rice. I said, 'I don't know any of those people.'
>
> He said, 'Well, if you won't tell us anything, we will kill you.'
>
> I said, 'If you are going to kill me, go ahead, and kill me because I don't know anything about this area.' We began walking together; suddenly they heard a radio nearby. One said, 'What about that radio making the noise?'
>
> I said, 'Yes, that's a radio making noise.' We walked, moving further down.

When Jola chooses to answer, *Yes, that's a radio making noise*, she knows that her statement may be construed by the rebels as a sign that she knew all along which homes had radios and had lied to them. But she takes the risk, making it look as if she, too, was finding out for the first time that some homes in the area indeed had radios. In the face of certain danger, Jola's burgeoning intuitiveness serves her well. It reassures her, just as it calms down the rebels, who might otherwise have taken rash action against the little girl. Her self-assured, extemporaneous performance is the product of her years growing up in an Acholi village where one learns how to speak respectfully to one's elders, to answer back without sounding cocky, arrogant, or deceitful. She is, one could argue, fashioning her survival strategies literally on the spot, creating a persona that is sweet and innocent yet not dumb enough to be disposed of by the rebels, who will only keep her as long as they think she is useful to them. A not-so-smart child cannot possibly be useful to the LRM/A.

Her quickness of mind may have again saved Jola's life that night when the rebels chose to raid a shopkeeper's home. The owner of the shop had refused to open the door, and the rebels were afraid of using their machine-guns to shoot the door open lest the noise attract unwanted attention from the NRM/A. The men then began cutting the window open using the machete they took from Jola's home. At some point, noting that they needed a better implement for the task of getting into the shop, one of the rebels asked Jola to fetch an axe. While the order was likely a genuine one, had Jola agreed to it, she could have come across as more knowledgeable of the area than she had let on. How else would she know where the shopkeeper kept his axe? In a most audacious exchange with the rebels, Jola Amayo knew what to say: 'I said, "Look, we came here together, I wouldn't know where the axe is kept." As soon as I said that, one of the men whacked me in the back with the machete. I cried out, "You are beating me for nothing. I really don't know this area, yet you are asking me for an axe."'

This is an important development in the abduction of Jola Amayo. The man, upset by Jola's sharp retort, could have easily used the sharp edge of the machete to split her head in half. But he did not. It could be argued that the men had no wish to kill her at that particular time because they needed her to lead them through the village. However, the second and more plausible explanation is that Jola Amayo, far from being a captive victim waiting for her fate, whatever that might be, was actively inventing, humanizing, and establishing herself as *dano adana*, a human person, in the minds of her abductors. One has to remember that this is a twelve-year-old child caught in the middle of a very violent war, where killing is routine and death is a matter of course. Intuitively, rather than remain a terrified faceless girl snatched from her bed in the middle of the night, Jola, through her dialogue with the men, made herself into a real person. Her actions are strikingly different from those of Victor Turner's liminal initiate, who is dependent, confused, and lacking a sense of self. It is this self-confidence and independence that the LRM/A seeks first to destroy in the process of transforming child abductees into soldiers, thereby training them to respond to violence as a way of life. But rather than remain passive victims of LRM/A's dehumanizing violence, abductees work to retain some control over the situation. Jola Amayo, in control of her emotions, has insinuated herself into the minds of her abductors. Though it was early in her abduction, she was engaged in a dialectic process of self-production in which she employed her understanding of relationships in Acholi culture in a new situation where violence is an ever-present reality. Through her quiet, self-confident manner, she created space for herself in the midst of two LRM/A soldiers. Her very survival depended not on playing dumb, or doing something stupid like trying to escape, but on being quick-witted and playing along. As she travelled farther and farther from her family and village, and became one of a growing number of LRM/A child abductees, Jola Amayo, more than ever, would need to depend on her inner resourcefulness if she was to have any chance of survival.

Separation: Goodbye Home, Hello LRM/A

In the course of the night of her abduction, Jola Amayo was initiated into the violence that characterized the dozen years she would spend with the LRM/A. When one of the many burglaries in which she was forced to participate went awry, she survived a shootout between the NRM/A and the two rebels. Although she had an opportunity to attempt an escape, she chose to stay calm, reasoning that she could easily be killed by bullets from the opposing armies. She also witnessed up close the execution of a village catechist whom she knew well. The man had refused to open the door, but when he finally did, he was immediately shot dead. His widow, who had just given birth, was abducted along with the baby and released only miles away from home. The killing would haunt Jola years after she returned to her village, with some accusing her of orchestrating it. At daybreak, as the rebels passed her compound, Jola asked to be freed, but the men refused. She had walked all night, and most of the morning, without resting, but the rebels pressed on, taking her to their jungle hideout. When they finally stopped to rest near a stream in late afternoon the following day, Jola Amayo was battered, bruised, and bloodied, but not bowed. Survival, she knew, depended on remaining alert and strong, not in playing victim. She was still as sharp-witted as in the beginning:

> The man left guarding me lay sleeping. I thought he was sleeping, but he was not; his eyes were open. When I got up, the river ran across this way; he was lying higher up the bank, and went to drink some water; he craned his neck to see if I was entering the river to escape. I drank water and returned back to resume sitting. He said, 'Had some foolish notion taken over your senses to attempt running away, I would have killed you.'
> I said, 'I am not going to escape, my feet are sore, I cannot walk.'
> *I am not going to escape, my feet are sore, I cannot walk.*

Jola Amayo, tantalizingly, is not ruling out the possibility of attempting to escape later. However, she is mature enough to know that her chances for escape range from very slim to none. She assesses her situation and determines that, in her current state of pain, she cannot possibly get far in an attempted escape. She states the obvious to the rebel guarding her. *I am not going to escape, my feet are sore, I cannot walk.* By stating openly her desire to remain where she is, Jola attempts to construct and establish an important element of survival – trust. Knowing that her very life depends on the rebels trusting her and dealing with her on the level of trustworthiness, she has to be completely transparent, open, readable, and, most important, believable. Anything that suggests the possibility of deception, cunning, or opposition, the very antithesis of being trustworthy, would jeopardize her chances of survival. So Jola states an obvious fact which she knows her captors can determine for themselves, namely, that she cannot escape because her feet are sore; she cannot walk. In doing so, Jola is demonstrating her realization that the long road to freedom requires that she continue to play along and do as the rebels command her to do.

The Vicious Beating and the Good Samaritan

As a newcomer among the LRM/A, Jola Amayo was neither immediately welcome nor accepted into the ranks of the rebel movement. In fact, after having mostly won the rapport of the two men who abducted her, she now had to start the process all over again with the larger group. She was treated with suspicion by the other abductees who preceded her into the bush. When she was ordered to clean up, she was accompanied to the riverside by a group of girls. At the river, as she bathed, a girl named Langwen hatched a conspiracy to murder her by throwing her in the river and claiming she escaped. Before the girls could carry out their plan, a sympathetic girl reported the matter to the camp, and the conspirators were summoned and punished. Jola Amayo now had to contend not only with whatever the LRM/A had in store for her but also with the hostility of some of her fellow abductees. When Langwen reported that Jola was planning to escape, she was ordered to stay in the rain all day, which left her thoroughly drenched not just in body but in spirit. After that incident, Jola attempted to keep to herself to avoid trouble, but that action brought suspicion and near-fatal consequences:

> Barely two days had gone by; the same girl reported that I wanted to escape. I was called and they began interrogating me. I said, 'I never said anything, I am new here, I don't know what this is all about.'

They said, 'You think you are stubborn; you will see what will happen if you do not tell the truth.'

I said, 'What I have told you is the honest truth, so help me God. It is now two weeks going on a month, you will never hear me speak about such things. Furthermore, I don't hang much around the girls, I keep mostly to myself.'

They said, 'That's it, you keep to yourself because you are planning to escape.' He said, 'Go cut some fresh sticks.' A bundle of sticks was cut. They got a real thick rope, and tied it around here [her waist], as well as tied my hands and pulled them behind me like this.

The beating began; I was beaten until all the sticks were shred to pieces. Once that was over, they cut over four hundred fresh sticks – they beat me until those too were gone. As the beating continued, I lost consciousness, no longer feeling any pain, no longer crying.

The incident of the beating was a milestone in Jola's journey into becoming a CI soldier. When the beating began, it was ostensibly to teach Jola a lesson. However, when prolonged to the point that she lost consciousness, it became likely that she was going to be killed. At the critical moment she survived as much by good luck as by the fact that she had endeared herself to some of the rebels, who took up her cause when, sprawled on the ground, bleeding and voiceless, she was no longer in a position to speak for herself. In our interview, remembering what seemed at the time to be an out-of-body experience, she described the haggling over her life between those supporting her and those against her:

One of the men came and said, 'Fellows, you will kill this girl for nothing. A person such as this, who cries in the name of God, such a person likely has never spoken a word of lie. Why are you hurting her? She is still a very young girl; such a plan [to escape] could not cross her mind. If she said anything it is likely because the older girls started such a conversation. Let the girl live.'

One person said, 'No, let's beat her some more.' They took the machete and hit my back, nine times in my back. Another person said, 'You will kill the girl for no reason, it has no benefit. Killing her will not make you famous because all you would have killed is an innocent little person.'

Those against killing Jola prevailed just in time, saving her from being beaten to death. When she regained consciousness, a sympathizer helped care for her, but her situation was dire. The group was ordered to abandon Jola at that campsite while the rest moved on to a new location. Yet, ignoring personal dangers, two rebels returned and carried Jola Amayo to the new site, helping to nurse her slowly back to health: 'I was brought to the new camp position where they had moved; they boiled water and washed my body with warm water. They took some liquid drug with which I was injected, feeling absolutely no pain, my entire body was numb.'

It is possible that, without the intervention by the two Good Samaritans, Jola Amayo would have died from her wounds. However, by rescuing Jola, the two rebels were likely placing themselves at some personal risk. That they were willing to take a chance on the new girl, and carry her to safety, clean her up, and give her a new dress to put on suggests a degree of rapport between Jola and her rescuers. In the short time that Jola had lived with the LRM/A in the bush, about three weeks at the time of the beating, she quickly sized up her captors and through her personal initiative created a sympathetic personal narrative with some of them. She likely understood that she could not possibly get everyone to be on her side, and she did not try.

Jola's beating also signalled the LRM/A's shifting attitude towards her. Before the beating, she was just another child abducted from the village, an outsider just as likely to survive as she was to die by being thrown into the river by a bunch of conniving girls. Whether or not she would live was a 50–50 proposition. The beating put her through a severe test of her will to survive. In Acholi tradition, which the LRM/A rebels were very much aware of, she is said to have escaped death just barely – *oloyo too cwii*. It is a phrase used to describe an edible rat that is being pursued by hunters and that at the last possible moment, before being clubbed or speared to death, disappears down a hole in the ground, thereby escaping its pursuers. The general belief among the LRM/A would have been that death spared Jola likely because she had a clean heart. The theme of clean heartedness versus dark heartedness was very often repeated in LRM/A narratives and appeared to guide many of the group's actions. It is also a common theme within Acholi oral tradition, as captured in p'Bitek's (1966) *Song of Lawino*, where Lawino speaks about the smallpox that killed so many because they were dark hearted:

The fiends found
Many people with bad hearts

There was much quarrelling
And jealously among women
And so many people perished
I lost my father too   (104)

Situated within the cultural context of *oloyo too cwii*, barely escaping death by a whisker, is the ever-present superstitious belief that fate favours those who narrowly cheat death. It is considered bad luck to tempt fate by trying to harm such a person a second time. Surviving the beatings likely increased Jola's chances of being accepted and no longer considered an outsider.

More importantly for Jola, *oloyo too cwii* also comes with an implicit determination by the collective not to allow the situation to repeat itself. There could be other life-threatening punishments farther down the road, but, for now, Jola cannot be beaten for the same issue, that of attempting to escape. At this stage, Jola is not yet a full-fledged LRM/A member, a successful initiate into the fold of the rebel movement. But the fact that she had survived a vicious beating raised her status just a bit.

Settling among the Rebels, Learning the Ropes

Those like Jola Amayo, who had been in captivity for over two years, were usually considered completely won over and did not require round-the-clock supervision. She was assigned to work in the LRM/A sickbay. Having looked after her siblings at home, Jola was a natural fit at the sickbay, where she helped to care for the wounded and assisted the doctors:

> When you were assigned a patient, it was your job to get up before dawn, around three in the morning to start the fire, boil water. As the sky reddened in the morning, you needed to have put out the fire; all that remained was hot charcoal. You should have also cooked food by then because there was fear that the smoke would give away the position of the rebels to the army.
>
> You took care of the patients as well as the doctor, the sick, and that's the way we stayed at the sickbay for two years. After spending time at the sickbay, we were ordered back into the convoy. We were returned to the convoy led by Kony. That was 1993.

For Jola, the three years spent away from home allowed her to establish her own surrogate family, one she cared about and shared good and bad moments with. She was not keenly thinking about escaping any more, but was simply doing the work assigned her. As a testament of her changing attitude, she was removed from the sickbay and asked to join a convoy led by Joseph Kony himself. This was a big increase in responsibility since it meant she was now considered part of an LRM/A operational team. She learned to walk long distances without food or water and take incoming fire from enemies, in this case, the NRM/A. For all practical purposes, Jola had become a full member of the LRM/A – perhaps not in the sense of identifying with all of the rebel movement's philosophy, but in the sense that her life as the young girl who was abducted several years prior had changed to that of someone who was now a soldier. For instance, in a combat engagement with the NRM/A, her status as a captive was now less apparent, replaced as it were by her demeanour as a combatant. She was as likely to draw the enemy's fire as to respond with fire herself.

In other words, even if Jola wanted to escape the captivity of the LRM/A at this point in her transformation, she would be at a loss as to where to start, how to negotiate the deadly terrain, escape villagers hostile to the LRM/A rebels since she would be identified as one, and survive a possible ambush by the NRM/A. Common sense would have suggested to her that the safest place at the moment was with the LRM/A itself. As a former CI soldier suggested, the irredeemability of the label of being *olum*, a LRM/A rebel, was perhaps the strongest deterrent for children contemplating escape from LRM/A captivity. As the informant put it:

> On reaching Uganda we started a campaign of deception – you know there are ways of deceiving people and especially since there was no option for amnesty – telling other abductees that when you spend a certain period in the bush, on returning home, you would be immediately killed. There would be no reason to let you live. Naturally, you would start thinking, 'Well, I am now one year in the bush, and have also fought battles, surely, returning home means certain death.' You begin thinking, 'How should I live? How should I protect my life in order to start living a life?' You begin to consider what to do when battles come. We stayed. Jola also stayed.

Training for the 1994 Peace Talks, and Prisoner of War

The 1993–4 peace talks between the government of Uganda and the LRM/A was the first serious effort to make peace between the warring parties. Implicitly, it was a tacit admission by the government of Yoweri Museveni that the LRM/A constituted a serious if not permanent threat to the security of northern Uganda. The peace talks themselves were initiated and led by the minister for pacification of northern Uganda, Betty Atuku Bigombe, and, according to my informants, were referred to by the LRM/A as the 'Atuku Peace Talks.' The first face-to-face talks between government representatives led by Bigombe and the LRM/A mid-level commanders took place on 25 November 1993 at Pagik village in the Aswa region in Gulu. Originally planned as a confidence-building exercise, the talks turned into negotiations aimed at the LRM/A's demobilization, an outcome that, according to rebel commander Cirilo Jurukadri Odego, should not be seen as 'surrendering' but as a 'return home' (O'Kadameri, 2002). The rebel delegation further articulated its view that those the LRM/A was fighting, including the NRM/A and UPDA, had rejected the way of God.

In the second session of talks, beginning on 11 January 1994 at Pagik, the LRM/A delegation was led by Joseph Kony himself, aided by his commanders Omona and Odego, while the government of Uganda delegation was led by Betty Bigombe (Dolan, 2009; O'Kadameri, 2002). The government army commanders who participated in the first meeting refused to attend the second because the LRM/A insisted on being solely responsible for choosing and securing the venue. Joseph Kony seemed eager to conclude peace with the government of Uganda and directed his most venomous remarks at Acholi elders, whom he accused of forcing his members to take up arms in the bush and then abandoning them there (O'Kadameri, 2002). The LRM/A leader wanted to be given time to gather together his soldiers, who were then scattered in various places, so that he could return the children to their homes.

Despite Kony's apparent eagerness to embrace peace, the government of Uganda suddenly developed cold feet towards the whole notion. There are likely many reasons for the about-face. What is certain is that on 6 February 1994, while speaking to the Acholi population in Gulu, President Museveni torpedoed the peace effort by calling the LRM/A 'bandits' and demanding that the rebels surrender within seven days (O'Kadameri, 2002). The peace talks essentially collapsed then, and war involving children would go on for another decade.

From her vantage point as an LRM/A foot soldier, Jola Amayo had not been an idle watcher of the peace talks. The LRM/A created a special force in late 1993 to act as security for the second negotiating session; its members would even be responsible for conducting body searches of government delegates. Among those chosen for this force was Jola Amayo, who at that point was just beginning military training but did not have combat experience: 'The peace talks began in 1993. When the peace talks began, we were selected for training close to a river. Through that time I was being trained on the use of the gun.'

By then, Jola Amayo was firmly embedded within the LRM/A, was trusted as one of their own, and did not attempt to set herself apart. The risky nature of the peace talks and the possibility that government forces could attack the LRM/A led Kony, in creating the special security force, to select those in whom he had confidence, people he could completely rely on not to betray him by defecting, showing fear, or failing on the job. Earlier, in the first few months of her bush life with the LRM/A, Jola had looked at the LRM/A in terms of 'me' versus 'them,' but three years on, at fifteen years of age, that separation was no longer apparent. She was now a combatant – still a child, to be sure, but one further removed from the life that she had experienced in her village. If in her past life as a child Jola had expressed fear of the LRM/A, now she had become the very kind of person whom she used to fear. The difference between then and now was that Jola possibly saw many things that were awry, amiss, wrong, or out of place in the LRM/A, but she accepted them as part of her new identity. If she had misgivings, she did not let on because she was focused on the task of being an LRM/A soldier, and survival.

As Joseph Kony had anticipated, the peace talks did not go well. The government of Uganda, from his point of view, was more interested in scoring political points than in reaching a final peace agreement, and would not commit to a formalized agreement of understanding (Dolan, 2009, 87–8). For Jola Amayo, these were very tense times, further complicated when her team was captured by NRM/A forces: 'Atuku came to us, we were placed in an ambush – we stayed four days in ambush. On the fifth day, we left for Lacek-Ocot. At Lacek-Ocot, we were captured. We were captured by government forces. Kony ordered the attack on Lacek-Ocot, saying that since we were captured there, everything should be destroyed even tiny ants; nothing should be left alive.' The LRM/A captives were later released without a fight on the intervention of Betty Bigombe.

The incident at Lacek-Ocot was a very important development in Jola's transition into the life of a child combatant. For the first time, she saw herself as non-LRM/A people saw her, an event that was truly transformative. Until then, her new identity as a child combatant had grown on her almost imperceptibly; it was not something she had consciously thought about. The incident at Lacek-Ocot changed that by providing her with double consciousness, that state of being aware of herself as a captive of the LRM/A yet equally aware that others now viewed her as part of the organization. The layered self-awareness that constitutes double consciousness was best described by W.E.B DuBois (1999) when he wrote about growing up black in America. DuBois recalled the moment when, as if watching himself from another level of consciousness, it dawned on him that he was now the other:

> It is in the early days of rollicking boyhood that the revelation first bursts upon one, all in a day, as it were. I remember well when the shadow swept across me. I was a little thing, away up in the hills of New England, where the dark Housatonic winds between Hoosac and Taghkanic to the sea. In a wee wooden schoolhouse, something put it into the boys' and girls' heads to buy gorgeous visiting-cards – ten cents a package – and exchange. The exchange was merry, till one girl, a tall newcomer, refused my card, refused it peremptorily, with a glance. Then it dawned upon me with a certain suddenness that I was different from the others; or like, mayhap, in heart and life and longing, but shut out from their world by a vast veil. I had thereafter no desire to tear down that veil, to creep through; I held all beyond it in common contempt, and lived above it in a region of blue sky and great wandering shadows. That sky was bluest when I could beat my mates at examination-time, or beat them at a foot-race, or even beat their stringy heads. (3–4)

DuBois's experience of being black in America in a time of racial segregation, of seeing his blackness in the eyes of others, as if shut off by a 'vast veil,' is ultimately liberating in that it freed him from the shadow of knowing, of suspecting without fully glimpsing the object of his tension and dilemma, and brought him face to face, as it were, with what he needed to know, that is, that he was different. On a similar level, a captive of an identity shift that she could not fully acknowledge or confront until the gaze of her community freed her at Lacek-Ocot, Jola Amayo became aware of who she had become. She may have been an unwilling captive of the LRM/A at the beginning, forcibly abducted from her own bed several years past, but now, in the eyes of the larger community, she wore the new label of rebel. She presumably could have screamed out loud that she was not what she appeared to be, an LRM/A rebel, but such indignant protestations would ultimately have been futile, leading to nothing but despair – the experience of other black boys of Dubois's youth in a segregated America, whose 'youth shrunk into tasteless sycophancy, or into silent hatred of the pale world about them and mocking distrust of everything white; or wasted itself in a bitter cry' (4). No, a return to the world in which she was just Jola Amayo and not 'Jola Amayo the LRM/A rebel' was not possible, because others had confirmed her new identity as a rebel combatant. The split consciousness and the dilemma it entailed further cemented her bond with the LRM/A rather than freeing her from the group. Conversely, it could also be argued that the knowledge that she was now regarded by the civilian community as a member of the LRM/A freed her from worrying about what she had become and how she should act. Instead, she was able to focus her mind on the small things that matter for survival, such as not eating too much when on standby. Jola Amayo, in other words, was ready for combat, to fight for the LRM/A and, if need be, to die for it as well.

After the failed peace talks in 1994, the rebel movement was drawn closer to the government of Sudan, even as the NRM/A (which became Uganda People's Defence Forces in 1995) pursued it more ruthlessly. Jola Amayo was among 250 combatants sent to Sudan for intensive six-month military training, lasting from December 1994 to June 1995, when she was deployed for combat operations inside Uganda. Freshly supplied by Sudan with guns and ammunition, the unit quickly engaged the UPDF. Over the next several weeks and months, Jola Amayo would see much combat, a typical clash occurring at Agoro, inside Uganda: 'In Agoro, the army followed and caught up with us at eight in the morning. We began fighting, shooting at each other from eight in the morning until six in the evening. You could not walk, you could not carry any load. With so many wounded and dead, there were now way too many loads to carry. One of the boys who lived with us died in that battle. Another boy who was the commander of the convoy was also shot, breaking his thigh. Their loads now became our responsibilities.'

By this time, Jola Amayo was a fully experienced combatant, and it showed in her description of the battle:

We were told to shoot until our ammunition was gone. We shot them and they scattered. Six lines, we shot them, they scattered. Another six lines entered the fray. That was a tough lot, we fought toe to toe with them – they were strong and would not run. On our side, the cry went up that if it was a fight to the death, so be it because there were way too many wounded to carry with us. Added to that all the loads previously carried by the wounded and the dead were now heaped together in three huge lots.

Jola Amayo was wounded in the thigh during one of the running battles with the UPDF. She could not walk, so she had to be carried by her colleagues. In one close exchange of fire with the UPDF, she was dumped by those carrying her. She crawled on all fours through the night until she located her team the following morning. Her bravery in battle brought her recognition from the leader of the LRM/A. Jola recalled that moment: 'Our unit finally connected with Kony's unit. Among those wounded, I was the only girl with injuries. Kony said, "You are a good role model to the other girls" – Kony is related to my father's side of the family. He asked me, saying, "Young girl, how are you?" "Are you wounded?" I replied, "I am wounded."' Jola was the first LRM/A girl soldier to be given a rank, something she remembered with some pride years later: 'I was the first among the girls to wear a rank, that is, among the women in Kony's household, and all the women in the bush, I was the first to be given a rank, and was appointed a second lieutenant.'

Jola discovered that not only was she not afraid to fight, she was also good at inspiring others to remain courageous in battle. Her role had changed completely; the child abductee clinging to life in LRM/A camps had become a confident, battle-tested child combatant whose growing importance made her the target of jealousy among her colleagues. She commanded both respect and fear. More important, she knew how to take care of herself, as she recalled:

As the jealousy grew there was a plot to shoot me mainly because I was seen as elevating the status of the leader [Kony] and he lavishly praised me. I should be shot and killed. On the way back to Sudan, we came under fire. An officer wanted to shoot me then, but alerted, I stepped away from the line of fire. Instead, he shot a young soldier who was part of the leader's escort. When we arrived, the shooter was jailed for six months, in which time he was not allowed to touch a gun, and required to walk bare-chested.

Jola Amayo not only stayed with the LRM/A, she had become one of its more important members.

Motherhood Intervenes: Baby on the Back, Machine-Gun in Hand

As she matured into a young woman, Jola Amayo found love. Unlike other young girls who were simply handed over to senior LRM/A officers as wives, Jola was wooed by a young man who became her first bush husband. This was important to Jola, who, in the midst of her own uncertain future as a child combatant, still retained the original, desired identity she had developed in her home village. She valued being able to say 'yes' to a suitor's advances. It confirmed a part of her Acholi upbringing, which said you don't throw yourself at a man, you allow him to approach you first. She may not have had the same setting for the wooing as she would have had at home, but she still went through the process, that satisfaction of being a girl pursued by a boy:

> When I left Uganda [to return to Sudan] the word went out that I was now having my menstrual period. Senior officers became interested in me as a woman. One officer was especially fierce in fending off other officers. He used to beat me badly, saying that I was unruly and wild.
>
> I began living with an officer, a boy from Alero. He wooed me instead of forcing me into the relationship. We began staying together, living together. We had a baby boy and named him Otim.

The birth of her son in 1996 meant that Jola Amayo could not actively participate in combat. In what seemed like the blink of an eye, Jola moved from being a child herself to being the mother of a child. Her son was deliberately called Otim, a Luo name that means a child born in the wilderness, in the diaspora, among aliens. She could have named him anything she wanted – Sam, Pedro, Andrew, James, or any number of other possibilities. But she still clung to Acholi customs, ultimately refusing to relinquish the very culture that had betrayed and abandoned her at the crucial moment of her childhood development.

She now focused on being a mother and a wife, but she was widowed early on when her bush husband was captured and killed during an operation inside Uganda. Alone, she worked her field, producing foodstuff that was sold in Juba. She met another man, who became her second bush husband; she would have two children with him and they live together today. But motherhood did not change Jola's stigmatized identity or status as a combatant since the LRM/A remained at war with UPDF. It meant that, instead of fending for herself alone, she now had to think about her children as well, as was the case, she said, in 1997 when the UPDF attacked the LRM/A base in Nisitu in southern Sudan. Jola Amayo was forced into combat with one-year-old Otim in tow: 'A fierce exchange of bullets ensued. Everywhere you turned, moving to the road, away from the road, bullets were flying. I began fighting with my baby son Otim tied to my back. I opened fire on the army position. Otim was asleep on my back. We fought a hard battle until the end, but we could not move along the road. We had dispersed government troops.' She adds: 'There was a wounded government soldier lying nearby, I thought he was dead, but he was alive. Another government soldier lay dead nearby; I searched his rank and found he was a captain. I had earlier shot and killed him. I plucked his rank and held it in my hand.'[3]

The unforgettable picture that Jola paints in this segment of her narrative, of a combatant wielding a machine-gun in battle with a sleeping baby tied to her back, is both heroic and tragic, leaving us to cheer her courage in facing the blazing guns of her enemies but also lament the inescapable reality of her new identity as a child combatant carrying a child of her own into combat.

In her village, she would have either gone ahead with her education, or been married in the traditional Acholi *nyom* ceremony. As a bride she would have gone on to establish her home at her in-laws, beginning the journey of motherhood within the new community. Here, in the wilderness, she became a mother with a gun in her hand. She killed without hesitation, and, as in the story just told, she could inspect the body of someone she had killed to see if there was anything on it worth taking, something that would have shocked most Acholi to their core. From the dead person, she yanked out the pip signifying that the dead soldier was a UPDF captain. Moments later, she herself was shot, the bullet shattering her wrist. Without yelping with pain, she walked for several miles before handing over her machine-gun to someone else to carry. She took care of her own wounds, and then tended to her sleeping son.

Viewed through the lenses of Acholi culture, in which killing and dying are extraordinary events regardless of the context, this story is striking. Yet the contradictory images that Jola offers, as a child mothering a child, as a child fighting a war, and as a child widow, are the least of her worries. She is fighting to survive and care for the child tied to her back. This was not something she had been trained for, but it was something she was forced to accept as part of her new identity. Her transformation from child to child combatant was complete. Abhorring introspection, second-guessing, and brooding about events over which she had little influence, she instead adapted, constructing and nurturing an identity that she had control over, that of a combatant, who acted deliberately and with confidence because that was the culture of war. In that environment, a moment's hesitation could be fatal. She did not question why she needed to kill the captain because, if she had not killed him (which she did), he would have killed her. The equation was fairly straightforward – kill or be killed, eat or be eaten.

Jola Amayo was a soldier now, self-assured with a gun in her hand, who would not necessarily kowtow to the demands of a man just because he was a man. She was a soldier whose values reflected warfare and combat, who was aware that those elements of her that long ago demanded that she look at the world from a certain cultural vantage point of obedience and meekness had been supplanted by a new self that spoke loudly of surviving the day so that tomorrow could take care of itself.

Return of the Living Dead: Home, Bitter Home

Jola Amayo's homecoming on 12 June 2002 was reminiscent of the manner in which she left in the first place. It was sudden, unexpected, and anti-climactic, a disorganized event that simply happened one night. She was part of the rebel movement one moment, fighting for her life and that of her children, if not for the cause for which she had been abducted more than a decade earlier. Then, the LRM/A, after using her for its purposes, spat her out, seeing her as a spent force, an unsuitable CI soldier on account of motherhood. As Jola herself put it, 'I stopped fighting when Otim grew up.' There was no letter of discharge that said so and so fought for such and such a cause and was now being honourably discharged. Instead, unless one was told her story, Jola was just another village mother, now with two children, one still nursing. Perhaps her scars could tell part of the story of what she had gone through all these years, what she had survived, and the battles she had fought.

But even at this crucial moment of liberation from her former abductors, she was not capable of crying. She was a soldier first. In fact, when her mother was moved to tears, wailing out aloud, Jola sharply rebuked her, an incident that she did not relish speaking about:

On arrival, my mother began wailing. I told her, saying, 'If you have come here to make me sad, then you had better go back. I have just come out of extreme difficulty, and here you welcome me by wailing? Here in the bush, there is no crying, go back home.'

Some people took my mother aside and calmed her down, telling her, 'Look, it is your daughter telling you to calm down, she should be the one crying, not the adult. Cry silently.' My mother went and sat alone, she calmed down, and then came to speak to me. We had a lot of catching up to do. I told her simply, 'I am alive, not dead.'

In the end, the child who was abducted years earlier was not the person who stood in front of her mother that day. The realization must have dawned on the sad mother that the little child she all along ached to touch and welcome back home was no more. In place of that child was now a grown woman with two children of her own, and many battle scars. So, as only a mother could, she cried for the loss she felt deep inside her. She also cried because Acholi culture demanded that one cries at the death of a child – the child who was once hers was no longer. She had died in the bush.

Jola Amayo is aware of the double existence she must continue to inhabit. In the bush she had lived the double life of a soldier and a child yearning to return home; now she has to live the life of returnee who is physically back in the community but whose very presence is denied by the community. That is because she is caught in a cultural grey zone where she is neither the person she used to be nor the person the community thinks she should be. Her stigmatized identity, that of a child who has fought in a war, is the one in plain view.

In the past, returning Acholi warriors were welcomed back into the community with ceremonies meant to cleanse them of evil spirits. The cleansing ritual would be accompanied with much ceremony and pride. If victorious, a warrior would almost certainly earn the *moi*, a title of praise reserved for the most courageous deeds. Whatever name he chose would end with *moi*; Lutanya-moi, Lwanya-moi, Luker-moi, Tweny-moi, Guru-moi, and so on.

But Jola is not seen as a warrior even though she fought many battles and showed extraordinary courage in the face of withering fire. Her return home is not a moment for celebration. Instead, there is shame attached to her return; she is a killer whose participation in war is akin to the role played by the village witches who danced at night and placed curses on innocent people. She is held both in contempt and fear for what she has done and what she is capable of doing. The fact that she is considered the 'walking-dead' only compounds the communal rejection of her presence. She can stay in the community only because nobody has the courage to ask her to leave. Her children can play with other children but must not touch them. She knows this: 'Even when my child was beaten, I held my tongue, merely watching what was going on. The antidote to that was to make sure your children did not go play near aggressive children. As soon as you spoke up because your child was beaten, you were derided as the mother of Lakwena responsible for massacring people. Where was your head at? You should be lynched by a crowd.'

The existential crisis that Jola Amayo now faces in her home village is exacerbated by her steadfastly held notion of being *dano adana*, a human person who survived years of abuse in LRM/A captivity. She is still a human being but not the person the community wants her to be. On her return, she was forced to accept her identity as a former CI soldier, and resolved to 'keep quiet' for fear of making matters worse. But today, Jola Amayo has chosen to speak up to teach others about who she is and, in so doing, to begin to negotiate her way back into the community: 'To those who knew I returned from the bush, [I say,] "Don't be afraid, let's stay on good terms, because I know what pain is and you know what pain is. So don't be afraid of me. If I have something you need, ask me, and I will not refuse to give it to you, and if you have something I need, I will also ask you, and I know you will not deny me."'

Jola Amayo is now beginning to show that she is still what she was all along, *dano adana*, a human person, one whose personhood has survived years in LRM/A bush camps.

Chapter Five

The Ringo Otigo Stories

I met Ringo Otigo for the first time on 17 July 2008 at GUSCO head office in Gulu. He was already waiting when I drove inside the gates of the GUSCO headquarters at about eight that morning. When he saw me, he quietly stood up from his perch on an embankment under the tree. He did so slowly, and walked towards me just as slowly, never giving the impression that he was in a rush to do something else, or that he could be rushed into something he did not want to do. He wore oily blue-jean coveralls, and dusted his right hand on his pants before offering it to me in a firm handshake. Ringo was a muscular man with a big chest, yet he was soft-spoken with an exceedingly polite demeanour. He was working as a bicycle mechanic at an open-air shop located at the north entrance of Gulu market in Gulu town. The location of the shop at a busy intersection ensured that he was a very visible man doing a visible job, and was constantly interrupted by passersby and acquaintances who wished him well. His job required that he welcome all walk-in customers who needed their bicycles repaired, chat with them as he did his work, and haggle a bit over how much the work was worth.

GUSCO had contacted him the day before, and he had come for the day. I apologized for the short notice and the fact that his day's work was ruined. He responded in English, 'It's okay.' At the time of our meeting, Ringo was twenty-six years old, living with a partner with whom he has three children. It had been six years and five days since the day he walked out of the bush as a child combatant with the LRM/A.

There was a formality in the way in which Ringo sat, hands neatly folded on his lap, back straight up on the chair, and head erect. When asked a question, he paused to consider it, and then proceeded to answer carefully. He employed Acholi proverbs often to illustrate a point, and executed precise use of the Acholi language in the same way elders do at gatherings of *kacooke*, meetings at which speakers are expected to use *lok mucwiny* (mature spoken words) to make their points. The ability to employ *lok mucwiny* in a conversation is considered an Acholi art form which one develops by listening to village elders and then uses skilfully to argue both sides of the issue. Persons with such skills are well regarded within the community when there are issues to be discussed. The person who possesses the skills for *lok mucwiny* is often called upon to *tweyo ter lok* (tie up the discussion) by summarizing and concluding it. It is foolhardy for a participant at such a communal meeting to reopen the discussion after the matter has been properly 'tied up.' The biggest public insult is for a speaker to be dismissively silenced for *loko lok me tino* (talking like an adolescent), instead of *lok mucwiny*.

When I asked him whether the publication of his story was a concern, Ringo answered that he would be most concerned if it was not published because, as he put it in Luo, *dong bene nongo loka oto nono* (my whole story would have died for nothing).

The Cultural Context of Ringo Otigo's Early Life in an Acholi Village

Ringo Otigo was born on 7 December 1981 in Labwoc village, Koro district, just outside Gulu town. His birthday came just three days before the first anniversary of the disputed national elections that returned Milton Obote to power. In fact, by the time Ringo was born, the insurgency that was founded by Yoweri Museveni to rid Uganda of Obote was almost ten months old. It would take a few more years before it could succeed in its objective of toppling the government, putting Museveni in power and thereby plunging northern Uganda into a new cycle of violence that would involve many Acholi children as child combatants. At the time of his birth, however, there was nothing in the life of his village that would suggest the turn of events five years later.

Ringo's father, a medical doctor at Gulu hospital, died before his birth. The boy's upbringing, however, emphasized family loyalty, a strong relationship with extended kin and the larger community in the village, thrift and hard work, respect for elders and people in positions of authority, and the value of being responsible and dependable, all of which were qualities exploited by the LRM/A in the transformation of many village children into child combatants. Ringo remembered that he grew up well liked by everyone because he did what was expected of him: 'Growing up, as young children, the way we lived with others, we lived in a large extended family, with many people living together. I was told that my grandfather and my father loved having people around them. Moreover, my father's job required him to be around people. He was a doctor at the main [Gulu] hospital. He had a good relationship with people.'

Having good relationships with others, or as Ringo puts it, 'good neighbourliness,' meant that a child was trustworthy, and Ringo seemed to work especially hard to cultivate and maintain such relationships. However, Ringo reserved a special affection for his old grandmother, whom he referred to as 'Big Mother.' In time, Ringo's grandmother became the most influential person in his life. He explained how the symbiotic relationship grew only stronger over the years: 'My grandmother was particularly fond of me, often remarking that she could never find another grandson like me. She said so because I was giving her a lot of help. She also had granddaughters, the children of her own son, but they tended to stay away from her, saying she was too old and useless … I would dig potatoes from the field and bring it in the house. All she did was peel the potato and boil it in the fireplace.'

In return for his help, Ringo's grandmother lavished attention on her grandson, showering him with the affection that he could never have received in his large household with so many children, something he acknowledged:

Grandmother had a special earthenware pot in which she would leave honey and simsim butter for me, which I enjoyed eating. She said she could not give the food to anyone else because nobody was giving her the kind of help I was providing her. The earthenware pot was an heirloom handed down by her mother who instructed her to allow only the most trusted grandchild to use it. She would pour simsim butter and add honey on top, which I then ate. Whenever hungry, I reached out to the hanging net in the ceiling in which the pot was placed, took it down and ate some of the sweet mixture.

Ringo's experience of bonding with many relatives is by no means unique to Acholi culture. In other African cultures, a child is expected to know his relatives, visit them often, and live with them (see, for example, Chinua Achebe's *Things fall apart*). The rationale is that a child who is acquainted with relatives can never be alone even when his immediate family members are away, dead, or otherwise unable to support him or her. The expression often used to describe the close ties of extended family is *wat aye yiki* (your relatives are the ones who will bury you). The extended family, in other words, will always support you, even in death. For Ringo, this was a normal part of developing his budding sense of identity, an identity rooted in and nurtured by the larger cultural web of extended relations.

But the strong family bond was tested often by the lack of money. To make ends meet, Ringo Otigo and his six brothers and five sisters worked the cotton field and the harvested cotton was sold to the ginnery to make some money. Ringo and his twin brother also worked long hours cutting and splitting firewood to be sold at the market for cash. Even that, however, was not enough money to pay for the basic necessities for school. Often, Ringo was suspended from school because he did not have money to pay the fees. His mother intervened from time to time, asking the school's headmaster to reconsider and take him back in. 'Sometimes, my mother would come and say, "I am poor, allow my child to attend school, debt has never killed anyone,"' he said.

Growing up poor in the village forced Ringo to mature quickly. Although he found time to engage in boyhood activities, like fashioning catapults from forked tree branches, going bird hunting, and swimming in the river, he also had to take on the adult responsibilities of tilling the land and picking cotton.

According to Ringo, he learned early on that adults could behave very badly. He specifically remembered two incidents. The first occurred when a boy accidentally threw a spear which pierced the face of another boy. The issue created tension in the extended family that became a running feud. And, perhaps as a continuation of the first incident, a second incident occurred that involved cattle eating the crops of another family. People in the village took sides in the dispute, some supporting the cattle owner and others the owner of the field. The fracas that ensued turned into an open fight that had to be broken up by the police. For Ringo, it became difficult to trust adults. He often declined to follow adults on hunting expeditions in the bush for fear that old enmities might surface and lead to the 'spilling of blood.'

Despite what he saw as life's many contradictions and challenges, he was shown early on how to cope and grow up to lead an honourable and useful life. Ringo recalled that most of his childhood education came from different elders in his community who taught him the meaning of life through Acholi traditional sayings. For instance, as a fatherless boy, Ringo was constantly reminded of the Acholi saying, *latin pa lacan winyo pwony ki ii bad deero* (the poor man's child takes lessons from the side of the granary). He explained what it meant to him:

> It meant that when adults were conversing, the smart child sat nearby, listening carefully to what was being said, never betraying his presence, but absorbing all the life's lessons. The elders also had a saying for the recalcitrant child. In the Acoli tongue, the way I recall it, the saying went, 'The recalcitrant child never gets a share of the wild cat's head,' meaning that when a child refuses to do an errand, but another does it, the one who was compliant gets a reward. But you, the recalcitrant child, get nothing, hence 'The recalcitrant child never gets a share of the wild cat's head.'

The ability to relate to his extended family went beyond the home into Ringo's school life, something he was proud to speak about. Though he spent only a short time in school before he was abducted by the LRM/A, Ringo seemed to have made a lifetime of friendships with some of the staff and students at the various schools he attended.

An Education in a Village School

Ringo Otigo started his primary education in the village in which he was born, Koro, but spent the last two years of school with his grandmother in Lakwat Omer. His school experiences were mostly positive because, as he put it, 'I was well liked by everyone.' He was always among the first to arrive in school in the morning, even ahead of the bell, a disused car-wheel rim banged with an iron bar. In class, his generosity extended to helping colleagues read, write, and study for tests. But it was his athletic ability that won him popularity beyond the classroom: 'The whole school looked to me when it came to sports, mainly two sports in track and field events, running and throwing shot put, all of which I excelled in with no problems.'

School was mostly an extension of the home, and Ringo, like his peers, was expected to relate to and respect teachers as he would his own parents. Two teachers stood out in Ringo's mind; one taught him mathematics while the other taught social studies. He remembered both as very kind, helpful, and always willing to spend time to explain new concepts to the students. Ironically, the day he returned from the bush, Ringo surrendered to his former social-studies teacher, Simon

Odong, who at the time was working as a social worker with GUSCO. Both teachers remained a part of his life when he returned home as a former child combatant: 'Odong worked as a staff member at GUSCO. Otto Leba is presently teaching in Abili. Whenever I go there, I spend time with him, and he likes to tell people, "This young man was my student, a student I truly loved, a good listener, punctual, and always respectful in the class." We have a good time together and to this moment he trusts me, such that whenever I get there – my mother resides in Koro Abili – and find them, and I have some money, I give them some [to buy beer], to relax.'

In school Ringo learned to resolve any conflicts that arose. He was especially afraid of a class bully called Abibu, whose vicious exploits left many children without lunch or with bumps on their heads. Abibu was a most dislikeable character: 'He was very nasty, yet he was so stupid and knew nothing. He hated whatever good things were happening in class. In class he was constantly disruptive and noisy. When you did something well, he would beat you up. He also intimidated others to try to take away whatever food he liked. His main preoccupation was making little children cry when they left the school ground.'

Ringo quickly sized up Abibu and concluded that the boy was angry because he was hungry. By offering food to him, Ringo solved the puzzle that had left many children in sheer terror: 'When we had food, and it was lunchtime, I would give him some of it, and he would then leave us alone to go and eat. For instance, when I brought mangoes, I would give him two. He would then go to harass other children; meanwhile, we went to eat somewhere else. That was how we managed to get around him because we did not give him opportunity to give us trouble.'

Being able to read people would become a very valuable life-saving skill when Ringo was abducted by the LRM/A. As he soon discovered while living with the rebels, a misreading of a situation, an intention, or the smallest cue could cost one one's life. In fact, whatever he did not learn in school, Ringo would learn the hard way during his life as a child combatant in both Uganda and Sudan.

Abduction in the Evening

Ringo Otigo says that he was abducted by the LRM/A just three days after his fifteenth birthday, on 10 December 1996. He spent the next six years with the insurgency, and coincidentally escaped from the bush on his birthday, 7 December 2002.[1] The abduction happened on a Tuesday evening at Lakwat Omer where he was living with his grandmother. He had been to the hospital in Gulu town early that day to have the doctor check on chest pain he had been experiencing. The doctor had prescribed medication which he had in a pocket of his shorts alongside the hospital medical form. He had returned home and gone straight to the stream to fetch water. On his way back from the stream, he met two armed LRM/A soldiers. The soldiers brandished their weapons at him, but Ringo acted calmly while answering their probing questions:

> They asked me, 'Boy, where are you coming from?'
> I replied, 'I am coming from the stream.'
> Then one said, 'Walk straight ahead, if you run, we will shoot you.' I walked with them, we arrived in our compound, and I put down the water. I was told to go sit down; I went and sat down. They asked me, 'Where are government soldiers stationed?'
> 'There are no government troops here; they are stationed in Labora, further away from here,' I replied. They went into the house where grandmother was sitting, and asked, 'Do you give permission for us to take the boy to go listen to some messages?' Grandmother did not answer.

Three characteristics made Ringo an especially good target for the rebel movement; he was a young boy between nine and sixteen, he was an Acholi, and he was living in a village which was virtually unprotected by the UPDF. He was young enough but not too young to be trained quickly for combat. Being an Acholi who spoke the Luo language and understood the Acholi culture meant that he could make meaning of and respond to the cultural manipulations of the LRM/A. Finally, Ringo was a prime candidate for abduction because the rebels did not expect much opposition from government troops who, as Ringo indicated in his answer to the two rebels, were stationed some distance away in Labora. To alert the army in an emergency such as the one the boy found himself in would have required someone to travel that distance on a bicycle or on foot. At least several hours would have passed before there was some kind of response from the UPDF, a fact the rebels seemed to acknowledge by their lackadaisical attitude. Many children were abducted from Acholi villages between 1989 and 2006 precisely because inadequate security facilitated quick access to the villages and clean exit for the LRM/A with relatively low risk of engaging government troops.

Ringo also possessed another quality that many young boys and girls the LRM/A rebels snatched from his village did not have – the ability to read and write fairly well. Being literate meant that he was a likely candidate for further training to serve the rebel movement in different capacities, for instance, as a secretary to senior officers, a medic, or even as an officer. Somehow his captors determined or grasped very quickly Ringo's potential, and he was separated at the outset from other abductees.

Ringo gained a vantage point from which to observe the dynamics of the abductees and their abductors. The LRM/A officers on location were always in control of the decision of what the next move ought to be. The group of abductees and rebels in which Ringo now found himself began walking towards Palenga, located about two hours away. Their path took them past Ringo's home where his grandmother had sat outside all night, waiting for him. She saw him, but neither spoke to the other. It could have been by design that Ringo was made to see his grandmother again yet not allowed to speak to her. There was, however, no doubt that this phase of walking in the bush, *wot ii lum*, was meant to break the physical and psychological attachment the children had to their homes.

The Abduction of the Aboke Girls and the Question of Memory

On the night of 10 October 1996, 139 nine girls were abducted from St Mary's Secondary School in Aboke, northern Uganda. The event would have likely gone relatively unnoticed and been relegated to the growing statistics of young victims of the long war but for the extraordinary courage of Sister Rachele Fassera, the Italian deputy headmistress at the school. She chose to follow the LRM/A into the bush at daybreak and demand the return of all her students, a perilous journey documented by Els de Temmerman (2001) and K. Cook (2007). The kidnapping of the 'Aboke girls' became an international issue, with the Vatican joining the campaign to have them released.

However, what is rarely mentioned in the media reports is that, on the night of the abduction, there were many newly kidnapped children from various villages in Acholi and in Lango. One of the abductees was Ringo Otigo, whose recollections of the event provide another vantage point from which to view the drama surrounding the abduction of the Aboke girls, and the process by which they, like many other child abductees, were slowly ground into the LRM/A rebel organization as child combatants. Given his detailed account of the incident, which is supported by independent sources (Cook, 2007, 6–16; de Temmerman, 2001), there is little doubt that Ringo Otigo had first-hand knowledge of the abductions at St Mary's Secondary School. But the date he gives for the Aboke incident contradicts the date he gives for his abduction in Lakwat Omer. According to the timeline cited in his story, the abduction of the Aboke girls occurred just days after his own abduction on 10 December 1996, probably on the 12th or 13th. He recalled: 'We walked to Lango within a day. I was not allowed to carry any load. They said that I would throw away the load and escape. I walked with the officers. On reaching Lango we went to Aboke School – I don't know whether you heard about the abduction of the Aboke students – where they began abducting Aboke students at night, and then we turned around and walked back. I witnessed the abduction of the Aboke girls.'

If he indeed witnessed the abduction of the Aboke girls, he could not have been abducted two months later, in December. However, Ringo's confusion about the date of his abduction and that of the Aboke students can be explained by his focus on the details, rather than the dates, of events. And, since Ringo's experiences with the LRM/A spanned many emotions and physical hardships, those events that had the most impact on or significance to him tended to stick in his mind years later. That is to say, when he remembered an event, the passage of time was not the essential marker of that event, but rather it was his immediate experience of the event itself in relation to another event that stood out. For example, he recalled being beaten while walking to Sudan, being shot at while raiding a shopping centre, being hungry and thirsty when food and water supplies ran out while on patrol, and so on. Life for Ringo, as for many LRM/A abductees, it seemed, was one long journey into an abyss of violence which, from time to time, was punctuated by jarring events or occurrences that were imprinted in his memory and that, by necessity, became markers of the passage of time in his new life as an LRM/A soldier.

In a sense, Ringo's use of memory is derived from the Acholi tradition of remembering in which life stories are wrapped around salient historical events that everyone can recall. For instance, the Acholi will speak of the time of *kec abongo wang dako*, the time of 'I-touched-my-wife's-face' famine, when a severe drought killed all the crops and many people died of hunger. The famine was so named because a man whose household was in the midst of the famine woke up in the middle of the night hungry and, hoping to eat whatever was left in the cooking pot, touched his wife's face to determine if she was sleeping. In Acholi culture, married men do not take food directly from the cooking pot, hence the man's cautious move to check whether the coast was clear.

The critical point, though, is that while the famine gained its name from the action of one hungry man, it also became a signpost in the collective memory, a point of reference against which other events such as births, deaths, wars, and conflicts were dated. On a cultural level, therefore, Ringo's selective use of memory to focus on conspicuous events served not only as a milestone for the time he spent in the bush but also as a cultural trigger to help him remember whatever happened around that time. The abduction of Aboke girls was such an event, and Ringo could remember that, up to that moment, he was relatively well treated by the LRM/A. He did not have to carry big loads and was allowed to stay close to the senior officers, which provided a rare opportunity to observe and learn what made them tick.

As he recalled it, after the raid on St Mary's Secondary School, the LRM/A manoeuvred the now very large group of abductees into the bush and retraced its steps, reaching the border of Lango and Acoli sometime in the morning. While traversing the terrain around a simsim field, rebel soldiers guarding the rear of the walking caravan radioed with walkie-talkie that there were some white people trailing the group. The senior officer responded that particular attention should be paid to the unidentified people, and if there were government soldiers with them, then the rebels should shoot the whites first, followed by the soldiers. However, if they were not accompanied by government soldiers, then they should not be harassed.

Soon after, the rear guards reported that the intruders were alone, unaccompanied by the UPDF, and the order was given to allow them through. The intruders turned out to be 'Sista Rakele' (Sister Rachele Fassera) and a male teacher from her school. The convoy was asked to set up a temporary camp in the bush and start cooking while the leader of the operation, Ocaya Lagira, and his deputy, Oyet Bur, discussed matters with Sister Rachele. Ringo and another unidentified boy abductee were ordered to sit next to the senior officers of the LRM/A, and not to get up. Other abductees could get up and walk freely as they cooked. Ringo listened carefully to the negotiations as Sister Rachele opened with a strong bid for freeing her students – she wanted all the girls back and, in return, she would become Lagira's wife. Lagira was not happy with such a demand, and made it known: 'When she put forward her proposal, Lagira asked her, saying, "Would you accept if only some of the students are returned to you?" At first she rejected that notion, saying she wanted all the students to be freed so she could return with them. She was asked again, "Why do you suppose we wasted time to go all the way to your school, what do you think that was for? We were specifically sent to go fetch these students."'

With the negotiations deadlocked, Lagira made a radio call to Sudan and spoke to LRM/A leader Joseph Kony. The order was given to release most of the Aboke girls into the care of Sister Rachele, but to keep the others. According to the literature, 109 students were freed, while thirty were retained by the LRM/A and marched to Sudan under physically demanding circumstances (Cook, 2007; de Temmerman, 2001). From his vantage point near the officers, Ringo noted the transaction: 'They discussed the matter on the phone, and an agreement was made, and they began separating the students – Sister Rachele would return with most of the students. In all, eighty six students had been abducted. He [Kony] ordered that forty-six students should be returned, and forty to remain with the rebels.'[2]

Privy to the discussion between LRM/A commander Lagira and the courageous Sister Rachele, Ringo continued to note other details of that morning. The deal had barely been reached when the group was attacked by a UPDF airplane. Everyone scampered into the bush for safety, including Sister Rachele. The attack by the plane went on for quite a while before everyone could emerge from hiding. Sister Rachele was covered with mud from head to toe, her white habit completely soiled. She was bleeding from a wound where a sharp stick had pierced her foot. Lagira selected the girls to be retained, and those to return with Sister Rachele. Once the list was completed, he ordered some of his soldiers to escort the returnees back to the road where Sister Rachele had parked her vehicle. The LRM/A escorts were to shoot at any approaching UPDF soldiers who might attack the nun and the students.

Over the next several days, the LRM/A rebels moved back and forth, traversing difficult terrain and covering long distances. Although he did not have a definitive explanation for why such manoeuvres were necessary, Ringo Otigo concluded that the long walks were probably deliberately designed as part of the process of integrating the abductees into the LRM/A:

> It appeared that they wanted to confuse the students before taking them to Sudan. They planned to move back and forth so that the students could not remember the direction being taken. After traversing the terrain three

times, each time taking a different direction, we returned to the river for the last time and began crossing it. Some people crossed first, including the students, while we remained on the other side. After they had all crossed, we crossed after them, and then walked to Kitgum where we stayed for a long time.

Ringo's memory of the incidents surrounding the abduction of the Aboke girls is important not only because it confirms most of the details that researchers later documented, but also because it enables him to reconstruct these events the way he witnessed them. It establishes his state of mind at the time as he attempted to comprehend what was happening to the girls and relate this to his own situation, especially his long-term chances for survival and, consequently, how he should act and behave in captivity. What is immediately and abundantly evident is Ringo's careful cataloguing of the details surrounding that event, his growing awareness of his environment, and his understanding of who was in control, what the ground rules of survival were, and what one needed to do to conform to those rules. Of prime importance was the need to be inconspicuous so as to avoid becoming the centre of attention, yet all the while remaining alert to the goings-on. The situation in which he found himself underlined the importance of the Acholi proverb that he had learned growing in the village – *latin pa lacan winyo pwony ki ii bad deero* (the poor man's child learns while hiding on the side of the granary). In the bush he was orphaned, but that did not mean he lacked a community from which to learn the lore and wisdom of the art of survival. Paying attention to little details became a very important skill in personal survival, and Ringo worked especially hard to learn what each gesture and body language meant, or as Acholi would say, *kit ma dano loko kwede* (how people talk).

Better to Kill Me Outright

The abductees were informed on reaching Palenga that the 'freshly abducted must move into the yard where our civilian mindset must be erased.' Ringo was among those chosen for *lwooko wii cibilan* (washing the civilian mind). By now Ringo Otigo had learned in the first few weeks of his life with the LRM/A that the rebel commanders were not always predictable, and something that seemed innocent at the beginning could prove fatal to the abductees. One needed to stay keenly aware of whatever was happening in order to stay alive. A moment of inattention almost cost Otigo his life: 'We were told, "If you were abducted, indicate if you were the only captive from your home. If two of you were abducted from the home, also say so. If you were abducted while sick, also let it be known."' Ringo still retained the piece of paper from the hospital on which the prescription for his chest pain was written on the day of his abduction. Such information, he reasoned, could help his cause, perhaps even gaining the sympathy of the rebels and persuading them to let him go free. He let the commanders know that he had had chest pain, and had the medical document to prove it. He was asked to move to one side. Others soon joined him, although it was unclear what rationale was being used to decide who was placed in which group. In the meantime, a group of rebels busied themselves cutting fresh sticks, which were piled by the hundreds in the yard. Ringo observed the activity with some interest, but he was not immediately alarmed about his own welfare. The purpose of the sticks soon became apparent: 'It was noon when they completed the cutting and bundling of sticks, and separating us into lots. Altogether, about thirty children were selected and thrown down in the sun. They kicked you, and sent you sprawling in the sun. We all lay down. We were then told that all of us were intending to escape, and we needed to be beaten, and if possible, killed.' The beating, carried out by almost half a dozen recruits for every abductee, was brutal and unrelenting. The beating went on even after the victims lapsed into coma. Ringo was beaten by five people: 'The two bundles were all used up, the sticks shredded to pieces, reaching a point when I felt my life was gone. My entire body had gone numb, and I no longer felt the sting of the sticks. They beat me until the two bundles were gone. Two people were chosen to return to carry out more beating. At that moment, a boy jumped up to run, and was cut down by a bullet, dying beside the house.' Barely clinging to consciousness, Ringo was given additional beatings by two others. This time the consequences were nearly fatal:

> So they beat me until all the sticks were gone, then they left me. They left us there, others were cooking. When they left me, I was told to get up and move to the banana plantation where food was being cooked. Mustering all my remaining strength, I straightened up; all of a sudden, blood broke free from my nose, my head was spinning, and I fell back to the ground. I remained sprawled in that position for some time. Blood flowed freely from my head until it stopped by itself, then slowly, I began to drag myself to the banana grove.

They left us there, others were cooking. For the LRM/A, the conspicuous ordinariness of cooking went in tandem with the inhumanely vicious business of beating the children to cleanse them of their civilian mindset. The LRM/A made it seem pedestrian that in the bush children's lives were balanced on a very thin edge between being *dano adana*, human persons who needed to be fed food one moment, and objects that were mercilessly flogged the next. The child going through this experience needed to decide early on how to live on either side of the equation. The fluidity of experiences, which ranged from being treated well to being handled harshly, necessitated the construction of a double identity, one capable of relating to others in the neighbourly fashion of village life, and the other characterized by a hardened, self-centred outlook geared towards personal survival to the exclusion of all else. Ringo, like most of the children who lived with the LRM/A, would in time learn to deploy one or the other of these identities based on the prevailing circumstances.

Seriously injured and weakened by the beating, which left his body covered with puffed bruises, Ringo was confused. Except for the beating he received days into his abduction, he had mostly been treated far better than the other abductees. While others suffered the indignity of carrying big loads on their heads, he walked freely without any encumbrance. Moreover, when the Aboke girls were abducted, he was able to sit beside the LRM/A officers to witness what was being discussed with the white nun. Yet, here, he was beaten to within an inch of his young life. His confusion deepened when a bush doctor approached him to offer treatment. Ringo's frustration exploded to the surface:

> At that moment a wave of anger overwhelmed me, making me cry. I said, 'First I was grievously injured, and now you want to treat me, what for? Better to kill me outright.' The doctor quietly told me two things. He said, 'Boy, here nobody cares about you, if you are begging to die, you will be killed this very moment. You should thank God that you are still able to drag yourself on your buttocks, perhaps your wounds will heal.' Then he fell silent, never repeating anything else. I took the drug he gave me, and then I began cutting banana barks, putting them on the fire and then placing them over my body.

The following morning, four children were discovered dead, having succumbed to their wounds from the beating of the previous day. The doctor again pointed out what Ringo already knew: 'That was when the doctor spoke to me again, saying, "Boy, yesterday, did I not tell you so? I told you to be thankful that you were able to drag yourself. Look at those who could not take it any more. Here, if you focus on being killed, then you will be killed, nobody cares. You have seen how a chicken is slaughtered, no? Here the death of a person is no different from a chicken's; at least a chicken is killed when a visitor comes, and is eaten. Here nobody cares about the death of a person."'

Ringo's budding self-reliance would prove crucial in the next few weeks when the LRM/A commanders chose to march hundreds of kilometres to Aruu inside Sudan. The long trek was physically taxing for any able-bodied adult, but for many of the abducted children, who were already weighed down with big loads on their heads and who lacked proper nutrition while nursing serious body wounds from the numerous beatings, it was fatal. At least a dozen children, including two of Ringo's relatives who could not walk any more, were clubbed to death before his very eyes. When the large party stopped to rest at the mouth of a river, the officers asked children unable to walk to step forward. Ringo hung back, his instinct for self-preservation fully deployed: 'They called out to any one who was badly off and could not walk to step forward. I decided that I would not step forward this time; however bad I felt, I would not get up. Seeing people being hacked with machetes, speared with bayonets, beaten with hideous looking sticks, and at time times whacked with an axe on the back of the head, made me resolve to hang tough, never to step forward. If I was going to die, I would die walking. I never stepped forward.'

Friendship on the Long Walk to Aruu Camp, Sudan

For many of the abductees, surviving the cruel transformation into child combatants involved finding a morsel of friendship amidst intense suffering, violence, and death. These moments of humanity and friendship afforded them some semblance of *dano adana*, human personhood. For Ringo, a genuine friendship seemed to develop between him and the doctor who treated him after the severe beating. As a senior officer with the LRM/A, the doctor was able to fend off any further attempts at mistreatment of Ringo. In some ways, he seemed to assume the role of a father figure for him. He ordered other boys to help with Ringo's bath and attend to his wounds. The doctor also ensured that Ringo got regular doses of antibiotics, administered through needles, to ensure that his wounds did not become infected.

A sure sign of the strength of the new relationship came when Ringo was afforded a luxury that other children did not have, hot tea:

The doctor had a bag in which he kept some sugar. He instructed his escort, telling him, 'You go and make some tea and give it to the boy to drink.' He came and prepared hot tea, one cup. I drank that. Sweat began pouring down my body. We stayed. When we woke up in the morning, I found my body stiff but I felt strong enough to walk. That morning, the doctor asked, 'Boy, how do you feel?' I replied, 'I am here, I don't feel too badly now.' I was afraid of what I had seen happen with my own eyes and I was afraid to tell him how I really felt. I responded with that simple statement: I am here, I don't feel too badly, I can walk. That morning, he gave me two more needles, and we began walking.

Despite his hesitation in trusting the doctor, Ringo had a growing sense of loyalty to him. On the long march through the arid desert of southern Sudan, the doctor entrusted Ringo with a jerry-can full of water. Ringo Otigo almost lost his life attempting to protect the water from another LRM/A officer who wanted it:

I walked along with the water; the water almost got me killed. Someone started beating me, demanding the water, and I said, 'Look, this water does not belong to me. The person who gave me the water made it clear that should I give it to someone, I would be killed here in the bush.' I said, 'This is not my water.' Still, I was beaten up, and my hand stabbed with a bayonet, the scar is right here. I was holding tight to the lid of the jerry-can so the soldier stabbed my hand, telling me to let go. 'This is not my water, I was simply ordered to carry it.' At that moment, the owner of the water showed up, and caught the soldier beating me, and said, 'You, why are you beating the boy? Do you know who gave him the water?'

The soldier was arrested, and taken to be beaten. Ringo, meanwhile, was now asked to walk with the senior officers for fear that the soldier who was beaten might carry out a revenge attack. By the time the caravan arrived at Aruu camp a few days later, Ringo Otigo seemed on the cusp of being absorbed into the LRM/A. What was left now was formal induction through the ritual of *moo yaa* and military training.

In Aruu, Ringo was allocated to serve under his officer-doctor friend, who was part of 'Control Altar,' the LRM/A high command set in Kony's compound. He was duly registered the following morning as a new arrival, and began training almost immediately. The formal induction into the LRM/A involving the *moo yaa* ceremony was conducted a few days after Ringo arrived. The ceremony was a crucial step in becoming a member of the LRM/A, and so Ringo paid close attention:

> During the purification ceremony, you took off your clothes, remaining bare-chested, and a gun [was] handed to you, before you stepped forward to be anointed. There were lines of people singing. The controller yard took some water, oil and a rock, and walked towards you, and circled you three times, put some water, placed the stone in the oil, then poured water on top, and then put the mixture on your body ... The stone was placed in the bottle, water added, and a string tied at the mouth, a plastic bottle. The ends of the string were tied together and then hung around your neck.
>
> During the rituals, only the controller yard spoke, saying, 'Today, you are being anointed with oil in front of the sacred home of Kony, and beginning today, you are a soldier for Kony, not anyone else.' This was repeated on the next person, and the next, until everyone was done.

After the *moo yaa* purification, the abductees were now considered part of the LRM/A and were expected to apply themselves fully to the training regimen. Ringo's career path with the rebels came as a result of a casual conversation with his benefactor, the doctor. Ringo recalled the conversation:

> The officer who picked me from the lot of new arrivals was a doctor in the camp. He asked me, saying, 'Young boy, did you attend school?'
> I said, 'I attended school.'
> He asked, 'To what grade did you attend?'
> I said, 'Grade Six.'
> He asked again, 'Can you listen to the BBC?'
> I replied, 'I can listen.'
> In the evening, he brought a radio and turned it on. He said, 'Listen to what is being said on BBC, then tell me.'
> After the BBC newscast ended, I told him what was said on the bulletin. He said, No problem. 'When the opportunity comes for further training, I will send you for it.' That was all he said, and that ended the exchange. That was the only time he spoke to me about it.

The conversation with the doctor about whether Ringo could under-stand the BBC newscast was a major turning point for the child abductee. Though at first fearful that he may have overexposed himself by demon-strating his grasp of the English language and, therefore, could be con-sidered a prime candidate for escape, Ringo soon learned that he was going to be sent to Khartoum for further training as *dakta mony* (war doc-tor). His status as *welo* (visitor), which he retained for the first few weeks of his arrival in Aruu, had slowly changed to that of *latin paco* (child of the home). His new identity was being built around the people in the rebel camp. This was his new home, and the doctor's family was his new family. He was on his way to becoming a full member of the LRM/A.

Dakta Mony (War Doctor)

In Khartoum, Ringo discovered that he was being trained to become not an actual doctor but rather a medic with knowledge of treating war wounds and administering certain drugs. He and four other trainees lived in Kony's official residence. Food was plentiful, and they had good beds to sleep on. Life generally was much better than in the bush and even at Aruu camp. The students travelled everyday from the house to the medical clinic where they were trained by Sudanese who spoke mostly Arabic intermixed with bits of English. They were taught to recognize different drugs, what they were for and how to administer them. The trainees also learned how to communicate with patients, how to find out what was wrong with them and make prescriptions. They were taught how to remove shrapnel and bullets from wounds, how to splinter broken bones, and how to administer first aid to those grievously wounded in battle.

A different dilemma now confronted the trainees, who were gener-ally well treated and not as closely watched by the LRM/A as the other abductees were. Should they try to escape from Khartoum? As Ringo put it, 'beatings and other mistreatments were unlikely. The way it looked, I had been accepted as part of the rebel group in the bush.' Besides, escape had its own risks and dangers. There were a number of factors to be taken into account, the main one being the inability to find one's way back to Uganda. There was also a language barrier because none of the trainees spoke Arabic. This would have reduced their abil-ity to ask for basic directions, food, and shelter.

As well, southern Sudan was hostile territory for the LRM/A. The geopolitics of the day that created an alliance between, on the one hand, the LRM/A and the Khartoum government of Omar al-Bashir, and, on the other, between the Sudan People's Liberation Army and the Kampala government of President Yoweri Museveni, meant that the LRM/A was at war with the SPLM/A. In a curious case of 'your enemy is my friend,' the national governments of Uganda and Sudan each sponsored and harboured rebels fighting the other, with Uganda supporting the SPLM/A and Sudan aiding the LRM/A. The LRM/A rebels, as we saw in chapter 2, referred to the SPLM/A simply as the 'Dinka'[3] and fought frequently with them. Former LRM/A child combatants had deep respect for the Dinkas' fighting prowess, and often spoke of avoiding contact with them whenever possible.

For Ringo and his colleagues, this meant that the idea of escape had to factor in the possibility not only of being discovered by the LRM/A but also of running straight into the LRM/A's mortal enemy, the Dinka. He recalled a story of six abductees who attempted to escape from Aruu camp. The escapees had not gone far when they ran into the Dinka and were captured. Four eventually escaped while two were immediately executed by the Dinka. On returning back to their barracks in Aruu, the four would-be escapees said that they had gone into the forest to hunt and collect a wild spinach-like vegetable called *adyegi* for cooking, and had encountered the Dinka. The rescue platoon, assembled to pursue the Dinka, found that the two captives had already been killed, disembowelled, and left near the forest path. In the end, Ringo decided that the risks of escaping far outweighed the benefits. As he put it, 'now I had to focus and work hard at my job so that, God willing, I could survive.'

As *dakta mony*, Ringo's job entailed accompanying expeditionary forces on field operations. His responsibility was mainly to care for the sick and wounded, but he always carried an assault rifle and occasionally engaged in firefights: 'The first time we came [to Uganda] and turned around, returned to base. Again, I was assigned; we came back to Uganda all the way to Kitgum. On that trip, we engaged the army in a fierce firefight on Lugaa road; many people were injured. I was asked to accompany the wounded to Sudan, and we went back. Forty six people were wounded. Some soldiers were selected among those to return to Sudan.'

Back in Sudan, Ringo was respected by the rank and file as *dakta mony* and given considerable prestige as a promising young officer. His daily duty at the sickbay was seeing the sick, prescribing medications, and attending to the wounded. Once or twice he treated one of the captured Aboke girls. The routine of life in the rebel camp was broken every so often when new abductees arrived with wounds and blisters from the long march from Uganda and had to be attended to immediately. He spent most of his spare time in his hut, listening to the radio or simply resting.

The LRM/A senior officers felt that Ringo should be given a wife to cook and care for him. Ringo was sixteen or seventeen at the time. However, he declined to take the proffered companion and, for his taciturn attitude, was given some beatings. He nonetheless preferred the beatings to taking a wife and essentially lied to the officers, telling them that he could not afford to have a wife at the time because he could not provide for her, much less dress her properly. 'I cannot stay with a woman without providing her with a dress to wear,' he told them. But, according to Ringo, the real reason for refusing to live with the girl was because she had recently been widowed after her husband was killed in a battle with the UPDF. Still steeped in Acholi beliefs about vengeance spirits and the idea that misfortunes happen for a reason, Ringo decided that he could not risk his good fortune by living with a woman whose life had been crossed by ill luck. He explained it this way: 'Essentially, I had difficulty with taking a woman whose husband was no longer there – she should not be the first to know my manhood [have intercourse with me], and should not be the first woman to live with me. My reservation came from knowing that the woman's husband was shot and killed, and the thought of taking over was something I could not do. My fear was that what happened to her husband could also happen to me because women come with different luck. That's why I refused her.'

Ringo clearly linked his refusal to take the widow for a wife to Acholi teachings that he had heard as a young boy growing up in the village, teachings that now guided how he constructed his new persona as an LRM/A child combatant:

That was in keeping with what I had heard much earlier while still at home, free of any problem, something elders would say, namely, that when travelling, particularly when going to the bush, say when a big hunt was called the following day, and everyone had been appropriately informed today about the hunt, there were certain rituals you, as a head of a house, were not allowed to perform. You could receive injuries should you perform them. That is, when you were married when you were going to the bush, you must not have intercourse with your wife. As well, there were certain foods that you were forbidden from eating when going on a hunt, such as sour vegetables. That I had heard.

In the bush, Ringo Otigo had retained the cultural identity formed in his village prior to abduction, and he would not take a woman already widowed and likely dogged by misfortune. It would not be long before he returned to his ancestral home where his original, desired identity would clash with his stigmatized identity as a CI soldier.

We Have Done Our Part

The chain of events that led to Ringo's eventual departure from the bush started sometime in 2000 when he accompanied another LRM/A expeditionary force to northern Uganda. This was his third trip from the LRM/A base in southern Sudan to northern Uganda and, as it turned out, his last expedition. The previous expeditions had seen the LRM/A take a number of casualties whom Ringo treated on the road back to Sudan. One of the goals of the new expedition was to raid shopping centres for medicine and food to be brought back to Sudan. But these trips were becoming more perilous as the UPDF monitored the movements of the LRM/A. Meanwhile, Dinka militias in southern Sudan were also becoming more menacing to LRM/A soldiers, often tracking them down and killing them. The LRM/A was feeling pressure from all sides, but the raid on the shopping centre went ahead anyway. According to Ringo, it did not go as planned: 'On this trip, we passed near the foothill of Ogili Hill in Kitgum. From there, the group went to loot the centre in Pajule. While looting the centre, a battle ensured with the [UPDF] army, and seventeen people were injured. With seventeen wounded, I was assigned to go care for them at the sickbay near Agago River.'

As time went by, with months turning into years and food supplies running low, all but six wounded soldiers got better and returned to Sudan. Ringo decided to shift base to Palabek, not far from Kitgum town. He was the most senior officer in the group and his decision could not be questioned. He had shown good leadership to his men, who now depended on him to lead them to safety. To avoid exposing their presence to the UPDF and the villagers, Ringo and the six wounded rebel soldiers shifted bases often, moving from one area to another, dodging possible UPDF traps.

During one such relocation, an LRM/A team from Sudan arrived at the sickbay where Ringo's group had been stationed, and found it empty. After searching for them for a while, the team returned to Sudan, leaving Ringo and his six wounded men behind. Until that point, Ringo and his men had been relying on food taken from gardens in nearby villages. The group also established a relationship with some of the villagers with whom Ringo bartered salt for food. But, as the salt supply ran low, it became harder to obtain food. One day, a peasant came across the footprints left behind by Ringo's team as they dug up sweet potatoes to augment their fast dwindling food supply. The peasant notified the UPDF, which set up an ambush for the team. The army pounced when Ringo's team, now weakened by hunger and isolation, returned to steal more sweet potatoes for food. In the fierce exchange of fire, two LRM/A young combatants were wounded, one sustaining a broken leg while the other was shot in the arm. Ringo's team quickly retreated with the wounded while the UPDF gave chase. In a cat-and-mouse game, the team hid their wounded in a cave, doubled back inside the UPDF circle, and ended up spending the night literally next to the UPDF detachment camp. As team leader, Ringo knew the situation had become dire: 'Early the next morning, we crossed the road and returned to the cave where we had left the two colleagues. We took them and crossed the Agago River. We came and camped between the Aswa River and Agago. We stayed there for a while. We would send civilians to get us food, and they did.'

But Ringo knew time was running out and soon he and his young combatants would find themselves in dire straits. He needed to act fast, and he did, initiating a conversation with a civilian about events around them. He recalled that day:

> One day, I asked a civilian, saying, 'We would like to get a clear picture. Those rebels who escape and return home into the hand of government, what happens to them?' The civilian replied, 'The escapees are cared for in two places. There is GUSCO and World Vision, and another possibility is CARITAS. It is not clear what else happens there. But it is certain that they are not hassled at all.'
>
> I said, 'What about trouble with the army? Is there trouble?'
>
> He said, 'No, trouble at all.'
>
> I said to him, 'Some of our colleagues escaped, one of my brothers was among them, and we wanted to ascertain that they were not harassed, and arrived safely. But if they ran into trouble then we wouldn't know how they arrived.'

They said, 'No, there is no trouble at all.'

I said, 'If so, that's good.'

At that moment, the civilians gave us flour, beans and peas. We gave them salt, eight packets. They returned back to the camp at Omel Kuru. As they departed, we told them, 'Go well; however, if the army asks you do not reveal that you saw us.'

Although his team was not aware of his plan, Ringo had laid the seed for defecting from the LRM/A. He was increasingly convinced that survival was most likely by getting out of the bush and returning to civilian life. However, he was not doing it because he thought that the LRM/A was evil or that its ideology was incompatible with his beliefs. He, after all, had become one of the LRM/A, a young combatant fighting for its cause. No, he was about to leave the bush because his survival and that of the young soldiers under his command was at stake. There was now no communication with the LRM/A base in Sudan. Further search for food only risked more firefights with the UPDF, which was closing in on the team every day. One day, with no more salt to barter for food from the villages, and the last of the beans cooked, Ringo's team roasted some measly fish they had caught from the river. Ringo spoke to his young charges, saying:

'Friends, we must travel to Gulu to go look for the big sickbay. At the time, we had been told that there were a lot of people [LRM/A rebels] in Gulu. If we go to the sickbay, we will look for people in Koich where we are told there is a big sickbay. Let's go and look for the others so that our life is improved. With the army now shooting at us while we look for food, life here is about to get tougher.'

When I made the comments, they said, 'Doctor, don't you think we will get killed?' I said, 'There will be no killing, we will walk, dodge the army, until we get there. There will be no trouble.'

They said as long as we know the way, there was no problem. I said, 'Let's go, we won't stay any longer. Life here has become difficult, and our presence is widely known, we cannot stay.'

That evening, however, Ringo changed his mind abruptly. Rather than wander through the bushes in search of another LRM/A sickbay, the team would simply walk out. He knew, however, that there was great risk in revealing his ultimate plan of escape to the boys. He had no way of knowing how they might react or what they might do when confronted with the choice of walking out free. To guard against an ugly dispute and a potential shootout among his team, Ringo waited until the boys were gone to the river to fish for supper and collected all their guns. He heaped the guns under his bedding, sat on them, and waited with his own machine-gun in hand. When the boys returned, Ringo called them and sat them down for a serious conversation. He recalled the tense and dramatic discussion that followed:

I took my gun and held it in my hands. I called out to them. When all six of them came, I told them to sit down. I began talking to them, saying, 'Friends, I want to tell you that we have endured enough working in the bush, we have done our part. We will leave this work for others. We are returning to Gulu. Our journey to Gulu is to return home and no where else. There is nothing you can say about this. But I want you to clean both your civilian clothes and soldiers' uniforms, they must be clean. Tomorrow, we are not sleeping here. We will begin our journey right away.

One of the boys said, 'Doctor, the words you have spoken are good, but there is a small problem. When we return home, we will all be killed. Presently, the army is killing many people. Even civilians, we understand when they leave the camps, are caught and killed with the claim that they are returning rebels. We are going to get hurt.'

I said, 'Look, death has been with us forever and when we were born, death was present on earth. How many have died in the bush such that family members had to make funeral arrangements without knowing where and how they died? At least if we are killed at home, people will know that the child of so and so was killed in this area. That is better than having wild pigs push your skull in the bush, which is tragic. Now that we have a chance to escape, let's leave.'

One of the boys was a Lango, and he said, 'Then give us back our guns.' I said, 'I won't return your guns. I don't have the power to return your guns at this time. What I have said I have said, and anybody not in agreement will remain here in the bush, unarmed. I will not kill anyone, but you will walk empty-handed. If you choose to report this to other Lakwena soldiers, then go ahead because I am now feeling the pain of this life in my skin, and won't tolerate it any longer. If we are caught along the way escaping, I will speak on your behalf, you will not respond. I will be the one to say why I am walking with you all, that's for me to say.'

They finally accepted. Once they accepted, a boy named Oraako from Palabek said there was no point in him going all the way to Gulu; he would instead take a direct route to return to his home; he was certain he would arrive safely. I said, 'It would be preferable to stick together, and then go our separate ways from the hand of the government.'

He said, 'No, I will reach home safely, I cannot return to Gulu.'

I said, 'No problem, I am releasing you this moment. If you can get to your home, arrive well. Take off your uniform, put on civilian clothes, and get started right away. If you meet Lakwena rebels, and you know some in the group, tell them that there was a shootout, everyone scattered from the sickbay, and you got separated from the others, and are now running around looking for other rebel units. If they ask, "What about your uniform?" Say only one thing, that "we had washed our uniforms, and we fled, leaving them behind, everyone is scattered in the bush, and I have no idea where everyone is. We were surprised while at the river, that's where the army found us."'

Ringo was just as concerned about being discovered escaping by the UPDF as by the LRM/A soldiers, whom he referred to as 'Lakwena,' the name that had stuck to the LRM/A insurgents since the early days of Alice Lakwena Auma and the Holy Spirit Movement in 1987. But he also had become a decisive leader who was in full control of the situation, instructing the 'boys' on what to do in order to navigate the dangerous transition from insurgent to former insurgent.

What is immediately evident from an Acholi cultural point of view is the manner with which he went about revealing his plan for deserting the LRM/A. Though he was roughly the same age as the others, he was also, by virtue of being the highest-ranking LRM/A soldier at that moment, the face of authority not only in military terms but also in the traditional Acholi sense, which explains why he was referred to as the *ladit* (elder). Tactfully, like the elder that he was in the eyes of the six young men, he asked them to come and sit down. When there is something important to say, Acholi elders don't say it 'on the run,' but always issue an invitation to the listeners to sit down first. It is a formal recognition that the persons being invited to sit down are worthy of consideration and respect. Quick repartee 'on the fly' is usually indicative of how those of the same age speak to each other, but when there is a serious issue to be discussed, with someone of authority present, the traditional approach is to sit down.

And as in many Acholi cultural settings, where there is a serious discussion, one takes issue with ideas by first acknowledging that whatever the last speaker said made some good sense, and then stating the nature of the objection. One of the young men noted that the idea of returning home was 'good'; however, he carefully phrased his objection by citing the possibility of being killed by the UPDF. For his part, Ringo responded to the objection by being philosophical about death and dying, a fate shared by all. However, his trump card was the image of death in the wilderness, where 'wild pigs push your skull in the bush.' To the Acholi, who believe that relatives cannot leave a person to die and rot in the bush without proper burial, this was a statement with many levels of meaning. Ringo was simultaneously reminding the young men, first, that they still had relatives at home who loved and cared for them, and, second, that they had the responsibility of ensuring that those at home knew what happened to them, even if that meant being killed close to home so 'people will know that the child of so and so was killed in this area.'

More important, Ringo skilfully exploited the young men's clear understanding of Luo kinship ties to rally them to his side of the argument, which was that it was better to escape and risk dying closer to home than to do nothing and die in the wilderness. Dying, according to his logic, was not the big thing to think about at that moment; rather, they should ponder the possibility of dying in such a manner that one's kin were not forever engulfed in the grief of not knowing what happened to their loved one who was taken to the bush by the LRM/A.

Ringo further injected wisdom into his response when asked by one of his young friends to return the confiscated guns. 'I don't have the power to return your guns at this time,' Ringo said. In fact, Ringo did have the power to return the guns to the boys, but because he had already made the decision to return home, he forestalled the potential for angry accusations from the team with a disarmingly ambiguous response. What he was telling them was that they should not blame or be angry with him for confiscating the guns because he was not the final authority in the matter. Technically, having committed himself to returning home, this was true because he no longer saw himself as an active LRM/A soldier. As a defector from the rebel movement, Ringo could not afford to return the guns to those who might still be committed to the LRM/A. He had effectively crossed to the other side of the divide from his LRM/A compatriots. Also, though he held a gun in his hands, Ringo realized that he was outnumbered. His refusal to return the guns to his friends was made in a manner that allowed him to come across as an ally rather than a foe, and he thereby persuaded the young men around him to continue looking up to him as a reasonable leader who knew what he was doing.

On the day of their defection, Ringo and the remaining LRM/A combatants slipped back into their combat uniforms and, using guile, wits, and skills acquired in their bush days, walked out into the open daylight. Ringo recalled this moment because he prayed to his ancestors for guidance (see, e.g., p'Bitek, 1971), knowing that he could be killed: 'I called the name of our grandfather who was in charge of the family shrine, saying, "Mzee Odonga, my day for leaving the bush has come. If you are ready, and my family shrine is strong, then I will arrive safely. If not, then that's the way it is; the death of a male child is such that one can die anywhere." I was imbued with boldness of inner strength, and prepared to leave.'

The impetus to leave was, in this case, not simply a physical preparation that demanded some military assessment of the outcome, but a spiritual one that required Ringo to feel firm in his resolve to leave and arrive safely. His resolution to walk out of the bush was underwritten by his prayers to his ancestors, and the knowledge that his ancestral spirits had never left him during the six years that he had been with the LRM/A. Interestingly enough, Ringo's prayer was similar to the kind made when someone was embarking on a long journey into the unknown. In this case, Ringo's homecoming was fraught with serious risks. The possibility that he might not survive the return home underlined the necessity of seeking spiritual connection with his ancestors.

With his prayer concluded, Ringo led his young combatants out, masquerading as UPDF soldiers on patrol along the main road to Gulu. The ruse worked so effectively that Ringo stopped occasionally along the road to chat with real UPDF soldiers who never suspected that the group belonged to the LRM/A. After a long walk, at last the group reached the outskirts of Gulu town. Ringo resorted to deception one last time by sending a bicycle courier to inform GUSCO staff that the UPDF had captured some LRM/A rebels who wanted to surrender, and asked that GUSCO send a vehicle to pick them up. Within the hour, Ringo and his soldiers were free:

> They came for us. The driver came with two [GUSCO] staff, one of them my former teacher I told you about earlier, Odong. As soon as he arrived and saw me, my heart skipped a beat. He said, 'Man is this you?' 'This is me in person!' I replied. He said, 'I thought you would never be seen again, and that your life had left this earth. No problem if you are still alive. Relax now, nothing will happen to you.'

At that moment we got into the vehicle, all of us. That was when people became aware that these were rebel escapees. People began gathering to see us. We were driven away and brought to GUSCO.

After being processed at GUSCO, Ringo and his colleagues were transferred to the UPDF barracks, where they were left to languish for a few days before his family was told that he had returned from the bush. Ringo's reunion with his mother at the barracks was very emotional as she fell on him, wailing at the top of her voice, and had to be calmed down. In the Acholi tradition, wailing at the return of someone who was away, and considered dead, is normal. It was a joyous occasion for everyone, but it was also a sad occasion because the physical and mental condition of the returnees was as yet unclear. Was this still a person who could be referred to as *dano adana*, or, after so many years in the bush, had he turned into a *bedo lee lee* (wild thing)?

When his mother was finally consoled and was able to speak to Ringo, she decided that he was still *dano adana*, and invited him to visit home. Permission was given for a military vehicle to take him to his village. Three army soldiers sat in the back of the vehicle. Ringo sat in front close to the passenger door, while his mother squeezed in between him and the driver. They drove in silence to the village, where many relatives had gathered in the compound. There was a mix of *kijira* (women's ululation) as well as more wailing by older women who performed *poto ikome* (falling upon him), a mixture of welcome, sympathy, and thanksgiving. Many could be heard saying, 'Latina maa doo, abila pa kwaru tek, oweko tin waneni' (My mother's child, your grandfather's ancestral spirit is strong; that's why we are seeing you today). Afterwards, a goat was slaughtered, and once the traditional rituals (fully explained in next chapter) that accompanied this act were completed, Ringo left, returning to the barracks. His family remained at home.

In days following the homecoming rituals, Ringo's mother visited him twice in the barracks. Ringo also felt something changing in him. He was reconnecting with a part of himself that had been suppressed during his years in the bush with the LRM/A, following the thread that led back to his childhood as a civilian:

I felt some change in my life. I had returned and seen home with my eyes, talked to my family, ate home cooking. I began to feel like a homebody person, and began using home things, and when I imagined home, the picture came to mind.

This after I had journeyed three times home, but some of the homes in the village had burned down, and some people were no longer alive. I had to think hard to remember that there used to be many homes in the village. When I returned these homes were gone, and the owners also gone. I had to imagine that this was where the home of this person was located, such a tree was standing here, and a papaya tree was at this location. All these I had to imagine before the pictures would come to my mind, and with time I became used to the new life at home, and began living again.

Returning home without being 'scratched even by a blade of grass' in battle after six years in the bush with the LRM/A, Ringo believed that his good fortune was partly attributable to military training and partly to the strength of his ancestral spirits, who looked after him, cared for him, and made sure that he returned home safely. Furthermore, the identity that Ringo crafted for himself in the bush was not created in isolation from the rebels, but rather was reproduced in spite of them and allowed him to continually find ways to survive and live. That is to say, his identity creation was accompanied by twin processes, namely, the LRM/A exploitation of Acholi culture as a mechanism for creating cohesion and control over its fighters, and Ringo's perpetual tapping into the cultural reservoir of his upbringing in an Acholi village as a means to understand, dissect, and make meaning of his bush environment. One could argue that his upbringing in the village was ultimately the most useful tool for his successful reproduction of an identity that could withstand the mental and physical rigour of being a child combatant. Yet it is this very same identity that was challenged by his family and community when he returned home. The angst of returnees, as it turned out, was occasioned not only by escaping the LRM/A camps but also by finding themselves again in communities which they left as little children but to which they were returning, in some cases, as adults with children of their own.

Dwoogo Paco (Returning Home)

Now, resilience could be something you are born with because learning something that you don't have is quite difficult. However, I should also say that it
can be taught. My father taught me in those days, and I kept in mind what my
father taught me. I took those teachings with me to the bush, and endured the
very kind of thing that my father was teaching me about. Whenever I became
bitter while I was there, I returned, reversed, came back to what my father had
taught me – that be tough, endure and you will get there. So, I endured, hanging in there until this very moment, I retain the same resilience.

Miya Aparo, 16 July 2008, Gulu

The above comment, made by Miya Aparo as we wrapped up our interview on a hot afternoon in Gulu town, provides a nuanced alternative
to the popular view – perpetuated by field reports and studies (e.g.,
Coalition to Stop the Use of Child Soldiers, 2001, 2004, 2008) – that CI
soldiers are victims pure and simple. At many levels, the comment flies
in the face of often graphic depictions of children as helpless war victims with horrific war-related injuries and mutilations, drug addic-
tions, and sexually transmitted infections, to say nothing of emotional
scars from the many other inhuman indignities they suffered in the
war.[1] These painful images of CI soldiers as victims of war have been
especially effective in mobilizing popular opinion against the exploitation of children as combatants in civil conflicts around the globe. They
have also prodded the UN, world leaders, and state policy makers to
enact laws that make it illegal to use children in war, and to take action
in enforcing the rights of children before courts tasked with investigat-
ing war criminality and atrocities.[2]

However, the narratives of returning CI soldiers as hapless and help-less child victims of war, some of which border on what A. Honwana (2006) refers to as 'exaggerated narratives of victimization' (15), have overshadowed the complexity of the coping strategies that child com-batants employ in order to survive war. For those in Western society eager to express shock that children can be used in such an horrendous manner, in such horrific settings, CI soldiers become the focus of our collective sympathy, victims upon whom we can shower our love and at the same time turn into heroic figures. In essence, by taking this ap-proach, we lose a fundamental recognition of the capacity of CI soldiers for growth in the face of adversity, for adapting to new situations, for fostering resilient selves such as when they 'construct their identities and develop their lives within the network of these dehumanizing rela-tions' (Martin-Baro, 1996, 125).

When I met her in Gulu, Miya Aparo, like the other former CI sol-diers, was on the path to repair, to a better image of herself in Acholi civilian society, where she had a new-found voice as a community counsellor for other child combatants who, like her, had returned home from the bush. However, in talking to Miya, it seemed as though the main challenge she faced in returning to civilian society was not forget-ting war and the violence associated with it. To the contrary, she still had vivid memories of war, and told of her participation in it as if it happened the day before the interview. She and the other former CI soldiers seemed to accept that war was a part of their life experiences, something they could not forget, unlearn, or let go of. Her principle struggle, rather, seemed to be in learning how to cope with a society that did not understand her and her colleagues from the war. All spoke sadly, even bitterly, about their reception back into civilian society. Rejection by family and by a society that viewed their former lives as stigmatized posed huge social and psychological barriers that many felt they had to overcome. Said Miya, 'For this reason, my children do not have a clan, they do not have extended family, I am now their fa-ther, aunt, and whoever else, all rolled into me.' Similarly, Ringo Otigo recalled the hostility he experienced from the community, 'The way people looked at me – truth be told, people talk too much and we all have different intentions – when I returned home was not always with good intentions, especially neighbours whose homes were nearby.'

Indeed, in this concluding chapter, I explore the idea that for many former LRM/A CI soldiers, *dwoogo paco*, translated as 'returning home,' expresses the deeply held desire to return to their ancestral homes. It is the place where ancestral kith and kin have lived over a period of time, and often it is where *abila pa kwaro* (shrine of the ancestors) is located (Ocitti, 1973, 13). It is at these shrines that people offer prayers for the welfare and well-being of family members as they travel away from home, asking the spirits of the ancestors to protect them and give them good fortune until they return safely.

I further suggest that it is critical for community providers (educators, social workers, policy makers, resettlement workers, community leaders, and the like) who are helping to reintegrate returning CI soldiers to recognize, support, and nurture the incredible personal resourcefulness that surviving former child combatants used as protective factors to overcome adversities of war (Werner, 2000; Werner & Smith, 1992; West, 2000). I also suggest that, as part of the process of returning home, Acholi cultural practices that survived the war ought to be revived to support and encourage former child combatants to reclaim their desired identities even as they shed their aggressive and violent stigmatized war identities. In this sense, *dwoogo paco* reverses the process of liminal repurposing of culture by which CI soldiers were forced to live as soldiers.

Kic ii Ogo (Honey in the Hollow Trunk of a Tree)

The Acholi phrase *kic ii ogo* expresses the possibility of overlooking or forfeiting something good because of its appearance. The inexperienced honey hunter who pays little attention to the bees hovering around a tree may not realize that rich honey is inside the hollow trunk. For my informants, and I suspect for many other CI soldiers who were abducted by the LRM/A, the years of precarious wandering in the bush and the horrendous violence to which they were subjected, and in which they participated, were bearable only because of the hope of *dwoogo paco*. Embedded within the notion of return was the idealized dream of a welcoming, loving, and supportive family and community waiting to reunite with the long-lost child; this dream became a source of hope in the midst of despair, constructing resilience in moments of grave self-doubt. As Jola Amayo put it, 'for the first six years, all I could think about was home.' Similarly, the thought that 'children my age are at school and here I am wasting away' prompted Payaa Mamit to embark on an ill-fated attempt to escape that almost got her killed by pursuing LRM/A.

The hope of returning home seemed to allow the abductees to sharpen their culturally endowed gift of resilience in the face of traumatic setbacks during the transitional period in the bush. These qualities have been observed and studied in different cultures and circumstances, such that children who bounce back from adversities to become well-adjusted adults are said to have resilient qualities (Antonovsky, 1987; Garbarino, Dubrow, Kostelny, & Pardo, 1992; Garmezy, 1985; Garmezy, 1991; Luthar & Zigler, 1991; Masten, Best, & Garmezy, 1990; Safyer, 1994). More recent studies have sought to link resilience to favourable outcomes among children confronting severe adversities or deprivation (Luthar, 2006; Masten, 2004; Masten & Coatsworth, 1998; Masten & Reed, 2002; Wright & Masten, 2005). Children who confront adversities and maintain self-esteem in the face of catastrophic events are also seen as survivors (Apfel & Simon, 1996; Cairns, 1996; Beristain, Valdoseda, & Paez, 1996; Masten, 1994; Masten, 2007). In the literature, resilience is, therefore, defined as the ability to control potentially life-altering adversities (Feldman & Masalha, 2007; Luthar, 2006; Masten, 1999; Masten & Obradovic, 2006) while 'achieving desirable outcomes in spite of significant challenges to adaptation or development' (Masten and Coatsworth 1995, 737) and as resistance to the adverse effects of risk experiences (Rutter (2000a, 2000b).

Acholi culture is especially rich with words and phrases like *kanyo* (coping), *ciiro peko* (overcoming problems), and *kayo lak* (gritting the teeth) to express the experiences of coping with and overcoming pain or setback. Meanwhile, *diiyo cwiny*, which literally translates as 'suppressing the heart or soul,' means keeping emotions under wraps, going into an existential cocoon to ward off further wounding to the soul in difficult times. Implicit in the act of *diiyo cwiny* is self-sacrifice, holding back the fulfillment of one's immediate needs either because of a lack of resources to fulfil those needs or because it is prudent and beneficial for the individual's overall welfare to defer fulfillment to a future time.

But *diiyo cwiny* also carries the message of hope in the sense that holding down one's heart allows it to be lifted up later. Acholi children are taught from a young age to learn the act of *diiyo cwiny*, suppressing the heart through the promotion of protective factors like *wat* (relational attachment), the ability to establish and sustain relationships with family members, caregivers, extended kin, and others; *tek cwiny* (self-regulatory skills), the ability to muster control over one's emotions such that one can act with courage when the occasion demands; and *kwiri* (self-efficacy), the confidence, independence, and keenness required to assess or size up situations, select the best possible options for overcoming an obstacle, and purposefully initiate action to achieve one's goal. Through communal play, children learn to negotiate, to give and take, to resolve conflicts, and even to identify danger such as *okutu lango* (needle tree), *twol* (snakes), and *ayila*, the tree whose hairy brown fruit causes a serious itch. Empathy and sensitivity towards the needs of others within the community is fostered through activities such as communal sharing of food from the same dish.

By anticipating, embracing, and accepting suffering through *diiyo cwiny*, so that their awful experiences could not affect their hope for tomorrow, the former child combatants in this book persevered and made their suffering a part of the daily rhythm of their lives. In this sense and meaning of survival, each of them gazed directly upon suffering without allowing it to affect their motivation to survive and return home. Miya, for instance, was able to survive when she was raped by a much older man to whom she was given for a wife. She also survived the most intense suffering when her bush husband was accused of trying to escape and was executed by firing squad. 'We were taken and divided up among senior officers. You went silently to live in his home. There was a lot of suffering. We lived a terrible life. After that, we were given to another officer. When your husband died in battle, suitors were allowed to woo you, instead of simply being handed over to an officer. In my case, I was given to another officer when the officer I was living with was executed. This was done by force, whether or not you agreed with it, you were given away to an officer.' This suffering almost broke her, but, through *diiyo cwiny*, she came through it.

Compelled by the need to survive captivity, but also imbued with the hope of *dwoogo paco*, the child abductees constructed dual identities, one rooted in the Acholi culture that the LRM/A manipulated and turned violent, the other stemming from their previous lives within the families they left behind in their villages. In effect, the separation of their bush identities from their home identities seemed to serve the psychological needs of child combatants by allowing them to retain their original, culturally constructed, and desired identities as *dano adana*, human persons, even as they deployed their stigmatized identities in the perpetration of extreme violence and atrocities. By keeping the two identities, they were able to rationalize their actions in the bush. In Acholi culture, after all, *dano adana* could not possibly inflict so much suffering on other human persons without simultaneously losing their humanity. Only a *lapoya* (pl. *lupoya*) (mad person) could commit such acts without feeling guilt or remorse.

In combat, their hidden home personas as *dano adana* enabled the CI soldiers to resolutely draw a tight veil of innocence around themselves in the face of mounting violence and atrocities. Whatever happened in the bush was divorced from who they felt they really were and how they were perceived back home. For Jola Amayo, dual identities enabled her to distance herself psychologically and emotionally from the violence of warfare by reminding her that she could never do such things back home. 'What you did at home was beneficial, but in the bush you were used – go and forcibly take someone's property, rob with violence. You realized you were being forced to act,' she explained.

Ringo Otigo elegantly contextualized his dual identities this way: 'In your normal existence as a person living where you were born, you could not stay from morning till noon without drinking water. There, however, you could stay from morning till sunset without putting water to your lips because there would be no place to collect water. I learned all that, withstood it, knew it, outlasted it, concluded it, until the moment when I got up and returned home in the manner that was planned for me.'

To the child combatants, therefore, returning home to a welcoming community would liberate them from their stigmatized existence as child combatants who committed crimes considered taboo within Acholi culture (killing, cutting off lips and limbs, burning homes, and in some cases rape). Yet, once back home, Ringo Otigo, like the rest of my informants who served as child combatants with the LRM/A, was confronted by a civilian population that viewed him not as a returning child survivor and hero but as a killer who committed atrocities. He discovered that the communal disdain for *olum*, those from the bush, ran deeper than mere anger directed at common criminals.

Invariably, former child combatants were blamed for all the atrocities and suffering that the Acholi had endured for so many years. Indeed, the persistent use of the stigmatized label of *olum* to refer to returning child combatants was itself a stark reminder that, in the eyes of Acholi civilian society, they were no longer *dano adana*. The subtext of the accusation was that only a *dano gang*, a home person who remained within the community, acting in a predictable manner that the community understood, and who was integral to the daily routines and rituals of that community, could pass as a human person. By being labelled *olum*, former LRM/A child combatants were rendered separate from the Acholi community's experience; they were relegated to the periphery as rejects, untouchables, discarded, as it were, on the *wii oduu* (garbage heap). Effectively, they had become strangers within their own families, community, and culture.

The realization that, in the eyes of their communities, they were considered outcasts created emotional turmoil for all my informants. Jola, for instance, was not prepared for her community's venomous attacks on her and her children. She was told to her face that she was an evil rebel who had done many bad things, and that she could not stay in the community because she was possessed by *cen*, the vengeful spirits of those she killed in battle: '[When] I got home, there was some anger directed towards me. When it happened, I mostly kept to myself, staying silent.'

Furthermore, the former child combatants felt especially bitter after experiencing rejection from family members whom they trusted and respected. Ringo Otigo, for example, was deeply hurt by the accusation from an aunt that his presence in the village was a liability since nobody could predict what he was capable of doing: 'My aunt said that nobody really knew my mind and nobody could predict how my life at home could turn out. Perhaps, with the type of life I had led in the bush, I could hurt someone or perhaps commit a serious act against neighbours, thereby creating enmity in the home.'

Far from being an isolated case, Ringo's experience with unwelcoming family members was a common one for the other former child combatants as well. Both Payaa Mamit and Miya Aparo experienced similar rejections from family members. Payaa was especially bitter about the attitude of her father, whom she had respected and idolized while growing up and, ironically, whose teachings had helped her through unspeakable suffering as a child combatant. She could barely hide her intense anger and sense of betrayal: 'What worries me the most and makes me very sad to this hour is the manner of my return. Instead of welcoming me home with [such words of] encouragement [as], "My child, now that you have returned, be firm, and take care of the three children you returned with," my father never said that. Instead he said, "You know what people say, that you have evil spirit inside your head. Because of the evil spirit that is said to be inside you, you cannot stay at home; you must return to the bush."' Moreover, without acknowledging her existence, Payaa's father showed up one day with Payaa's siblings, who were born after she was abducted and had been orphaned when Payaa's mother died: 'When my father saw that I was settling well, and living peacefully, no fights, no evil spirit to disturb me, he showed up with the two children, my two brothers that my mother left behind as orphans. He left my brothers in my hands.'

Miya Aparo faced a similar situation in the village where she grew up. She was looked upon as a returning rebel rather than as a child who had been forcibly removed from her home. The hatred was so intense that she beat a hasty retreat to an anonymous existence in the community on the outskirts of Gulu town: 'I went home to my mother, and found unwelcoming stares. Some people hated me; others hated the children that I returned home with. Truly, life was very hard. It finally dawned on me that I needed to live independently by myself. I started living in Ariya-Agaa, not far from here, all by myself.'

For Miya Aparo and former child combatants like her, rejection by family was the ultimate act of betrayal within a culture that already viewed her and other former child combatants as unclean, unstable, and possibly possessed by *cen*. In essence, the community had turned its back on her and those like her. It had deliberately chosen not to honour her as *dano adana*, pushing her away to live alone like a person without *wat* (extended family and kin). Left searching for new identities because the ones which they held close to their hearts for many years as child combatants, and which they had imagined as legitimate, were contested and rendered invalid in the eyes of the communities to which they had returned, most former child combatants reacted with anger and confusion.

Miya, Ringo, and Jola felt betrayed twice. The first time was when they were abducted by the LRM/A and grievously harmed and placed in harm's way. The second was when, upon return to the village, having come through what many described as the jaws of death, they discovered that society no longer cared or wanted them.

The rejection of returning former child combatants can be rendered meaningful only when understood as one of the outcomes of a war that caused total devastation to traditional institutions of community and family. In essence, by rejecting returning child combatants because of fear that they harbour the dreaded *cen*, which could also be interpreted in terms of individual trauma, Acholi society exposes its own cultural trauma and its resulting impotence in dealing with social issues arising from the war. It is this uncertain terrain of cultural trauma with shifting meanings of victims and perpetrators that CI soldiers encounter upon returning home.

Acholi Cultural Trauma

Acholi society, I would argue, is experiencing severe cultural trauma today. This trauma denotes both the shared sense of collective suffering that has been experienced over the last two decades in Acholi society, and the profound impact that the war has had on the way the Acholi think of themselves as a distinct cultural entity. To qualify as cultural trauma, according to N.J. Smelser (2004), the event must be remembered, the memory must be 'culturally relevant, that is, represented as obliterating, damaging, or rendering problematic something sacred' (36), and, finally, the memory must be associated with a 'strong negative affect, usually disgust, shame or guilt.' J.C. Alexander (2004) argues that cultural trauma comes about when the victimized group not only becomes aware of the impact of the trauma on them, but is also alerted to the dangers that it poses to their 'collective identity' as a group or as a people. He writes: 'For traumas to emerge at the level of the collectivity, social crises must become cultural crises. Events are one thing, representations of these events quite another. Trauma is not the result of a group experiencing pain. It is the result of this acute discomfort entering into the core of the collectivity's sense of its identity' (10).

The cultural trauma in this case affects the collective by inflicting damage on the basic tissue of social life, destroying the bond between people and creating a deepening awareness of their shared suffering. Acholi society itself is wounded, not in the organic sense of physical trauma, but in terms of broken social connectedness; the familial bonds that formed the basis of the smallest social units, radiating outwards to connect members of communities into tight cohesive groupings, have waned, setting children against parents, and siblings against each other.

The social condition arising from cultural devastation over the last two decades is best illustrated by the old Acholi proverb, *Pe iput te okono* (Do not uproot the pumpkin).[3] The warning not to uproot the pumpkin plant is both literal and symbolic. It is literal because the pumpkin survives on its own even when the old homestead is abandoned for a new one; and, so long as it is not uprooted, it can be harvested again and again to sustain life, especially in times of famine. Because it requires minimal intervention and upkeep, often surviving wildfires and drought on its own, the pumpkin is considered an essential part of an Acholi homestead, readily available when needed. In almost all Acholi homesteads, including my own in Pamin-Yai, the large round vegetable was often planted in the *wii oduu* (garbage dump), where it flourished in the rich composted soil and, year after year, produced nutritious crops that were harvested as needed and prepared as part of a larger meal or by itself for breakfast. The pumpkin leaves, *pot okono*, make a tasty soup.

Looked at in the context of the two decades of violence in Acholi, to extend the metaphor one step further, the old homestead is left barren, strewn with old broken pots, overgrown weeds, and shrivelled pumpkin roots. That is to say, the situation is so critical that the old Acholi adage, *Pe iput te okono*, no longer applies because, metaphorically speaking, the war has uprooted the pumpkin, leaving it in danger of wilting altogether.

Within a generation, the very fabric of family that articulated social roles by gender and by age has largely disappeared; men are no longer able to provide for their families, women abandon their children, and children ignore their elders. The institution of marriage is now seen not as a lifetime union of a man and a woman, but as a vehicle for survival in the moment. A 2001 report by the U.K.-based Agency for Cooperation and Research in Development (ACORD, 2001) warned of 'cultural demoralization' in displaced-persons camps in Acholi where 'prostitution, divorce, and early sexual relationships among young children have become another way of earning income to survive' (17). Suicide, a serious taboo in Acholi culture, has become commonplace (Dolan, 2009, 165–6). The despair among the Acholi, in other words, is so catastrophic and complete that death, a much feared concept in Acholiland, is a welcome alternative.[4]

Because of the long, culturally destructive war, living has become a speculative ritual where problems are either ignored altogether or attributed with a sense of resignation to the supernatural world of spirits. For example, an often repeated refrain I heard while visiting the displaced-persons camps in 2005, 2006, and 2007 was that perhaps the Acholi were suffering so much because the *jok* (gods or spirits) were angry and wanted to punish the entire ethnicity collectively. As Ocitti (1973) explains, in traditional Acholi culture, these deities were dominant figures to whom 'sacrifices and prayers were offered whenever the whole chiefdom was faced with threats such as war, drought, epidemic, famine, plague or when people were asking for fertility in women' (13).

In fact, though the idea of a vengeful god might sound far-fetched to an Acholi living in North America or Europe, the notion of collective punishment was well entrenched in some of the camps. In July 2006, for instance, I had a dramatic encounter with this world while visiting the Anaka camp, located about thirty-five kilometres west of Gulu town. I arrived in the camp in a pick-up truck around midday and parked in front of the small building that served as the police station. The overhead sun was intolerably hot. I was met by David Okot, a camp leader. After we greeted each other, he began telling me about the mysterious fires that burn homes everyday without any apparent reason. Arson was often ruled out because many of the homes tended to burn during the day when people were around to watch for suspicious activities. Moreover, recently, fully expecting the fires, homeowners had begun removing all belongings from their homes in the morning.

Coincidentally, almost on cue, as Okot told the story, a fire started about two hundred metres from where we stood in the shade of a big mango tree. 'There is a fire just starting right now, and it will burn the house to the ground,' he said excitedly, pointing to white smoke billowing from a grass-thatched house. We piled into the truck and raced to the scene. The fire had begun at the top of the roof, and was fast spreading downwards. A quick inspection indicated that the house was empty, and there was no fireplace where the flame could have accidentally ignited. The gathering crowd confirmed that the house was used only as a sleeping place and not as a kitchen. In the next twenty minutes, we raced around trying to save the next building, which housed a milling machine. Water was brought and poured on the building even as the doomed house burned to the ground. I took many dramatic pictures, including one of a schoolgirl in her uniform who was now rendered homeless.

In the aftermath of the fire, concerned camp residents crowded around me to tell me their stories of encounters with spontaneous fires. One man recounted how his own trousers once caught fire all on their own, burning the pocket. Another told how a sleeping baby caught fire and barely survived. Then there was the *munnu* (white man), whose camera spontaneously combusted. These incidents, according to the assembled crowd, were compelling evidence of something supernatural haunting the community. Okot later told me that, according to rumour, an evil spirit from across the Nile River was responsible and could be appeased only by the sacrifice of a beautiful young girl's blood. Uganda government officials whom I later spoke to, meanwhile, merely laughed at the idea of fire starting by itself or chalked it up to carelessness or even arson. But, when I did further research into the phenomenon of spontaneous fires, I discovered that it was entirely plausible that the grass-thatched homes in the camps were indeed spontaneously com-busting, but the devil had nothing to do with it. The problem was the hot grass itself.[5]

The response of Anaka camp residents to the fires was another reminder of how the devastating war ominously weakened the self-healing capacity of Acholi culture, a capacity that studies of cultures in other jurisdictions (Espino, 1991; Eyber, 2001; Garbarino, 1995; Garbarino & Kostelny, 1996a; Garbarino & Kostelny, 1996b; Garbarino, Kostelny, & Dubrow, 1991; 1997) suggest is crucial for maintaining social order and sustaining resilience in children facing catastrophic events. The incapac-ity to respond to social crises such as those arising from the return of child combatants, I would argue, is a manifestation of the larger failure of traditional institutions that collapsed as a result of the war.

Today, the traumatized Acholi culture not only lacks the capacity to support returning child combatants saddled with their own individual traumas but is afflicted with what Martin-Baro (1996) terms 'seriously damaged roots of social co-existence' (114) and, consequently, rejects former child combatants, consigning them, as it were, to their own in-dividual suffering. The rejection of returning child combatants that I explore below should, therefore, be seen not as a reflection of the atti-tudes of individual families but rather as a symptom of a society caught in the throes of cultural trauma. The collective, in other words, is aware of its own pain insofar as it affects its identity as a people, and yet indi-vidually, as families, the community is unable to deal with this pain because it lacks the cultural resources to do so, thereby perpetuating the vicious cycle of trauma in which both the collective and the indi-viduals within it cannot find resolution.

Cultural and Personal Resurgence

As used in this book, the expression *pe iput te okono* is also hopeful in that it teaches the importance of remembering one's roots, one's old friends and family, kin and community, of maintaining a connection with the past, especially when times are hard and the future is bleak. It is a reminder of the need to return to those roots, to reconnect with an-cestors in order to foster a supportive environment that continually nourishes the culture and the individuals that are integral to it. It is an acknowledgment of the role of tradition in shaping how a people sees itself and acts, of what culture regards as important and what is dis-carded as spent by-product.

Though devastated by the war, many elements of Acholi culture survive today within the collective memory of the elders who were old enough when the war started to know how to use different cultural elements for individual and collective healing. Like the tender green shoot of the *okono* plant that defies the parched earth and is protected from total decay, this knowledge can be reclaimed. All is not lost, so to speak.

According to sociologist Emile Durkheim, and further elaborated by M. Halbwachs (1992), collective memory plays a major role in how a people recount and mythologize their past. As used in this book, collective memory is conceived of as the memories of a shared past 'that are retained by members of a group, large or small, that experienced it' (Schuman & Scott, 1989, 361–2) and transmitted through time and space in publicly sanctioned commemorations and group-specific discourses. The sharing of memories among the Acholi people presents a huge opportunity in helping returning CI soldiers reintegrate into the community. In this sense, metaphorically speaking, the Acholi must return to the old homestead to rummage in the ruins for salvable cultural resources that can be employed to help returning CI soldiers as well as rebuild society.

I am not suggesting a form of collective amnesia that denies that significant suffering ever took place in Acholi. Many communities, in any case, still bear the scars of years of atrocities; graves abound in the villages; victims whose lips, limbs, and ears were chopped off still struggle to survive openly; evidence of the LRM/A's and NRM/A's violent handiwork is amply and readily available in the form of burnt-down homes, schools, and churches. The failed Uganda government policy of mass uprooting and relocation of Acholi into overcrowded internal camps exacted an unimaginable human toll.[6] Indeed, as an Acholi proverb puts it, *pii pe mol dok cen* (water does not flow backward). Not only is a denial of widespread suffering impossible in the face of the evidence of destruction, but ultimately it is self-defeating.

At the same time, as Jola Amayo put it unflinchingly, *Gwok ka dong ongok pe dok nago ngoke* (When a dog vomits, it will not lick back its vomit). What has happened cannot be undone. In other words, Acholi society, has, in its returning CI soldiers, the opportunity to look beyond its despair – with its corollaries of anger, pessimism, and social discord – to find a new kind of radical hope by choosing to remember those cultural resources that bring healing and repair to individuals and society as a whole. C.L. Oryem (2008), an Acholi academic, frames the issue this way: 'We are either victims or perpetrators and members of a community enmeshed in the cycle of violence, so as stakeholders we all must do our part and meet the needs of each category. What do victims need? How about the perpetrators and the community?' (5).

The issue that Acholi like Oryem are wrestling with in the wake of a war that devastated and traumatized Acholi culture is how to reconcile the two parts of the survivor-perpetrator dichotomy (Mamdani, 2002) under which many returning CI soldiers fall. I maintain that looking for transformative resources in their cultural past, those cultural resources with the capability of freeing individuals from their divergent status as survivors and perpetrators, and uniting them as co-existing members of a harmonious society, is the best way for Acholi society to deal with collective and individual trauma. There are many of these cultural resources, some particular to certain Acholi communities, and others universal to the Acholi people. For the purpose of this book, I examine four such Acholi cultural resources, namely, *tumo kiir* (cleansing the curse), *culo kwor* (restorative restitution for loss of life), *mato oput* (the drinking of bitter roots), and *yweyo kom* (cleansing the body), that could be used to reconcile former CI soldiers to their communities, enabling them to embark on the process of healing.

Tumo Kiir (Cleansing the Curse) and *Culo Kwor* (Restorative Restitution for Loss of Life)

Traditionally, Acholi culture was predicated on shared communal responsibilities such as *pur awak* (communal tilling of land) and *kayo kac aota* (communal harvest) and *laro lok* (communal resolution of conflict). A conflict emanating out of everyday living was quickly settled by elders, *wek pe obal kin dano* (so that it does not ruin the relationship between people). Ocitti (1973, 17), for instance, notes that the offence of *kiir*, disturbing the spirits by acts such as throwing food at another in anger, a mother lifting her breasts to curse her child, or committing arson, was considered serious enough that 'a cleansing ceremony [would] be performed immediately.' The communal ritual of *tumo kiir*, cleasing the curse of *kiir*, required that a goat be slaughtered and the contents of its innards smeared over the hearts of those present. The elders portioned out the meat of the goat which was communally cooked and shared by all. The contrite perpetrator of *kiir* was now safe from spirits who had hitherto been angered but were now mollified.

In the more serious case of murder or manslaughter, something that became commonplace during the war, *culo kwor*, restorative restitution for loss of life, was based on the cultural understanding that the loss of life affected not only the immediate family of the deceased but the entire community in which the dead person lived. The concept of *culo kwor* extended to the perpetrator's clan, which was deemed morally and socially responsible for the crime committed by their son or daughter. A child, after all, is brought up by the village and so his or her behaviour reflects his or her upbringing by that community. The arrangement for *culo kwor* is an Acholi cultural mechanism for bringing the two clans, that of the perpetrator and that of the victim, towards a harmonious co-existence (Dolan, 2009, 172; Girling, 1960, 66–7; Finnstrom, 2008, 219–20). It is restorative at its essence in that, without devaluing the humanity of the perpetrator, it allows compensation to satisfy the community of the victim. Acholi traditional justice, in this sense, was not vengeful but oriented towards maintaining social connectedness between society's members, who make mistakes but should, after making restitution, be accepted back by the community at large. Perpetrators reclaim their status as *dano adaana* once the appropriate compensation is made. It is within such traditional Acholi practices that returning CI soldiers can find redemption and the cultural resources to rebuild their lives in a peaceful manner, in essence, returning to the land of the living. This is not to be interpreted as a cure, for what ails them is not an illness that needs to be cured; rather, what they need most is recognition that they retain their human personhood despite many years in the bush.

Mato Oput (Drinking Bitter Roots)

One of the cultural resources that would enable returning CI soldiers to be reconciled with their communities so that they are finally looked at again as *dano adana* is the ritual of *mato oput*. Traditionally, *mato oput* was used to engender reconciliation between clans, even families. It usually followed a period of feuding which had simmered between two parties or a precipitous action which resulted in manslaughter. To ensure that the matter was settled amicably, six elements were adhered to. First, everyone, victim and perpetrator included, came forward freely for the meeting of the court. Second, the meeting was held in the open where everyone could hear what was being discussed. Third, the perpetrator, if known, willingly told the truth and acknowledged the alleged wrongdoing in public. Fourth, *ludito kaka* (clan elders) discussed the problem and came up with a solution agreeable to both parties. Fifth, the perpetrator had to pay restorative restitution or compensation to the victim's family. Sixth, once the punishment was accepted, and restitution made, the two sides of the disputes drank a liquid made from bitter *oput* roots. Drinking the bitter roots signalled the burying of the conflict since everyone had symbolically swallowed the bitterness. Life could proceed as before without any more finger pointing, isolation, or repercussions.

The concept of *mato oput* as an alternative mechanism for creating resolution for returning child combatants was proposed in 1997 by Denis Pain in a widely circulated document titled *The bending of the spears*. In another document, *Roco wat i Acoli* (Re-Establishing Kinship in Acholi), the Liu Institute for Global Issues, the Gulu District NGO Forum, and Ker Kwaro Acholi (2005) elaborated the steps needed to complete the ritual of *mato oput*. As traditionally conceived and practised by the Acholi, *mato oput* involved known actors. This, however, is not possible in the current conflict in northern Uganda, given the scale of the war and the atrocities committed over the last twenty years. It may never be possible to identify all the victims. There are instances where some of the abducted children were killed in the bush and, to paraphrase Ringo Otigo, their skulls were left to be pushed by wild pigs. Meanwhile, the confusion over victims' identities is irresolvable in cases like the Corner Kilak Massacre,[7] where hundreds were mowed down in a lopsided battle in which inexperienced and sometimes unarmed HSM fighters, while singing hymns, faced NRM/A bullets. Most of the victims were buried in mass graves.

Even in cases where it is possible to know the identities of the victims, as in the cases of the Atiak, Mucwini, and Bar-Lonyo massacres, the killers may never be identified. Except for vague allusions to crimes committed during the war, neither the LRM/A nor the NRM/A (now UPDF) has admitted responsibility for atrocities. This very point is emphasized by O. Lucima (2007), an Acholi academic living in London, who rejects *mato oput* as a mechanism for achieving justice and reconciliation in the northern Uganda war. He writes:

> To apply mato oput and partial ICC indictments to end the northern Uganda conflict and as a basis for a just peace, is tantamount to consciously promoting impunity and acquiescing in state-led propaganda that seeks to absolve the Ugandan state from responsibility to protect, and its own unjustifiable counterinsurgency strategies that, like the LRM/A's insurgency methods, victimised unarmed women and children;

targeted entire ethnic groups for collective punishment in order to dis-
courage support for insurgency. (para. 8)

Nonetheless, despite its obvious limitations, *mato oput* provides a
framework for reconciling former CI soldiers to their communities. The
ritual could, for example, be used to drive home the reality, in the minds
of victims and returning CI soldiers alike, that the war is over and that
there is now a need to move forward. As Pain argues, this imperfect
process of *mato oput* needs to take into account the 'impossible task of
differentiating the coerced from the instigators of violence' and, further,
the fact that returning fighters lack 'the means to pay compensation'
(Pain, 1997, 3). While it cannot be a silver bullet, *mato oput*, when combined with *yweyo kom* rituals, has the potential to move former CI soldiers and the Acholi community beyond remembering the war with all
its atrocities and suffering to learning to live with those memories.

Yweyo Kom (Cleansing the Body)

Unlike the more elaborate *mato oput*, hybridized Acholi traditional rituals collectively known as *yweyo kom*, also known as *yubo kom* (repairing
the body), have been used by different families and communities to
welcome back returning CI soldiers. These include rituals such as *nyono
tong gweno* (stepping on an egg), *kalo opobo* (stepping over the *opobo*
branch), and *tumu dyel* (sacrificing a goat).[8] These ceremonies are performed mostly to welcome the returning child combatants, cleanse
them of contaminants, and reconcile them to the community. But, in a
study conducted in all Acholi districts, the Liu Institute for Global
Studies (2005) concluded that almost half of returnees did not go
through cleansing and purification rituals. The authors noted:

> Interviews with returnees found that just over half (50 per cent) went
> through a family level 'Stepping of the Egg' ceremony before being
> welcomed back into the family home. Usually this is done at the entrance
> of the home to chase away anything bad encountered while in the bush.
> One Elder also described it as a message to the returnee that the door of
> the family is open, encouraging the returnee to pass through it and join the
> family again: 'Stepping on the egg means that the relationship that once
> existed between a child and family has not yet been broken.' By reunifying
> the person and their family, the returnee is encouraged to contribute to the
> health and productivity of the community. (39)

According to the study by the Liu Institute, when returning CI soldiers went through the communal cleansing rituals, they 'felt more accepted' and 'better able to communicate and socialise with community members' (45). The feeling of acceptance was starkly demonstrated in the way Ringo Otigo and Payaa Mamit were received at home. When Ringo's mother learned that her son had returned, she immediately arranged to take him home from the army barracks where he was being kept, in order to complete the cleansing ceremonies. Six years later, Ringo could still recall the episode as if it had happened the day before our interview in July 2008:

> A vehicle was provided at that moment, and a driver asked to take me home. Three army soldiers went in the back of vehicle to go along with us. With my mother, we were driven to the village. Once we got home, the vehicle stopped some distance from the homestead, and I was asked to get out. Fresh branches of the opobo tree were split and some chicken eggs provided. Water was poured in the courtyard. I stepped on the eggs and the opobo tree and then entered our home. Afterward, a goat was slaughtered and all the traditional rituals that went along with it were completed, and then we left, returning to the barracks. My family remained at home.

Ringo was asked to disembark several hundred metres from the entrance of the ancestral home so he would not bring contaminants into the homestead. Fresh branches of the *opobo* tree were split and some fresh chicken eggs provided for traditional ritual cleansing. The breaking of the egg signifies a new beginning, the spilling of whatever evil contaminants might have inhabited his body. The stepping over the *opobo* branch symbolically marked the demarcation point between the violent, stigmatized identity Ringo knew in the bush as an LRM/A operative and the one he was about to reacquire at home as a civilian, the desired identity. He explained, referring to himself in the third person: 'The goat was sacrificed to wash away whatever bad deeds that Ringo Otigo committed as a CI soldier. He was a new person again.'

By contrast, Payaa Mamit felt rejected outright by her father, who did not go through the rituals. She was bitter and could not hide her deep disappointment: Although she had physically left the bush, Payaa's homecoming was unremarkable and unmarked by a cultural sign that said she was finally home. Feeling alone, alienated, and unwanted, Payaa Mamit suffered from not knowing whether she could ever relinquish her stigmatized identity and restore fully the desired identity she had had before she was abducted by the LRM/A. As she put it, 'This makes me remember the past, and think, had I not gone to the bush, I would not be like this.' Moreover, the rejection by her family and community confused Payaa about the nature of forgiveness as a process for burying her stigmatized war identity:

> Before I went to the bush I was young, and you could fight with your best friend, you hit your friend or step on her leg, and later say, 'Please, pal, forgive me, I did not mean to …' But at this moment that I am a grown up, understanding the meaning of forgiveness is a lot more difficult because I still understand it the same way as in the past. When I say, 'Please forgive me, look, I did not know that this was a bad thing, so forgive me,' [this] means that the action was not deliberate and if the person could forgive then he or she should forgive your action. But at this time, I do not understand the deep meaning of forgiveness.

It is not that Payaa cannot forgive, or is unable to forgive; rather, she is searching for a forgiveness that has deeper meaning for herself and for the community to which she has returned. In this sense, Payaa, like the other informants in the book, recognizes the impossibility of returning to the life she led as a child before being abducted by the LRM/A – so much has happened since then. Yet, at the same time, she has no wish to drown in the shame and guilt of having been one of the CI soldiers who caused so much pain in the community. She is seeking cultural absolution, a discharge from the suspended purgatory to which she was forced to reside as a CI soldier who committed certain acts of violence. She wishes to leave behind her identity as the guilty person she was in the bush, in order to find forgiveness, to forgive, and eventually to live free of guilt.

Payaa, I would argue, like the other returning former CI soldiers, is willing to engage in the process of personal renewal by accepting responsibility for her role in the war, as well as by forgiving the community that failed to protect her in the first place. Embedded within Payaa's doubt about the meaning of forgiveness is a space where fellow CI soldiers and the community can sit down and engage in a dialogic process of defining the terms and meanings of post-war healing and repair. She acknowledges the possibility that this soul-searching process is messy, difficult, and rife with uncertainty and indecisiveness. Yet she is optimistic about the prospects for a renewed relationship with her community.

Pito Lwit Okono Odoco (Replanting the Pumpkin Roots)

It is a reality that the dilemmas confronting returning child combatants are not entirely metaphysical, or concerned mainly with their conflicting identities, their images of themselves and how we see them. These dilemmas also involve their physical needs, including their grumbling stomachs and uncertainty about where they will sleep at night. As noted by N. Boothby, L. Crawford, and J. Halperin (2006) in a study of reintegration of child combatants in Mozambique, there cannot be a return to the status quo that existed prior to the war. In the case of the Acholi, so many have lost their homes, lives, families, relatives, even whole villages during the war. Furthermore, the difficulty for returning former LRM/A child combatants seeking their homes was compounded by the creation in 1996 of camps for the internally displaced in Acholiland. At the height of the LRM/A war and the counterattacks by the UPDF between 2002 and 2004, an estimated 1.5 million Acholi were living in camps, depopulating the countryside and turning villages into what the Acholi refer to as *paco wii obuu* (abandoned decrepit homesteads). The haphazard manner with which the Uganda government forced the population to relocate to the camps meant that scant or no records were kept of which families lived in which camps.

For many returning child combatants, tracking down families often involves painstaking research by non-governmental agencies. For over a decade, the reunification of returning child combatants with their families has been carried out by three NGOs, World Vision and GUSCO in Gulu and Kitgum Concerned Women's Association (KICWA) in Kitgum town. When the returnee can recall where his or her family originally lived, field workers are given the job of locating the family home, if it still exists. In cases where family members cannot be readily tracked down, the agencies have used mass media, mostly radio. When Radio Mega FM 102.1, which broadcasts all over northern Uganda, went on air in August 2002, it quickly became an avenue for returning child combatants to alert family members that they had come back home (Otim, 2009).

In addition to the problem of finding their families, many former CI soldiers were abducted in their early years of formal education, before they had developed a level of literacy beyond the ability to read and write simple sentences in the Acholi language. Almost none of my informants spoke English, which is the official language of Uganda and a prerequisite for employment in large centres like Kampala and Jinja.

And, despite carrying out initial assessments of returnees, providing for their temporary upkeep, and furnishing them with skills training and other educational resources, non-governmental services are generally hard-pressed financially, continually searching for sources of funding to keep programs running. Many of the returning CI soldiers, consequently, must eke a living tilling the land and selling what they produce. As one put, it, 'it makes me feel that maybe living in the bush was better.'

Aside from their immediate basic needs, CI soldiers must worry about the lack of a comprehensive peace agreement between the government of Uganda and the LRM/A. Officially, as of December 2011, the war remains an unfinished business. International Criminal Court indictments of five senior LRM/A officials for war crimes and crimes against humanity (ICC, 2002; Lee, 1999) have further complicated the process of reconciliation in northern Uganda (Allen, 2005; Hovil & Lomo, 2005; Li, 2005; Lomo & Hovil, 2004). The ICC prosecutor, Luis Moreno Ocampo, has insisted that there cannot be impunity in the conduct of the war. He has argued vociferously for the prosecutions of Joseph Kony, Vincent Otti, Okot Odhiambo, Raska Lukwiya, and Dominic Ongwen.[9] The ICC, however, withdrew the warrant against Raska Lukwiya in March 2007 when it was confirmed that the LRM/A officer was killed in a firefight with the UPDF in August 2006.[10] Pending as well is confirmation of the death of the LRM/A's second-in-command, Vincent Otti, who is believed to have been executed on the orders of Joseph Kony in December 2007, and whose death was confirmed by the LRM/A in January 2008.[11]

The LRM/A, for its part, has tendered the argument that reconciliation cannot occur so long as the threat of ICC prosecution remains. This was a major issue for discussion during the 2006–8 Juba Peace Talks and likely prompted the LRM/A not to sign the final peace agreements in April 2008. What this all means is that resolving the social dilemma faced by returning former LRM/A CI soldiers demands a multifaceted and complex social, moral, political, and cultural approach that must consider the wider contexts of Acholi society today, Uganda national politics, and, indeed, the international political landscape. It requires the engagement of actors and resources at many levels so as to address not simply the pressing issues facing the child combatants but also those issues being experienced by families, communities, and Acholi society as a whole.

Notwithstanding the above concerns, much like *pito lwit okono odoco*, which I translate as 'replanting the pumpkin roots,' what is much needed is an ambitious process to restore Acholi cultural stability, re-establish social connectedness where individuals relate to one another as *dano adana* (McCallin, 1998), and create a robust self-sustaining economy in which returning former LRM/A child combatants can thrive again. To explain the process of healing using the pumpkin metaphor, just as returning to the old homestead requires clearing the bushes, re-planting the uprooted pumpkin, and re-establishing a habitable community, so does healing the wounds of war demand the inclusion of the affected individuals, Acholi society, and Uganda as a country. As out-lined in the *Roco wat i Acoli*, a good starting point for this exercise is the regeneration of Acholi culture itself after the war. There is urgent need for the restoration and rehabilitation of the various Acholi traditional leaders such as *rwodi-moo* (anointed chiefs), *ludito kaka* (clan leaders), and *ludito* (elders). The main tasks of the traditional leaders will be to guide and lead the cultural rebirth in Acholi, and, especially, to help with the difficult task of sorting out and addressing the numerous claims, grievances, anger, trauma, and unresolved spiritual issues pertaining to those who died in the war but who were not given proper customary burials, orphans born during the war as a result of rape, children of returning child combatants who were born in the bush ... the list goes on.

The restoration of traditional leaders was given a boost in 1995 when the government of Uganda included a provision in the constitution formally recognizing their existence. The following year, Rwot David Acana I was nominated and elected by various Acholi elders as *lawi-rwodi* (paramount chief) of the Acholi. He died, however, before his official coronation, and was immediately replaced by his son, David Onen Acana II. The young leader was elected by the Acholi and his peers as *lawi-rwodi* in August 1999 and was crowned at a large ceremony held in Gulu on 17 January 2005.[12] The impact of the election of the paramount chief gave the Acholi people renewed confidence in their traditional institutions and cultural practices, crucial for their recovery from the war. Notably, when the Juba Peace Talks stalled in late 2006, the call to restart the negotiations came from Rwot David Onen Acana II at the Juba Peace Conference in February 2007.[13] The peace talks resumed a month later in Juba.

There is a also need for persuasive narratives about the scale of the suffering of the people of Acholi and CI soldiers. Although there are signs of change, one of the most surprising elements of the two-decades war is how very little is known about it in the rest of Uganda and internationally. In November 2003 the UN under-secretary for humanitarian affairs, Jan Egeland (2008), indicted the national and international media when he described the situation in northern Uganda as 'worse than Iraq' and was quoted by the British Broadcasting Corporation (BBC) as saying, 'I cannot find any other part of the world that is having an emergency on the scale of Uganda, that is getting such little international attention.'[14] Indeed, while the atrocities in Rwanda in 1994 (Human Rights Watch, 1999) and Darfur (2003–7) gained the international spotlight, relatively little is known about what has happened in northern Uganda since 1986. And, because the casualties of the war are largely unknown outside the families immediately affected, the perpetrators have not been made to account for their actions.

The failure to acknowledge the suffering of the people of northern Uganda and specifically the pain of the CI soldiers has perpetuated a sense of neglect. Today, there is not a single public event in Uganda that memorializes the children who lost their innocence, and in many cases their lives, as LRM/A combatants. The only memorial of any significance to the children who fought in the war is a monument erected by the government of the Netherlands in July 2009. It is located at the main intersection in the middle of Gulu town. Called the Pillar of Peace, it depicts two children, with dismantled guns at their feet, reading a book. This is, as the Acholi like to say, *loyo nono* (better than nothing). Though small, even insignificant, the monument serves to remind, not only the former CI soldiers themselves, but also the population as a whole, of what the war did to thousands of children who became soldiers against their free will.

There is a need, too, for more comparative studies that look at the experiences of Acholi children and children elsewhere around the globe that are caught in civil conflicts as CI soldiers. Specifically, as the findings in this study suggest in a limited way, more research is needed on how culture might be subverted, manipulated, and deployed in the destructive dynamics of making children become part of the machinery of war. Moreover, such research could delve into the notion of whether children are clueless, helpless, and incapable victims caught in the midst of violent and disruptive conflicts or, as the experiences of LRM/A CI soldiers demonstrate, survivors who utilize various elements of their own culture to survive the experience of war. In fact, while the LRM/A created an Acholi community within which it subverted Acholi culture for war and violence, it also, perhaps unwittingly, simulated relationships of families and community in a manner that enabled its child combatants to retain the desired identity developed prior to abduction (Bruner, 1985; Lave & Wenger, 1991; Wertsch, 1985; Wertsch, 1991). The web of relationships that the CI combatants established while in LRM/captivity allowed them to retain their sense of themselves as *dano adana*.

In concluding, as they return home, one by one, the former CI soldiers who fought for their lives in the bush as part of the LRM/A have little education, no skills to get good jobs, and plenty of war wounds. Yet they have not given up hope either. After their bitter experiences of suffering in the bush, all my informants are working to better their lives and those of their dependants. 'Suffering,' Payaa said, 'taught me how to endure living on this earth, anywhere.' Indeed, a case can be made that, in reconnecting with their communities, they are learning to live with death and destruction, pain and suffering. These CI soldiers are practical examples of living with hope without forgetting the past. Their optimism about the future is also the Acholis' hope for regeneration, renewal, and return to a vibrant culture in which children are children.

Notes

Introduction

1 The Lord's Resistance Movement/Army is one of numerous insurgencies that arose after President Yoweri Museveni captured power in 1986. Based in southern Sudan and operating mostly in eastern and northern Uganda, the LRM/A is reported by UNICEF to have abducted as many as 20,000 children over a period of ten years.
2 My father would later add two more wives to his household, but this happened after I had left home and was already either studying at Makerere University in Kampala or living in exile in Canada.
3 Likely a derivative of 'Trigger,' a nom du guerre.
4 The World Vision Center is run by the international-based, non-profit, non-governmental organization (NGO) World Vision. It receives and cares for former CI soldiers who were either captured from or released by the LRM/A, or escaped, prior to reuniting them with family members.
5 I was struck by the absence of anger among the CI soldiers and their somewhat fatalistic attitude about what had happened to them. *Jami time ku meno* (That's how it is) was a phrase repeated by many of the children we spoke to at the time.
6 Beyond the battlefield, the fate of CI soldiers is fiercely contested by international organizations such as Coalition for Child Soldiers and UNICEF which champion their immediate and unconditional release from captivity and military service, even as rebel and military and paramilitary organizations claim de facto control over them. In the case of Uganda, the government of President Yoweri Museveni has recruited into the national army CI soldiers who escaped or were rescued from the LRM/A.

7 Cape Town Principles and Best Practices on the Prevention of Recruitment of Children into the Armed Forces and on Demobilization and Social Reintegration of CI soldiers in Africa were adopted in April 1997 at a symposium held in Cape Town, South Africa, that was organized by UNICEF and other NGOs working on behalf of CI soldiers. See Kendra E. Dupuy and Krijn Peters, *War and children: A reference handbook* (ABC-Clio 2010), and a pamphlet by Jean Claude Legrand (1997) titled *Cape Town principles and best practices* (New York: UNICEF).

1. Conceptual and Practical Challenges

1 Tekidi is believed to have been located in present-day Sudan and to be the first major settlement of the Luo, who would later give rise to the Acholi people.
2 'Kuturia' is likely a vernacularized corruption of 'Equatoria,' a province of the Egyptian empire which extended through Sudan to northern Uganda in the 1800s, and which enabled Arab slave traders to extend their hold on part of Acholiland, plundering, taking slaves, and levying taxes. The brutal period that saw much of Acholi in turmoil and in constant war was ended when the British explorer Sir Samuel Baker reached Acholiland in 1864, stopping the slave trade and generally bringing some measure of peace, albeit for a short time.
3 'Bantu,' according to the colonial ethnic typology, covers most part of south, western, and eastern Africa.
4 According to the colonial classification, 'Nilotics' or Nilotes, people living along the Nile, were generally tall and lean; they are predominantly found in northern Uganda and southern Sudan. Although there are many different languages and cultures among the Nilotes, there is a tendency to regard them as one homogenous group. The resentment that built up against Idi Amin, during his years in power from 1971 to 1979, was later directed at the Acholi, who were seen as 'Amin's people' because of the geographical proximity of Acholi to Arua, Amin's hometown.
5 The constitutional crisis of 1966 marked the beginning of an enduring enmity between the Baganda and the Luo generally; Obote was a Luo. The writer made notes of Oyite Ojok's speech in his diary, and later discussed the implications of the general's claims in two public addresses on the same day in Gulu town, at Sacred Heart Secondary School and Alokolum Seminary. An address at Layibi College was cancelled when some students threatened violence.

2. *Gwooko Dog Paco* (Defending the Homestead), Cultural Devastation, and the LRM/A

1 Shaka, king of the Zulu, is described as a military genius who, between 1788 and 1828, built an empire in southern Africa that stretched from the Cape to the Zambezi. He kept a standing army and made many changes in the way war was fought in Africa, including the use of *assegai* (short spears) and shields. His soldiers were also known for wearing slippers on long marches.

2 Sundiata Keita (c. 1210–60) was the founder of the Mali empire. He is now regarded as a great magician-king, the national hero of the Malinke-speaking people, and one of the greatest empire builders in West Africa.

3 Mutesa I (c. 1838–84) was a kabaka, or monarch, of Buganda in the nineteenth century. Under his leadership, Buganda became a powerful and influential kingdom in East Africa.

4 Olara Otunnu, UN under-secretary general for children and armed conflict, in a lecture titled 'Innocent victims: Protecting children in times of conflict,' in London, Wednesday, 20 October, 1999. Retrieved from http://www.un.org/children/conflict/english/20oct1999millenn.html (14 February 2009).

5 Observers believe that this was one of the most bizarre battles ever fought, with HSM soldiers spending much of their time singing rather than fighting, and, although this initially confused the NRA soldiers, many HSM soldiers were killed.

6 In an interview in March 2000 with a group of freed former child combatants in Gulu Army Barracks, several informants reported that Kony, when referring to Museveni, often used the president's first name and incorrectly claimed that 'Yoweri' meant *lating opoko* (carrier of the gourd). Before Museveni's coming to power, cattle herders from western Uganda found employment in Acholiland as herders, generally caring for livestock in the community in return for selling the milk. Though generally respected by the Acholi community, these itinerant herders were sometimes looked down upon, seen as good for looking after cattle and nothing else; hence the reference to 'opoko carriers.' The *opoko*, a long-necked gourd, is used by herders to carry milk to market. The LRM/A likely used the image of the *opoko* carrier to convince its child fighters that the resistance war against Museveni would be short and successful, presumably because a cattle herder could not possibly be a good soldier.

3. Culture, Identity, and Control in the LRM/A

1 In the now well-publicized video of the failed 1993–4 peace talks, the appearance of LRM/A leader Joseph Kony was heralded by a group of young rebel fighters singing Christian hymns while a catechist dressed in a white robe and wearing a large cross sprinkled unknown liquids on the ground on which the leader later walked. Kony spoke at length at the gathering, referring often to God and making biblical references such as 'the time will come when lamb with lie down with the leopards.'

2 After she was abducted on 4 February 1974 in Berkeley, California, by a black radical group known as the Symbionese Liberation Army (SLA), Patricia Hearst adopted the name 'Tania,' wielded machine-guns to help rob banks and convenience stores, and appeared ready to kill to defend the members of the radical organization (Graebner, 2008, 159–61; Hearst, Reeves, & United States District Court for California Northern District, 1976).

3 Fourteen-year-old Elizabeth Smart of Federal Heights, Salt Lake City, Utah, was snatched from her bedroom in the early hours of 5 June 2002 and kept in captivity for nine months by Brian David Mitchell and his wife, Wanda Ileen Barzee. When questioned by suspicious authorities in March 2003, Smart, who was veiled and wearing a wig, denied her identity and instead claimed that her name was Augustine, and seemed concerned about what would happen to Mitchell and Barzee (Haberman & MacIntosh, 2003; Grady, 2003; Krakauer, 2003).

4 Shawn Hornbeck, who was abducted by Michael Devlin on 6 October 2002, lived in captivity for four and a half years and eventually adopted his abductor's last name and became Shawn Devlin. Although he reported a stolen mountain bike to police, Hornbeck never revealed to them that he was the missing boy from Richwoods, Missouri (Sauerwein, 2008).

5 Jaycee Lee Dugard was kidnapped on 11 June 1991 in South Lake Tahoe, California, while on her way to school (Schneider, 1991), remained in captivity for almost eighteen years, and revealed her true identity only when she was confronted by campus officers at the University of California at Berkeley in August 2009. By then, she had had two children with her abductor, Philip Garrido, aged eleven and fifteen (Young & Bane, 2009).

6 'Battle of the Bank Vault,' *Time 82* (18 October 1973): 38–9.

7 In 'The Six Day War in Stockholm' (*New Scientist*, 61, no. 886 [1974]: 486–7), Nils Bejerot reveals that the pressure from the public was intense to give in to the demands of the hostage takers. It would appear, therefore, that Enmark seemed to reflect the public mood that authorities were being unreasonably firm in not giving in.

8 'Battle of the Bank Vault,' *Time*, 38–9.

9 In the 1990s, dreadlocks became a fad for some Uganda musicians who mostly lived in the larger cities like Kampala and Jinja. In Acholi villages, however, dreadlocks are seen as unhygienic and have an aura of mystery.

10 Behrend (1999) notes the special purification ritual undertaken after such a killing: 'The warriors, who were considered impure, sacrificed a black and white billy goat in the bush by running it through with a spear. The men present then collected firewood with their left hands, to make a fire on which they roasted the animal without adding salt. After the meal, they gathered up the bones, threw them in the fire, laid twigs over them, and stamped out the flames until they were extinguished. I was told that the sacrificial animal was killed to pacify the cen, the evil, vengeance seeking spirits of the enemies, who had been killed' (42).

11 The controller yard, or the one who controls the yard, was usually a senior member of the LRM/A. According to Dolan (2009), the controllers are chosen by 'the holy spirit' and are 'always men' (303).

12 For the U.S. military's perspective on fraternization, see Major Kevin W. Carter, 'Fraternization,' *Military Law Review*, 113, no. 61 (1986): 77–135.

13 It is interesting to note that, during the 1993–4 peace talks between the LRM/A and the government of Uganda, rebel leader Joseph Kony respectfully referred to government negotiator Betty Bigombe as 'Mami' (mother).

14 My informants told me that girl-child abductees were married soon after experiencing their first menstrual cycles, and many became pregnant as teens.

4. The Jola Amayo Stories

1 A form of hide and seek usually played in the evening where the 'it' is blindfolded and his/her back is rhythmically thumped, while all the other children look for safe hiding places. When the thumping ends, the 'it' must now search for the hidden playmates – the first person the 'it' discovers becomes the 'it,' and the game continues.

2 Kabir is a millet type used in the making of Acholi drinks such as *kweete* and *lacooyi*. *Radio kabir* refers to rumours that are fuelled by a drink or two, and that often are greatly exaggerated depending on how much the storyteller has drunk.

3 The battle between the UPDF and LRM/A in Nisitu took place not in 1997, as Jola Amayo says, but in early 2002. Uganda formally signed an agreement with Sudan in 2002 allowing the UPDF to pursue the LRM/A inside

Sudan in what became known as Operation Iron Fist. The Uganda *Monitor* of 23 March 2002 reported that a Captain Nsereko of 4 Division Gulu was missing in southern Sudan and was 'feared dead or captured' (Kibirige, 2002a). Later, on 28 March, the *Monitor* stated that Captain Ssekabojja was 'among Uganda soldiers killed in Sudan' in firefights with the LRM/A (Kibirige, 2002b), and on 31 March it reported that earlier in February UPDF Captain Bbosa was killed in southern Sudan. It is possible that one of these officers was the casualty Jola Amayo refers to in her narrative. If so, this brings into question when her son Otim was actually born and how old he was when she shot a UPDF captain with Otim tied to her back.

Another possibility is that the 1997 battle refers to a clash between the LRM/A and the SPLM/A, when the latter overran the position of the former at Aruu Junction (Schomerus, 2007, 21). The question then would be about the identity of the dead captain whom Jola Amayo killed, whether he was part of the SPLM/A or a UPDF officer who had accompanied SPLM/A fighters into Sudan. The latter scenario, though unlikely because of the later date of the official agreement allowing Uganda troops in Sudan, is not inconceivable.

5. The Ringo Otigo Stories

1 As discussed below, the date of Ringo's abduction conflicts with a key event in which he was both a witness and a participant. The abduction of 139 girls from St Mary's Secondary School in Aboke occurred on the evening of 10 October 1996, about two or three days after Ringo's own abduction. His detailed eyewitness account of the key events that happened when the Aboke girls were abducted provides support for his claim that he was physically present at the time. The date he gives for his own abduction could therefore be a slip of memory or simply a wishful attempt to bring it closer to another key event in his life, his birthday. A more probable explanation is that children undergoing the transformation into soldiers are subjected to the most intense emotional and psychological stresses that make them oblivious to all but the most salient events during that period.

2 It is not surprising that Otigo's figures conflict with those given in de Temmerman's *Aboke Girls: Children Abducted in Northern Uganda.* The account by Otigo is mostly from the point of view of an abductee who was privy only to some of the details of the transaction.

3 The Dinka, one of the main ethnic groups in southern Sudan, made up the bulk of the SPLM/A, which was fighting the Khartoum government. In 1995 an agreement signed in Nairobi, Kenya, between the government

of Sudan and the SPLM/A, led by Dr John Garang, created the semi-autonomous Government of South Sudan (GOSS). In 2011, after a referendum, the Republic of South Sudan became a fully independent state.

Conclusion

1· The movie *Blood Diamond*, for example, does end on a positive note as the main character escapes the killing field, but, generally, it stereotypes the child combatant as a victim.
2 Strong and sustained advocacy has resulted in hard-won rights for children, starting with the UN's enactment of the Convention of the Rights of the Child (CRC) in 1989 and its adoption of the optional protocol on the involvement of children in armed conflict in May 2000. According to the Coalition to Stop the Use of Child Soldiers (2004), the adoption of the optional protocol by the General Assembly was a clear signal that 'it was no longer acceptable to use children in war.'
3 Sverker Finnstrom, in chapter 6 of his book *Living with Bad Surroundings*, discusses in detail the uprooted pumpkin proverb in context of the Acholi crisis today (Finnstrom, 2008, 197–232).
4 I witnessed first-hand the degradation of Acholi culture in March 2000 when I visited Pagak camp for the burial of a Gulu city councillor. I did not know the deceased but the occasion provided me an opportunity to visit the displaced-persons camp near Awer, twelve kilometres west of Gulu town. On arrival, the Catholic Mass conducted near the graveside was already in progress. What struck me was the total lack of concern of other camp dwellers whose homes were contiguous to the home of the deceased. Instead of responding with what is known as *ringo koko* (running to cry on the grave of the deceased) (Ocitti, 1973, 23), most seemed unmoved and uninterested. This was the first indication I had that life in the camp was different from the life that I had experienced growing up in the village of Pamin-Yai.
5 The answer to the problem of spontaneous fires in the Anaka camp, and in other camps for displaced persons, may actually be found on North American farms where hay is grown to feed livestock. Two weeks after my trip to the Anaka camp, I spoke by phone with Professor Lester Vough, a specialist in 'forage crops extension' and a leading expert on hay fire at the University of Maryland, who told me that the fires in Anaka are similar to hay fires on North American farms. He explained that, when freshly cut wet and green grass is piled in a heap, chemical reactions produce a steady amount of heat that is released into the bale. American farmers describe the rising

temperature inside the pile of hay as 'sweating' or 'going through a heat.' Over time, especially when the moisture cannot escape, heat is trapped inside the hay and the temperature may build dangerously. At about 150 degrees Fahrenheit, the hay turns black and spontaneous fire can begin in the haystack. Vough speculated that the people of the Anaka and other camps were thatching their homes with wet fresh green grass, which indeed was true. 'When you think about it, green grass does not usually burn by itself, but when left in a thick mat, the green grass begins to decay thereby releasing heat which builds in six to eight weeks into the potential for fire,' he told me.

6   The camps mostly disappeared after May 2008, when many of their inhabitants began to return to their former villages. Yet today, with peace and security now firmly in place, returnees continue to struggle to re-establish themselves after so many years away.

7   See an account of this war in Behrend (1999).

8   See Liu Institute for Global Studies (2005), *Roco wat i Acoli*, for a complete list of other rituals used for reconciling and cleansing returning former child combatants.

9   Statement by the ICC Chief Prosecutor on the Uganda Arrest Warrants, The Hague, 14 October 2005.

10 ICC document no. ICC-02/04-01/05, 22 March 2007.

11 BBC World News, 23 January 2008. Retrieved on 31 December 2009 from http://news.bbc.co.uk/2/hi/africa/7204278.stm.

12 *Roco wat i Acoli* gives comprehensive detail on the succession and selection of Paramount Chief Rwot David Onen Acana II.

13 I was chosen as a delegate to the conference from the Acholi diaspora and was one of a half a dozen people given the task of drafting the final resolutions, which I then read out in front of Paramount Chief David Onen Acana II, Riek Machar, vice-president of the government of South Sudan, and assembled delegates at the Juba Raha Hotel.

    Also, see Justice and Peace Commission of the Diocese of Gulu (2007), 'What Acholi Juba meeting would have focused on,' *Justice and Peace News*, 7, no. 21 (2007): 5–8.

14 The BBC interview with UN Under-Secretary for Humanitarian Affairs Jan Egeland appeared on the BBC website on 10 November 2003. Retrieved on 31 December 2009 from http://news.bbc.co.uk/2/hi/africa/3256929.stm.

References

Abdullah, I. (Ed.). (2004). *Between democracy and terror: The Sierra Leone Civil War*. Johannesburg, SA: UNISA Press.

Abu-Lughod, L. (1986). *Veiled sentiments: Honour and poetry in a Bedouin society*. Berkeley, CA: University of California Press.

Abu-Lughod, L. (1993). *Writing women's worlds: Bedouin stories*. Berkeley, CA: University of California Press.

Achebe, C. (1958). *Things fall apart*. London: William Heinemann Limited.

ACORD (2001). Research report on internally displaced persons (IDPs), Gulu District. (ACORD Report No. 29). Retrieved from ACORD website: http://www.acordinternational.org/

Adebajo, A. (2002). *Liberia's civil war: Nigeria, ECOMOG, and regional security in West Africa*. Boulder, CO: Lynne Rienner Publishers.

Adimola, A.B. (1954). The Lamogi Rebellion, 1911–12. *Uganda Journal: The Journal of the Uganda Society, 18*(2), 166–77.

Adyanga, C.O. (2006, November 07). The politics of mass death: Human body parts, human remains and war propaganda in Museveni's Uganda [Web log post]. Retrieved from http://stginu.blogspot.com/

Alasuutari, P. (1995). *Researching culture: Qualitative method and cultural studies*. Thousand Oaks, CA: Sage Publication Inc.

Alexander, J.C. (2004). Toward a theory of cultural trauma. In J.C. Alexander, R. Eyerman, B. Giesen, N.J. Smelser, & P. Sztompka (Eds.), *Cultural trauma and the collective identity* (1–30). Berkeley, CA: University of California Press. http://dx.doi.org/10.1525/california/9780520235946.003.0001

Allen, T. (1991). Understanding Alice: Uganda's Holy Spirit Movement in context. *Africa, 61*(3), 370–99. http://dx.doi.org/10.2307/1160031

Allen, T. (2005). *War and justice in Northern Uganda. An assessment of the International Criminal Court's intervention* (Crisis States Research Centre,

London School of Economics Draft Report). Retrieved http://www.dfid
.gov.uk/r4d/PDF/Outputs/CrisisStates/AllenICCReport.pdf

Amnesty International. (1990). *Uganda: Death in the countryside* (AI Index:
AFR 59/15/90). Retrieved from Amnesty International website: www
.amnesty.org

Amnesty International. (1991a). *Uganda: Human rights violations by the National
Resistance Army* (AI Index: AFR 59/20/91). Retrieved from Amnesty
International website: www.amnesty.org

Amnesty International. (1991b). *Uganda: Army violates human rights, government evades responsibility* (AI Index: AFR 59/24/91). Retrieved from Amnesty International website: www.amnesty.org

Amnesty International. (1992). *Uganda: The failure to safeguard human rights*
(AI Index: AFR 59/05/92). Retrieved from Amnesty International website:
www.amnesty.org

Amnesty International. (1997). *Breaking God's command: The destruction of
childhood by the Lord's Resistance Army*. London: Amnesty International.

Amnesty International. (1999). *Uganda: The full picture: Uncovering human rights
violations by government forces in the northern war* (AI Index: AFR 59/05/99).
Retrieved from Amnesty International website: www.amnesty.org

Antonovsky, A. (1987). *Unravelling the mystery of health. How people manage
stress and stay well*. San Francisco: Jossey-Bass, Inc.

Apfel, R.J., & Simon, B. (1996). *Minefields in their hearts: The mental health of
children in war and communal violence*. New Haven: Yale University Press.

Appadurai, A. (1998). Dead certainty: Ethnic violence in the era of globaliza-
tion. *Development and Change, 29*(4), 905–25. http://dx.doi.org/10.1111/
1467-7660.00103

Appadurai, A. (2006). *Fear of small numbers: An essay on the geography of anger*.
Durham, NC: Duke University Press.

Arts, K. & Popovski, V. (Eds.). (2006). *International criminal accountability and
the rights of children*. Cambridge: Cambridge University Press.

Atkinson, R. (1989). The evolution of ethnicity among the Acholi of Uganda:
The precolonial phase. *Ethnohistory and Africa, 36*(1), 19–43. http://dx.doi
.org/10.2307/482739

Avirgan, T., & Honey, M. (1982). *War in Uganda: The Legacy of Idi Amin*. Dar es
Salaam: Tanzania Publishing House.

Baker, S.W. (1874). *Ismailia: A narrative of the expedition to Central Africa for the
suppression of the slave trade* (Vol. 1). London: MacMillan & Co.

Barry, D. (2006, 31 August). Uganda signs truce with LRM/A [Web log post].
Retrieved from http://nebuchadnezzarwoollyd.blogspot.com/2006/08/
uganda-signs-truce-with-LRM/A.html

Battle, M. (2009). *Ubuntu: I in you and you in me*. New York: Seabury Books.

Beah, I. (2007). *A long way gone*. Vancover, B.C: Douglas and McIntyre.

Beary, B. (2010). Religious fundamentalism: Does it lead to intolerance and violence? In D. Repetto (Ed.), *Global Issues: Selections from CQ Researcher* (107–37). Thousand Oaks, CA: Pine Forge Press/Sage Publications.

Behrend, H. (1998). War in northern Uganda. In C. Clapham (Ed.), *African guerrillas* (pp. 107–18). Bloomington, IN: Indiana University Press.

Behrend, H. (1999). *Alice Lakwena and the Holy Spirits: War in northern Uganda, 1985–1997* (M. Cohen, trans.). Athens, OH: Ohio University Press.

Bejerot, N. (1974). The Six-Day war in Stockholm. *New Scientist, 61*, 486–7.

Bennett, O., Bexley, J., & Warnock, K. (1995). Uganda. In O. Bennett, J. Bexley, & K. Warnock (Eds.), *Arms to fight, arms to protect: Women speak out about conflict* (pp. 90–109). London, UK: Panos Publications Ltd.

Beristain, C.M., Valdoseda, M., & Paez, D. (1996). Coping with fear and loss at the individual and the collective level: Political repression in Guetamala indigenous communities. In G. Perren-Klinger (Ed.), *Trauma: From individual helplessness to group resources*. Berne: Paul Haupt Publishers.

Bettelheim, B. (1943). Individual and mass behavior in extreme situations. *Journal of Abnormal and Social Psychology, 38*(4), 417–52. http://dx.doi .org/10.1037/h0061208

Bohannan, P.J. (1995). *How culture works*. New York, NY: Free Press.

Boothby, N., Crawford, J., & Halperin, J. (2006). Mozambique child soldier life outcome study: lessons learned in rehabilitation and reintegration efforts. *Global Public Health, 1*(1), 87–107. http://dx.doi.org/10.1080/ 17441690500324347 Medline:19153896

Bradburd, D. (1998). *Being there: The necessity of fieldwork*. Washington, DC: Smithsonian Institute.

Brett, R., & Specht, I. (2004). *Young soldiers: Why they choose to fight*. Boulder, CO: Lynne Rienner Publishers.

Bromley, D.G., & Silver, E.D. (1995). The Davidian tradition: From patronal clan to prophetic movement. In S.A. Wright (Ed.), *Armageddon in Waco: Critical perspectives on the Branch Davidian conflict* (pp. 43–74). Chicago, IL: University of Chicago Press.

Brown, P.R. (1969). *Augustine of Hippo: A biography*. Berkeley, CA: University of California Press.

Brownmiller, S. (1975). *Against our will: Men, women, and rape*. New York: Simon & Schuster.

Brownmiller, S. (1994). Making female bodies the battlefield. In A. Stiglmayer (Ed.), *Mass rape: The War against women in Bosnia-Herzegovina* (pp. 180–2). Lincoln: University of Nebraska Press.

Bruner, J.S. (1985). Vygotsky: A historical and conceptual perspective. In J.V. Wertsch (Ed.), *Culture, communication and cognition: Vygotskian perspectives* (pp. 21–34). Cambridge: Cambridge University Press.

Burgess, A.W., & Regehr, C. (2010). Victimology: concepts and theories. In A.W. Burgess, C. Regehr, & A.R. Roberts (Eds.), *Victimology: Theories and applications* (pp. 31–66). London: Jones and Bartlett Publishers.

Buzacott, M. (1991). *The death of the actor: Shakespeare on page and stage*. London: Routledge Publisher.

Cairns, E. (1996). *Children and political violence*. Oxford: Blackwell.

Carter, W.K. (1986). Fraternization. *Military Law Review, 113*, 77–135.

Chang, I. (1997). *The rape of Nanking: The forgotten holocaust of World War ll*. New York: Basic Books.

Cheney, K.E. (2007). *Pillars of the nation: Child citizens and Uganda national development*. Chicago, IL: University of Chicago Press.

Chidester, D. (2003). *Salvation and suicide: Jim Jones, the Peoples Temple, and Jonestown*. Bloomington, IN: Indiana University Press.

Churchill, W.S. (1989). *Memories and adventures*. New York: Weidenfeld and Nicolson.

Clodfelter, M. (2002). *Warfare and armed conflicts: A statistical reference to casualty and other figures, 1500–2000*. Jefferson, N.C.: McFarland & Company Inc.

Coalition to Stop the Use of Child Soldiers. (2001). *Child soldiers: Global report 2001*. London: Coalition to Stop the Use of Child Soldiers. Retrieved from www.child-soldiers.org

Coalition to Stop the Use of Child Soldiers. (2004). *Child soldiers: Global report 2004*. London: Coalition to Stop the Use of Child Soldiers. Retrieved from www.child-soldiers.org

Coalition to Stop the Use of Child Soldiers. (2008). *Child soldiers: Global report 2008*. London: Coalition to Stop the Use of Child Soldiers. Retrieved from www.child-soldiers.org

Cohn, I., & Goodwin-Gill, G. (1994). *Child soldiers: The role of children in armed conflicts*. Oxford: Clarendon Press. http://dx.doi.org/10.2307/20047146

Cook, K. (2007). *Stolen angels: The kidnapped girls of Uganda*. Toronto: Penguin Books.

Cornell, S., & Hartmann, D. (1998). *Ethnicity and race: Making identities in a changing world*. London: Pine Forge Press.

Crazzolara, J. P. (1950). *The Lwoo, part 1: Lwoo migrations*. Verona, Italy: Museum Combonianum/Instituto missioni africane.

Crisp, J. (1986). Ugandan refugees in Sudan and Zaire: The problem of repatriation. *African Affairs, 85*(339), 163–80.

Curtus, A. (2005, January). Demonstrators push for UN resolution to Uganda Crisis. *New People: Pittsburg's Peace and Justice Newspaper*, 35(1), 11.

Daily Monitor (2002, March 31). Sudan: UPDF Captain killed in Khartoum. Retrieved from http://allafrica.com/stories/200203310125.html.

Dawes, A., & Cairns, E. (1998). The Machel Study: Dilemmas of cultural sensitivity and universal rights of children. *Peace and Conflicts: Journal of Peace Psychology*, 4(4), 335–48. http://dx.doi.org/10.1207/s15327949pac0404_3

de Berry, J. (2004). The sexual vulnerability of adolescent girls during civil war in Teso, Uganda. In Boyden & de Berry (Eds.), *Children and youth on the front line (45–61)*. New York: Berghahn Books.

de Temmerman, E. (2001). *Aboke girls: Children abducted in northern Uganda*. Kampala: Fountain Publishers.

Denov, M., & Maclure, R. (2006). Engaging the voices of girls in the aftermath of Sierra Leone's conflict: Experiences and perspectives in a culture of violence. *Anthropologica*, 48(1), 73–85. http://dx.doi.org/10.2307/25605298

Derrida, J. (1988). *The ear of the other: Otobiography, transference, translation: Texts and discussion* (P. Kamuf, & A. Ronell, Trans.). Lincoln, NE: University of Nebraska Press.

Dolan, C. (2000). *What do you remember? A rough guide to the war in northern Uganda, 1986–2000.* COPE Working Paper No. 33, ACORD, 15–19.

Dolan, C. (2002). Collapsing masculinities and weak states: A case study of Northern Uganda. In F. Cleaver (Ed.), *Masculinities matter!: Men, gender, and development* (57–83). London: Zed Books Ltd.

Dolan, C. (2009). *Social torture: The case of northern Uganda, 1986–2006.* New York: Berghahn Books.

Doom, R., & Vlassenroot, K. (1999). Kony's message: A new Koine? The Lord's Resistance Army in northern Uganda. *African Affairs*, 98(390), 5–36. http://dx.doi.org/10.1093/oxfordjournals.afraf.a008002

Dörmann, K. (2003). *Elements of war crimes under the Rome Statute of the International Criminal Court*. London: Cambridge University Press. http://dx.doi.org/10.1017/CBO9780511495144

Druckman, D. (2005). *Doing research: Methods of inquiry for conflict analysis.* Thousand Oaks, CA: Sage.

DuBois, W.E.B. (1999). *The souls of black folks* (L.H. Gates Jr. & T.H. Oliver, Eds.). New York: Norton. First published in 1903.

Dupuy, Kendra E., & Krijn Peters. (2010). *War and children: A reference handbook.* Santa Barbara, CA: ABC-Clio.

Dutton, D.G., & Painter, S.L. (1981). Traumatic bonding: The development of emotional bonds in relationships of intermittent abuse. *Victimology: An International Journal*, 6(1–4), 139–55.

Egeland, J. (2008). *A billion lives: An eyewitness report from the frontlines of humanity*. New York: Simon and Shuster.

Eggers, D. (2006). *What is the what*. New York: Vintage Books.

Eisner, J. (1980). *The survivor*. New York: William Morrow.

Erhlich, S. (1989). *Lisa, Hedda and Joel: The Steinberg murder case*. New York, NY: St. Martin's Press.

Espino, C.M. (1991). Trauma and adaptation: the case of Central American children. In F. Ahearn & J.L. Athey (Eds.), *Refugee children: Theory, research and services* (pp. 106–24). Baltimore, MD: Johns Hopkins University Press.

Eyber, C. (2001). *Alleviating psychosocial suffering: An analysis of approaches to coping with war-related distress in Angola*. Unpublished doctoral dissertation, Queen Margaret University College, Edinburgh.

Fabiani, M., Nattabi, B., Pierotti, C., Ciantia, F., Opio, A.A., Musinguzi, J., …, & Declich, S. (2007). HIV-1 prevalence and factors associated with infection in the conflict-affected region of North Uganda. *Conflict and Health, 1*(3), 3. Retrieved from http://www.conflictandhealth.com/content/1/1/3. http://dx.doi.org/10.1186/1752-1505-1-3 Medline:17411455

Feldman, R., & Masalha, S. (2007, Winter). The role of culture in moderating the links between early ecological risk and young children's adaptation. *Development and Psychopathology, 19*(1), 1–21. http://dx.doi.org/10.1017/S0954579407070010 Medline:17241481

Finnstrom, S. (2003). *Living with bad surrounding: War and existential uncertainty in Acholiland, northern Uganda* (Doctoral dissertation). Philadelphia, PA: Coronet Books Inc.

Finnstrom, S. (2008). *Living with bad surroundings: War, history, and everyday moments in Northern Uganda*. Durham, NC: Duke University Press.

Fitzpatrick, P.L. (2009, August 31). Brief history: Stockholm Syndrome. *Time Magazine*. Retrieved from http://www.time.com/time/nation/article/0,8599,1919757,00.html

Franklin, B. (2007). *The autobiography of Benjamin Franklin*. New York: Cosimo Classics. [Original work first published in 1868]

Frie, R. (2003). *Understanding experience: Psychotherapy and postmodernism*. New York: Routledge.

Fuselier, D. (1999). Placing the Stockholm Syndrome in perspective. *FBI Law Enforcement Bulletin, 68*(7), 22–5.

Garbarino, J. (1995, December). The American war zone: what children can tell us about living with violence. *Journal of Developmental and Behavioral Pediatrics, 16*(6), 431–5. Medline:8746554

Garbarino, J., & Kostelny, K. (1996a). What do we need to know to understand children in war and community violence? In R. Apfel & B. Simon (Eds.),

Minefields in their hearts: The mental health of children in war and community violence (pp. 33–51). New Haven, CT: Yale University Press.

Garbarino, J., & Kostelny, K. (1996b, Feb). The effects of political violence on Palestinian children's behavior problems: A risk accumulation model. *Child Development, 67*(1), 33–45. http://dx.doi.org/10.2307/1131684 Medline:8605832

Garbarino, J., Dubrow, N., Kostelny, K., & Pardo, C. (1992). *Children in Danger: Coping with the consequences of community violence.* San Francisco: Jossey-Bass Publishers.

Garbarino, J., Kostelny, K., & Dubrow, N. (1991). *No place to be a child: Growing up in a war zone.* Lexington, MA, and Toronto: Lexington Books.

Garmezy, N. (1985). Stress resistant children: The search for protective factors. In J.E. Stevenson (Ed.), *Recent research in developmental psychopathology. Journal of Child Psychology and Psychiatry Book Supplement No. 4* (213–33). Oxford: Pergamon Press.

Garmezy, N. (1991, Sep). Resilience in children's adaptation to negative life events and stressed environments. *Pediatric Annals, 20*(9), 459–60, 463–6. Medline:1945543

Geertz, C. (1973). *The interpretation of cultures: Selected essays.* New York: Basic Book, Inc.

Gersony, R. (1997). *The anguish of northern Uganda: Results of the field based assessment of the civil conflict in northern Uganda* (USAID & United States Embassy Report, Kampala). Retrieved from http://www.internal-displacement.org

Ginyera-Pinycwa, A.G.G. (1989). Is there a northern question? In K. Rupesinghe (Ed.), *Conflict resolution in Uganda* (44–64). Oslo: International Peace Research Institute.

Girling, F.K. (1960). *The Acholi of Uganda.* London: Her Majesty's Stationary Office.

Glaser, B.G., & Strauss, A.L. (1980). *The discovery of grounded theory: Strategies for qualitative research.* New York, NY: Aldine Publishing Company.

Goodwin-Gill, G., & Cohn, I. (1994). *Child soldiers: The role of children in armed conflicts.* Oxford, UK: Clarendon Press.

Grady, D. (2003, March 15). End of an abduction: Coercion; Utah girl may have suffered from Stockholm Syndrome, experts say. New York Times. Retrieved from nytimes.com/2003/03/15/us/end-abduction-coercion-utah-girl-may-have-suffered-stockholm-syndrome-experts.html.

Graebner, W. (2008). *Patty's got a gun: Patricia Hearst in 1970s America.* Chicago, IL: University of Chicago Press.

Graham, D.L.R., Rawlings, E., & Rimini, N. (1988). Survivors of terror: Battered women, hostages and the Stockholm syndrome. In K. Yllo & M.L. Bograd (Eds.), *Feminist perspectives on wife abuse* (217–33). Newbury Park, CA: Sage Publications Inc.

Gutteridge, W.F. (1969). *The military in African politics*. Suffolk, UK: Chaucer Press Ltd.

Haberman, M., & MacIntosh, J. (2003). *Held captive: The kidnapping and rescue of Elizabeth Smart*. New York, NY: Harper Collins Publishers.

Halbwachs, M. (1992). The social frameworks of memory. In Coser, L.A. (Trans. Ed.), *On collective memory* (37–175). Chicago, IL: University of Chicago Press. (Original work published 1925).

Hall, J.R. (1995). Public narratives and the Apocalyptic sect: From Jonestown to Mt. Carmel. In S.A. Wright (Ed.), *Armageddon in Waco: Critical perspectives on the Branch Davidian conflict* (pp. 203–35). Chicago, IL: University of Chicago Press.

Hall, J.R. (2002). Mass suicides and the Branch Davidians. In D.G. Bromley & J. Gordon Melton (Eds.), *Cults, religion and violence* (149–69). New York, NY: Cambridge University Press. http://dx.doi.org/10.1017/CBO9780511499326.009

Hammersley, M., & Atkinson, P. (2007). *Ethnography: Principles in practice* (3rd ed.). New York, NY: Routledge.

Hansen, H.B. (1977). *Ethnicity and military rule in Uganda: A study of ethnicity as a political factor in Uganda*. Uppsala: Scandinavian Institute for African Studies.

Harkness, S., & Super, C. (1991). East Africa. In J. Hawes & N.R. Hiner (Eds.), *Children in historical and comparative perspective* (217–240). New York: Greenwood Press.

Hearst, P., Reeves, K.J., & United States District Court for California Northern District (1976). *The trial of Patty Hearst*. San Francisco, CA: Great Fidelity Book.

Honwana, A. (1997). Healing for peace: Traditional healers and post-war reconstruction in Southern Mozambique. *Peace and Conflicts: Journal of Peace Psychology, 3*(3), 293–305. http://dx.doi.org/10.1207/s15327949pac0303_6

Honwana, A. (2006). *Child soldiers in Africa*. Philadelphia: University of Pennsylvania Press.

Hough, P. (2008). *Understanding global security* (2nd ed.). New York: Routledge.

Hovil, L., & Lomo, Z. (2005).*Whose justice?: Perceptions of Uganda's Amnesty Act 2000, the potential for conflict resolution and long-term reconciliation* (RLP Working Paper No. 15). Retrieved from Refugee Law Project website: http://www.refugeelawproject.org

Human Rights Watch. (1997). The scars of death: Children abducted by the Lord's Resistance Army in Uganda. *New York: Human Rights Watch.* Retrieved from http://www.hrw.org/en/reports/1997/09/18/scars-death

Human Rights Watch. (1999). *Leave none to tell the story: Genocide in Rwanda.* Index No. 1711. Retrieved from http://www.hrw.org/legacy/reports/1999/rwanda/

Human Right Watch. (2003a, March). Stolen children: Abduction and recruitment in northern Uganda. *Human Right Watch, 15*(7). Retrieved from http://www.hrw.org/reports/2003/uganda0303/uganda0403.pdf.

Human Rights Watch. (2003b, July). Abducted and abused: Renewed conflict in Northern Uganda. *Human Rights Watch.* Retrieved from http://www.hrw.org/en/reports/2003/07/14/abducted-and-abused

Human Rights Watch. (2005, 20 September). Uprooted and forgotten: Impunity and human rights abuses in Northern Uganda. Human Rights Watch. Retrieved from http://www.hrw.org/node/11614/section/1.

Human Rights Watch. (2009). *The Christmas Massacres: The LRM/A attacks on civilians in northern Congo.* New York: Author. Retrieved from http://www.hrw.org/en/reports/2009/02/16/christmas-massacres

Hunter, E. (1951). *Brainwashing in Red China: The calculated destruction of men's minds.* New York: Vanguard.

Hunter, E. (1956). *Brainwashing: The story of men who defied it.* New York: Farrar, Strauss, and Cudahy. http://dx.doi.org/10.1037/13189-000

Husserl, E. (1970). *The crisis of European sciences and transcendental phenomenology.* Evanston, Illinois: Northwestern University Press. http://dx.doi.org/10.1002/9780470755501.ch9

Ibingira, G.S.K. (1973). *The forging of an African nation.* New York: Viking Press.

Ingham, K. (1990). *Politics in Africa: The uneven tribal dimension.* London: Routledge Press.

International Criminal Court (2002). Rome Statute. Retrieved from http://www.icc-cpi.int/NR/rdonlyres/ADD16852-AEE9-4757-ABE7-9CDC7CF02886/283503/RomeStatutEng1.pdf.

Isis-Women's International Cross Cultural Exchange (2001). Women's experiences of armed conflict, Gulu District 1986–1999 (An Isis-WICCE Research Report, Part 1). Retrieved from Isis-WICCE Online Library website: www.isis.or.ug

Iweala, U. (2005). *Beasts of no nation.* New York: HarperCollins Publishers.

Jonte-Pace, D.E. (2001). *Speaking the unspeakable: Religion, misogyny and the uncanny mother in Freud's cultural texts.* Berkeley, CA: University of California Press. http://dx.doi.org/10.1525/california/9780520226005.001.0001

Jorgensen, J.J. (1981). *Uganda: A modern history.* London, UK: Croom Helm Ltd.

Junger, S. (2000, August). The terror of Sierra Leone. *Vanity Fair*, 480: 110–17; 169–73.

Justice and Peace Commission of the Diocese of Gulu. (2007, March). What Acholi Juba meeting would have focused on. *Justice and Peace News*, 7(21), 5–8. Retrieved from http://www.archdioceseofgulu.org/JPC/Newsletter0703_a.pdf.

Justice and Reconciliation Project. (2007). *Remembering the Atiak massacre, April 20th 1995*. (JRP Field Notes No. 4). Retrieved from Justice and Reconciliation website: http://justiceandreconciliation.com/.

Justice and Reconciliation Project. (2008). *Massacre in Mucwini* (JRP Field Notes No. 8). Retrieved from Justice and Reconciliation website: http://justiceandreconciliation.com/

Justice and Reconciliation Project. (2009). *Kill every living thing: The Barlonyo massacre*. (JRP Field Notes No. 9). Retrieved from Justice and Reconciliation website: http://justiceandreconciliation.com/

Karugire, S.R. (1980). *A political history of Uganda*. Nairobi, London: Heinemann Educational Books.

Kasekende, L.A., & Atingi-Ego, H. (2008). Restarting and sustaining growth in a post-conflict economy: The case of Uganda. In B.J. Ndulu, S.A. O'Connell, J.P. Acam, R.H. Bates, A.K. Fosu, J.W. Gunning, & D. Njinken (Eds.), *The political economy of economic growth in Africa, 1960—2000* (244–83). Cambridge: Cambridge University Press.

Kasozi, A.B.K., Musisi, N., & Sejjengo, J.M. (1994). *The social origins of violence in Uganda, 1964–1985*. Montreal and Kingston, ON: McGill-Queen's University Press.

Kasozi, W.K.L. (2001). *Assault on the spying church in Uganda: The violation of the right to freedom of religion and worship*. Maseru, Lesotho: GWKLK.

Keitesi, C. (2004). *Child soldier*. London: Souvenir Press.

Kibirige, D. (2002a, 23 March). Sudan: Captain Nsereko missing in Sudan. *The Daily Monitor, Uganda*. Retrieved from http://allafrica.com/stories/200203230066.html.

Kibirige, D. (2002b, 28 March). Uganda: Capt. Ssekabojja killed. *The Daily Monitor, Uganda*. Retrieved from http://allafrica.com/stories/200203280490.html.

Kiwanuka, M.S.M. (1971). *A history of Buganda: From the foundation of the kingdom to 1900*. London: Longman.

Klare, M. (1999). The Kalashnikov age. *Bulletin of the Atomic Scientists*, 55(1), 18–22. http://dx.doi.org/10.2968/055001009

Klineman, G., Butler, S., & Conn, D. (1980). *The cult that died: The tragedy of Jim Jones and the Peoples Temple*. New York, NY: Putnam Press.

Krakauer, J. (2003). *Under the banner of heaven: A story of violent faith*. New York, NY: Anchor Books (Random House).

Kuepper, W.G., Lackey, G.L., & Swinerton, E.N. (1975). *Ugandan Asians in Great Britain: Forced migration and social absorption*. London: C. Helm.

Kuper, J. (1997). *International law concerning child civilians in armed conflict*. Oxford, UK: Clarendon Press.

Kutesa, P. (2006). *Uganda's revolution 1979–1986: How I saw it*. Kampala, Uganda: Fountain Publishers/Michigan: University Press.

Lamphear, J. (1976). *The traditional history of the Jie of Uganda*. Oxford: Clarendon Press.

Lamphear, J., & Webster, J.B. (1971). The Jie-Acholi war: Oral evidence from two sides of the battle front. *Uganda Journal, 35*, 23–42.

Lamwaka, C. (2002). The peace process in northern Uganda, 1986–1990. Conciliation Resources. Retrieved from http://www.c-r.org/accord-article/peace- process-northern-uganda-1986-1990-2002.

Lave, J., & Wenger, E. (1991). *Situated Learning: Legitimate peripheral participation*. New York: Cambridge University Press. http://dx.doi.org/10.1017/CBO9780511815355

Lear, J. (2006). *Radical hope: Ethics in the face of cultural devastation*. Cambridge, MA: Harvard University Press.

Lee, R. S. (1999). The International Criminal Court: The making of the Rome Statute: Issues, negotiations and results. Leiden, The Netherlands: Martinus Nijhoff Publishers.

Leggett, I. (2001). *Uganda: OXFAM country profile*. Oxford, UK: OXFAM.

Legrand, Jean-Claude. (1997). *Cape Town principles and best practices* [pamphlet]. New York: UNICEF.

Li, K. (2005). *Children bear the brunt of Uganda's 19-year conflict* (UNICEF Online article). Retrieved from UNICEF website: http://www.unicef.org/protection/uganda_25704.html

Lifton, R.J. (1961). *Thought reform and the psychology of totalism: A study of "brainwashing" in China*. New York: W.W. Norton & Co. Publishers.

Lionnet, F. (1989). *Autobiographical voices: Race, gender, self-portraiture*. Ithaca, NY: Cornell University Press.

Liu Institute for Global Issues, Gulu District NGO Forum, & Ker Kwaro Acholi (2005). *Roco wat i Acoli, restoring relationships in Acholiland: Traditional approaches to justice and reintegration*. Vancouver: Liu Institute for Global Issues.

Liu Institute for Global Issues & The Gulu Justice Forum. (2006, September). Young mothers, marriage, and reintegration in Northern Uganda: Considerations for the Juba Peace Talk. *JRP Field Notes, 2*.

Lomo, Z., & Hovil, L. (2004). Behind the violence: Causes, consequences and the search for solutions to the conflict in Northern Uganda. Refugee Law Project Working Paper No. 11. RLP, Kampala, Uganda.

Lucima, O. (2007). *Mato oput is a cloak for impunity in northern Uganda*. Retrieved from http://kwotkaka.wordpress.com/mato-oput/

Luthar, S.S. (2006). Resilience in development: A synthesis of research across five decades. In D. Cicchetti & D.J. Cohen (Eds.), *Developmental psychopathology: Vol. 3. Risk, disorder, and adaptation* (2nd ed., pp. 739–95). New York: Wiley.

Luthar, S.S., & Zigler, E. (1991, January). Vulnerability and competence: A review of research on resilience in childhood. *American Journal of Orthopsychiatry, 61*(1), 6–22. http://dx.doi.org/10.1037/h0079218 Medline:2006679

Lynn, S.J., & Rhue, J.W. (1994). *Disassociation: Clinical and theoretical perspectives*. New York: Guilford Press.

Machel, G. (1996) *Impact of armed conflict on children: Report of the expert of the Secretary General, Ms Graca Machel*. (UN Report submitted pursuant to General Assembly Resolution 48/157). Retrieved from UNICEF website: http://www.unicef.org/graca/

Machel, G. (2001). *The impact of war on children*. New York: Palgrave.

Mamdani, M. (2002). *When victims become killers: Colonialism, nativism, and the genocide in Rwanda*. Princeton, NJ: Princeton University Press.

Marsella, A.J. (1990). Ethnocultural identity: The "new" independent variable in cross-cultural research. *Focus: Newsletter of the American Psychological Association Minority Division, 3,* 3–8.

Martin-Baro, I. (1994). *Writings for a liberation psychology*. Cambridge, MA: Harvard University Press.

Masten, A.S. (1994). Resilience in individual development: Successful adaptation despite risk and adversity. In M. Wang & E. Gordon (Eds.), *Risk and resilience in inner city America: Challenges and prospects* (3–25). Hillsdale, NJ: Erlbaum.

Masten, A.S. (1999). Resilience comes of age: Reflections on the past and outlook for the next generation of research. In M.D. Glantz, J. Johnson, & L. Huffman (Eds.), *Resilience and development: Positive life adaptations* (289–96). New York: Plenum Press.

Masten, A.S. (2004, June). Regulatory processes, risk, and resilience in adolescent development. *Annals of the New York Academy of Sciences, 1021*(1), 310–19. http://dx.doi.org/10.1196/annals.1308.036 Medline:15251901

Masten, A.S. (2007, Summer). Resilience in developing systems: Progress and promise as the fourth wave rises. *Development and Psychopathology, 19*(3), 921–30. http://dx.doi.org/10.1017/S0954579407000442 Medline:17705908

Masten, A.S., Best, K.M., & Garmezy, N. (1990). Resilience and development: Contributions from the study of children who overcome adversity. *Development and Psychopathology, 2*(04), 425–44. http://dx.doi.org/10.1017/S0954579400005812

Masten, A.S., & Coatsworth, D. (1995). Competence, resilience, and psychopathology. In D. Cicchetti & D.J. Cohen (Eds.), *Developmental psychopathology Vol. 2. Risk, disorder, and adaptation* (715–52). New York: Wiley.

Masten, A.S., & Coatsworth, J.D. (1998, February). The development of competence in favorable and unfavorable environments: Lessons from research on successful children. *American Psychologist, 53*(2), 205–20. http://dx.doi.org/10.1037/0003-066X.53.2.205 Medline:9491748

Masten, A.S., & Obradovic, J. (2006, Dec). Competence and resilience in development. *Annals of the New York Academy of Sciences, 1094*(1), 13–27. http://dx.doi.org/10.1196/annals.1376.003 Medline:17347338

Masten, A.S., & Reed, M.J. (2002). Resilience in development. In C.R. Snyder & S. Lopez (Eds.), *Handbook of positive psychology* (74–88). Oxford, UK: Oxford University Press.

Mawson, A. (2004). Children, impunity and justice: Some dilemmas from northern Uganda. In Boyden & de Berry (Eds.). *Children and youth on the front line* (130–41). New York: Berghahn Books.

Mazrui, A.A. (1975). *Soldiers and kinsmen in Uganda: The making of a military ethnocracy.* Thousand Oaks, CA: Sage publications.

Mazrui, A.A. (1976). Soldiers as traditionalizers: Military rule and the reafricanization of Africa. *World Politics, 28*(2), 246–72. http://dx.doi.org/10.2307/2009892

Mazrui, A.A. (1977). The Warrior tradition and the masculinity of war. In A.A. Mazrui (Ed.), *The warrior tradition in modern Africa* (69–81). Leiden, The Netherlands: E.J. Brill Publishers. http://dx.doi.org/10.1177/002190967701200105

McCallin, M. (1998). Community involvement in the social reintegration of child soldiers. In P.J. Bracken & C. Petty (Eds.), *Rethinking the trauma of war* (60–75). London: Free Association Books Ltd.

McDonnell, F.J.H., & Akallo, G. (2007). *Girlsoldier: A story of hope for northern Uganda's children.* Grand Rapids, MI: Chosen Books.

McDougal, M.S., & Reisman, W.M. (1981). *International law in contemporary perspective, the public order of the world community: Cases and materials.* New York: Foundation Press.

McQuillan, M. (Ed.). (2000). *The narrative reader.* London: Routledge.

Melady, M., & Melady, T. (1977). *Idi Amin Dada: Hitler in Africa.* Kansas City: Sheed Andrews & McMeel.

Merleau-Ponty, M. (1962). *Phenomenology of perception*. New York, NY: Routledge & Kegan Paul.

Mills, J. (1979). *Six years with God*. New York, NY: A&W Publishers.

Muleme, G. (2004, 27 September). War boosts HIV/AIDS in Northern Uganda. *Associated Press*. Retrieved from http://www.ap.org/

Museveni, K.Y. (1997). *Sowing the mustard seed: The struggle for freedom and democracy in Uganda*. London: Macmillan Education Ltd.

Mutibwa, P. (1992). *Uganda since independence: A story of unfulfilled hopes*. Trenton, NJ: African World Press.

Nantulya, P. (2001, July). *Exclusion, identity and armed conflict: A historical survey of the politics of confrontation in Uganda with specific reference to the independence era*. Paper presented at the conference on Politics of Identity and Exclusion in Africa: From Violent Confrontation to Peaceful Cooperation. University of Pretoria. Retrieved from http://www.kas.de/suedafrika/en/publications/5094/

Ngoga, P. (1998). Uganda: The National Resistance Army. In C. Clapham (Ed.), *African guerrillas* (91–106). Bloomington, IN: Indiana University Press.

Nietzsche, F. (1992). *Ecce Homo: How one becomes what one is* (R.J. Hollingdale, Trans.). New York: Penguin Books. (Original work published 1908).

Nikolić-Ristanović, V. (2000). *Women, violence, and war: Wartime victimization of refugees in the Balkans*. Budapest: Central European University Press.

Nsamenang, B.A. (1992). Perceptions of parenting among the Nso of Cameroon. In B.S. Hewlett (Ed.), *Father-child relations: Cultural and biosocial contexts* (321–43). New York: Aldine de Gruyter.

Nyakairu, F. (2008, January 6). The making of LRM/A's Joseph Kony: The enigmatic rebel leader. *The Sunday Monitor*, editorial page.

Nyeko, B., & Lucima, O. (2002). Profiles of the parties to the conflict. In O. Lucima (Ed.), *Protracted conflict, elusive peace: Initiatives to end the violence in northern Uganda*. 16–23. London, UK: Coalition Resources and Kacoke Madit.

Obita, J. (1997, June). *A case for national reconciliation, peace, democracy and economic prosperity for all Ugandans*. Paper presented at the conference of Kacokke Madit, London, UK. Paper retrieved from http://www.km-net.org.uk/conferences/KM97/papers_htm/casefor.htm

Ochberg, F.M., & Soskis, D.A. (1982). Concepts of terrorist victimization. In F.M. Ochberg & D.A. Soskis (Eds.), *Victims of terrorism* (105–35). Boulder, CO: Westview Press, Inc.

Ocitti, J.P. (1973). *African indigenous education: As practised by the Acholi of Uganda*. Nairobi: Kenya Literature Bureau.

Ockslong, M., ... (Producers), & Zwick, E. (Director). (2006*). Blood diamond* [Motion picture]. United States of America: Warner Brothers.

Odonga, A.M. (1999). *Ododo pa Acoli, Vol. 1. Kampala.* Uganda: Fountain Publishers.

Odonga, A.M. (2005). *Lwo-English Dictionary. Kampala.* Uganda: Fountain Publishers.

Ogunbanjo, M.B. (2002). *African military unprofessionalism: Roots and results.* Ibadan, Nigeria: Oputoru Books.

O'Kadameri, B. (2002). LRA/Government negotiations 1993–94. In O. Lucima (Ed.), *Protracted conflict, elusive peace: Initiatives to end the violence in northern Uganda* (34–41). London, UK: Coalition Resources and Kacoke Madit.

Okpewho, I. (1992). *African oral literature: Backgrounds, character and continuity.* Bloomington, IN: Indiana University Press.

Okuku, J. (2002). *Ethnicity, state power and the democratisation process in Uganda.* Uppsala, Sweden: Nordic Africa Institute.

Oliver, R.A. (1986). The East African interior. In R. Oliver (Ed.), *The Cambridge history of Africa: From c. 1050 to c. 1600* (Vol. 3, 621–69). New York: Cambridge University Press.

Oloya, O. (2005, 14 September). Political thuggery should not be allowed this time. *The New Vision, Uganda,* Editorial page.

Onyango-ku-Odongo, J.M. (1976). The early history of the Central Lwo. In J.M. Onyango-ku-Dongo & J.B. Webster (Eds.), *The central Lwo during the Aconya.* Nairobi: East African Literature Bureau.

Onyango-Obbo, C. (1997, November 10). One day partyists will be butchered. *The Monitor,* Uganda. Retrieved from http://www.newsafrica.com/

Oryem, C.L. (2004). Breaking the cycle of violence. In M.L. Klassen (Ed). *Fighting history in Uganda* (4–6). (Mennonite Central Committee (MCC) Peace Office Publication Report 34, 2). Retrieved from Mennonite Central Committee website: http://www.mcc.org/whatwedo/peace/pon.

Oruni, P. (1994). *What is right for Uganda.* London: Local Government Publication.

Oryem, C.L. (2008). Internally displaced persons in northern Uganda: A challenge for peace and reconciliation. In D. Hollenbach (Ed.), *Refugee rights: Ethics, advocacy, and Africa* (195–204). Washington, DC: Georgetown University Press.

Otim, P.W. (2009, March). An interactive media: Reflections on Mega FM and its peacebuilding role in Uganda. *Conflict Resolution Information Source.* Retrieved from http://www.crinfo.org

Otunnu, O. (2002). Causes and consequences of war in Acholi. [Special Issue]. *Accord, 11.* London: Conciliation Resources.

Otunnu, O. (2006, 9 June). The secret genocide. *Foreign Policy, 155,* 44–6.

OXFAM (2006). *The AK-47: The world's favourite killing machine.* London: OXFAM. Retrieved 6 December 2007 from http://www.oxfam.org/en/policy/bn0606_ak47

Pain, D. (1997). *The Bending of the spears: Producing consensus for peace and development in Northern Uganda*. London: International Alert & Kacoke Madit.

Parsons, T. (2003). *The 1964 army mutinies and the making of modern East Africa*. Westport, CT: Greenwood Publishing Group.

p'Bitek, O. (1966). *Song of Lawino*. Nairobi: East African Publishing House Ltd.

p'Bitek, O. (1971). *Religion of the Central Luo*. Nairobi: East Africa Literature Bureau.

p'Bitek, O. (1974). *Horn of my love*. London, UK: Heinemann.

Peters, K., & Richards, P. (1998a). Fighting with open eyes: Youth combatants talking about war in Sierra Leone. In P.J. Bracken & C. Petty (Eds.), *Rethinking the trauma of war* (76–111). London: Free Association Books Ltd.

Peters, K., & Richards, P. (1998b). Why we fight: The voices of youth combatants in Sierra Leone. *Africa, 68*(2), 183–210. http://dx.doi.org/10.2307/1161278

Petraitis, R. (2003). *Joseph Kony's spirit war*. Retrieved from http://www.infidels.org/library/modern/richard_petraitis/spirit_war.html.

Portelli, A. (1991). *The death of Luigi Trastulli and other stories: Term and meaning of oral history*. New York: SUNY Press.

Postlethwaite, J.R.P. (1947). *I look back*. London: T.V. Boardman and Company Ltd.

Prunier, G. (1996). *Update on the border crisis with Uganda* (UNHCR Report, 1 April 1996). Retrieved from UNHCR website: http://www.unhcr.org/refworld/docid/3ae6a6b614.html

Raundalen, M., & Dyregrov, A. (1991). War experiences and psychological impact on children. In C.P. Dodge & M. Raundalen (Eds.), *Reaching children in war: Sudan, Uganda and Mozambique* (21–38). Bergen, Norway: Sigma Forlag/The Scandinavian Institute of African Studies.

Ressler, E., Boothby, N., & Steinbock, D. (1988). *Unaccompanied children: Care and protection in wars, natural disasters and refugee movements*. New York: Oxford Press.

Rice, A. (2006, July). The book of Wilson. *Paris Review, 177*. Retrieved from http://www.theparisreview.org/letters-essays/5644/the-book-of-wilson-andrew-rice.

Richards, P. (1996). *Fighting for the rain forest: War, youth and resources in Sierra Leone*. Oxford: James Currey.

Richards, P. (2002). Militia conscription in Sierra Leone: Recruitment of young fighters in an African war. In L. Mjøset & Stephen van Holde (Eds.), *The comparative study of conscription in the armed forces, 20* (255–76). Oxford: Elsevier Science Ltd. http://dx.doi.org/10.1016/S0195-6310(02)80031-X

Roberts, J.P. (2003). *Glitter and greed: The secret world of the diamond cartel.* New York: The Disinformation Company.

Rosen, D.M. (2005). *Armies of the young: Child soldiers in war and terrorism.* New Brunswick, NJ: Rutgers University Press.

Ruganda, J. (1980). *The floods.* Nairobi, Kenya: East African Publishing House.

Rutter, M. (2000a, Summer). Psychosocial influences: Critiques, findings, and research needs. *Development and Psychopathology, 12*(3), 375–405. http://dx.doi.org/10.1017/S0954579400003072 Medline:11014744

Rutter, M. (2000b). Resilience reconsidered: Conceptual considerations, empirical findings, and policy implications. In J.P. Shonkoff & S.J. Meisels (Eds.), *Handbook of Early Childhood Intervention* (2nd ed., 651–82). New York: Cambridge University Press. http://dx.doi.org/10.1017/CBO9780511529320.030

Safyer, A.W. (1994). The impact of inner-city life on adolescent development: Implications for social work. *Smith College Studies in Social Work, 64*(2), 153–67. http://dx.doi.org/10.1080/00377319409517406

Salopek, P. (2002, February 27).The guns of Africa: Violence-wracked nations are dumping grounds for world's arsenals. *Seattle Times.* Retrieved from http://community.seattletimes.nwsource.com/archive

Sanders, W.B. (1980). *Rape and woman's identity.* Beverly Hills, CA: Sage Publications.

Sandywell, B. (1996). *Reflexivity and the crisis of Western reason.* London: Routledge. http://dx.doi.org/10.4324/9780203420171

Sathyamurthy, T.V. (1986). *Political development of Uganda 1900–1986.* Brookfield, VT: Gower Publishing Company.

Sauerwein, K. (2008). *Invisible chains: Shawn Hornbeck and the kidnapping case that shook the nation.* Guildford, CT: Lyons Press (Globe Pequot Press).

Sayndee, T.D. (2008). Thugs' paradise, agencies' guinea pig, and the natural resource intrigue: The civil war in Liberia. In K. Omeje (Ed.), *Extractive economies and conflicts in the global South: Multi-regional perspectives on rentier politics* (149–60). Burlington, VT: Ashgate Publishing, Ltd.

Schabracq, M.J. (2007). *Changing organizational culture: The change agent's guidebook.* Chichester, West Sussex: John Wiley and Sons Ltd.

Schadt, C. (Director). (2001). *Soldier boys* [Motion picture]. Canada: Paradox Productions Film.

Schafer, J. (2004). The use of patriarchal imagery in the civil war in Mozambique and its implications for the reintegration of child soldiers. In J. Boyden & J. de Berry (Eds.), *Children and youth on the front line* (87–104). New York: Berghahn Books.

Schein, E. (1961). *Coercive persuasion: A socio-psychological analysis of the "brain-washing" of American civilian prisoners by the Chinese communists.* New York: W.W. Norton & Co. Publishers.

Schneider, K.S. (1991, 25 November). Too cruel a theft. *People, 36* (20), 158–63.

Schuman, H., & Scott, J. (1989). Generations and collective memories. *American Sociological Review, 54*(3), 359–81. http://dx.doi.org/10.2307/2095611

Seidman, I. (2006). *Interviewing as qualitative research: A guide for researchers in education and the social sciences* (3rd ed.). New York: Teachers College Press.

Singer, P.W. (2006). *Children at war.* Berkeley, CA: University of California Press.

Singh, J. (Ed.). (1995). *Light weapons and international security.* New Delhi: British American Security Information Council and Indian Pugwash Society.

Smelser, N.J. (2004). Psychological trauma and cultural trauma. In J.C. Alexander, R. Eyerman, B. Giesen, N.J. Smelser, & P. Sztompka (Eds.), *Cultural trauma and the collective identity* (31–59). Berkeley, CA: University of California Press. http://dx.doi.org/10.1525/california/9780520235946.003.0002

Smith, G.N. (2008). *They come back singing: Finding God with the refugees.* Chicago, IL: Loyola Press.

Spiegel, P., & Harroff-Tavel, H. (2006). *HIV/AIDS and internally displaced persons in 8 priority countries* (UNHCR Report). Retrieved from UNAIDS website: http://data.unaids.org/pub/Report/2006/idp_hiv_paper.pdf

Stohl, R. (2002). Targeting children: Small arms and children in conflict. *Brown Journal of World Affairs, 9*(1), 281–92.

Stohl, R., & Smith, D. (1999, April). *Small arms in failed states: A deadly combination.* Paper presented at the Failed States and International Security Conference at Purdue University, West Lafayette, Indiana. Retrieved from http://www.cdi.org/issues/failedstates/march99.html

Strauss, A., & Corbin, J. (Eds.). (1997). *Grounded theory in practice.* London: Sage Publications.

Strentz, T. (1980). The Stockholm syndrome: Law enforcement policy and ego defenses of the hostage. *Annals of the New York Academy of Sciences, 347* (1 Forensic Psyc), 137–50. http://dx.doi.org/10.1111/j.1749-6632.1980.tb21263.x Medline:6930893

Swidler, A. (1986). Culture in Action: Symbols and strategies. *American Sociological Review, 51*(2), 273–86. http://dx.doi.org/10.2307/2095521

Symonds, M. (1975, Spring). Victims of violence: Psychological effects and aftereffects. *American Journal of Psychoanalysis, 35*(1), 19–26. http://dx.doi.org/10.1007/BF01248422 Medline:1155652

Taylor, K. (2006). *Brainwashing: The science of thought control.* New York: Oxford University Press.

Thompson, C.P., Skowronski, J.J., Larsen, S.F., & Betz, A.L. (1996). *Autobiographical memory: Remembering what and remembering when.* Mahwah, NJ: Lawrence Erlbaum Associates, Publishers.

Turner, V. (1995). *The ritual process: Structure and anti-structure.* New York: Aldine de Gruyer.

Twaddle, M. (1985). The nine lives of Semei Kakungulu. *History in Africa, 12,* 325–33. http://dx.doi.org/10.2307/3171726

Twaddle, M. (1993). *Kakungulu and the creation of Uganda, 1868–1928.* London: James Currey.

UNICEF (1997). *Cape Town principles and best practices.* Retrieved from http://www.unicef.org/emerg/files/Cape_Town_Principles(1).pdf

Van Gennep, A. (1960). *The rites of passage.* London: Routledge.

Van Manen, M. (1990). *Researching lived experience: Human science for an action sensitive pedagogy.* London, ON: University of Western Ontario.

Vuckovic, G. (1997). *Ethnic cleavages and conflict: The sources of national cohesion and disintegration. The case of Yugoslavia.* Aldershot, UK: Ashgate Publishing Ltd.

Weisner, T.S. (1984). The social ecology of childhood: A cross-cultural view. In M. Lewis (Ed.), *Beyond the Dyad* (43–58). New York: Plenum Press.

Werner, E.E. (2000). Protective factors and individual resilience. In J.P. Shonkoff & S.J. Meisels (Eds.), *Handbook of early childhood intervention* (2nd ed., 115–32). New York: Cambridge University Press. http://dx.doi.org/10.1017/CBO9780511529320.008

Werner, E.E., & Smith, R.S. (1992). *Overcoming the odds.* Ithaca, NY: Cornell University Press.

Wertsch, J.V. (1985). *Vygotsky and the social formation of mind.* Cambridge, MA: Harvard University Press.

Wertsch, J.V. (1991). *Voices of the mind: A sociocultural approach to mediated action.* Cambridge, MA: Harvard University Press.

Wessells, M.G. (1997). Child soldiers. *Bulletin of the Atomic Scientists, 53*(6), 32–9.

Wessells, M.G. (2006). *Child soldiers: From violence to prevention.* London: Harvard University Press.

West, C.D. (2000). *Pathways of thriving and resilience: Growth responses to adversity and trauma in two Cambodian communities: A Comparative study between Lowell, Massachusetts, and Phnom Penh, Cambodia* (MA thesis, University of Massachusetts, Lowell). Retrieved from Eric Database. (ED461073)

West, H.G. (2004). Girls with guns: Narrating the experience of war of
FRELIMO's 'female detachment. In J. Boyden & J. de Berry (Eds.), *Children
and youth on the front line* (105–29). New York: Berghahn Books.

Witzsche, R.A.F. (2003). *Crimes against humanity*. North Vancouver, BC: Cygni
Communications Ltd.

Woodward, P. (1991). Uganda and southern Sudan, 1986–9: New regimes and
peripheral politics. In H.B. Hansen & M. Twaddle (Eds.), *Changing Uganda:
The dilemmas of structural adjustment and revolutionary change* (178–86).
Athens, OH: Ohio University Press.

Wright, M.O.D., & Masten, A.S. (2005). Resilience processes in development:
Fostering positive adaptation in the context of adversity. In S. Goldstein &
R. Brooks (Eds.), *Handbook of resilience in children* (17–37). New York: Kluwer
Academic/Plenum Press. http://dx.doi.org/10.1007/0-306-48572-9_2

Young S. & Bane, V. (2009, 29 August). Inside story: How Jaycee Dugard
finally escaped her captor. *People Magazine*. Retrieved from http://www
.people.com/people/article/0,,20301301,00.html.

Yow, V.R. (2005). *Recording oral history* (2nd ed.). New York: Rowman Altamira.

Zolberg, A.R., Suhrke, A., & Aguayo, A.S. (1989). *Escape from violence: Conflict
and the refugee crisis in the developing world*. New York: Oxford University
Press.

Index

abductions: of Aboke schoolgirls,
62, 131–5, 182n1; famous, 69–70,
180nn2–5; LRM/A's rationale for,
60–2; risk of, 130; testimonies of
former CI soldiers, 7–9, 78–80,
104–8, 129–31; total number of
LRM/A, 62, 177n1. *See also* child
abductees; Stockholm Syndrome
abila pa kwaro (shrine of the ancestors), 155
'Aboke girls,' 62, 131–5, 182n1
Abu-Lughod, L., 26
Acana, Rwot David Onen, II, 174
Acholi culture: ancestral *(paco)* and
residential home *(ot)*, 80–1;
centrality of livestock in, 50–1,
179n6; communal responsibilities
in, 166; courtship traditions, 119;
dual character of the bush and, 80;
folktales *(ododo)*, 42–3; food, 10,
14, 56, 86–7, 90–1, 181n2; importance of the pumpkin, 161–2;
killing taboo, 84–6; liminal
repurposing of, 24, 66, 74, 90, 155;
LRM/A exploitation of, 10, 13,
24–5, 66, 84, 152; marriage
ceremony *(nyom)*, 120, 162; night

and darkness significance, 79;
NRM/A destruction of, 46–51, 61;
protection of home and family
values, 43–6, 51; rape and incest
taboo, 48–9, 92; regeneration of,
174; resources, 166; restorative
restitution for loss of life *(culo
kwor)*, 166–7; self-healing capacity
of, 164; symbol of victory *(oboke
olwedo)*, 5; traditional cures, 99;
traditional justice, 167; tradition
of remembering life stories, 132–3;
trauma and devastation of, 47–51,
160–6; wild fruits, 22; youth
dances *(laraka-raka)*, 14–15. *See also*
Acholi people; Acholi sayings and
phrases; rituals; spirits
Acholiland: business and economy,
56–7; cattle rustling, 50–1, 179n6;
colonial policy in, 36; context of
war in, 6; displaced-persons
camps, 172; Lamogi Rebellion
(1911–12), 36–7; NRM/A invasion
of, 45–52, 57, 60; rape reports, 49;
slave trade in, 178n2
Acholi people: children, 156–7;
collective identity, 46; collective

doctor, 137–9; full membership in LRM/A, 140–1; homecoming, 151–2, 170; identity, 144, 152, 158; job as bike mechanic, 124; leadership, 144–5, 148–9; mistrust of adults, 127; plan for desertion, 145–9; recollection of Aboke girls' abduction, 82, 131–5, 182nn1–2; referred to as *ladit* (elder), 148; refusal to take a wife, 94, 143–4; rejection by family and community, 159–60; return to civilian society, 154, 158; sexuality in the bush, 8; survival skills, 129, 135; thoughts of escape, 141–2; training and duties as war doctor *(dakta mony)*, 141–3

Otti, Vincent, 91, 173

Otunnu, Olara, 44, 179n4

Oyite-Ojok, David, 39, 178n5

paco (ancestral home), 43, 80–1. See also *dwoogo paco* (returning home)

Pagik village, 114

Pain, Denis, 168–9

Pamin-Yai: author's upbringing in, 10–15, 17, 22, 42; remains of, 4; spirits of, 12–13

p'Bitek, Okot, 22, 32, 79, 84; *Song of Lawino*, 18–19, 50, 111

peace talks, 114–15, 173–4; in Juba (2006–8), 173–4; at Pagik village (1993–4), 58, 114–15, 180n1, 181n13

pe iput te okono (do not uproot the pumpkin), 161–2, 164–5

Peters, K., 70

Petraitis, R., 67

pito lwit okono odoco (replanting the pumpkin roots), 172–4

politics of 'otherness,' 38

Popular Resistance Army (PRA). *See* National Resistance Movement/ Army (NRM/A)

Portelli, Allessandro, 30

Postlethwaite, J.R.P., 37

poto ikome (falling upon him), 151

poverty, 21, 33, 51, 57

prayer, 88, 150, 155

proverbs, 27, 135; pumpkin, 161–2, 164–5, 172–4, 183n3

Prunier, G., 68

purification: anointing with shea butter ritual *(wiiro kom)*, 69, 86–9, 139–40; of *cen* (evil spirit of the dead), 83–4, 181n10; cleansing ceremony for returning CI soldiers *(yweyo kom)*, 151, 169–70

pwonyo mony (military training), 93–4

Radical Hope: Ethics in the Face of Cultural Devastation (Lear), 53–4

radio kabir, 103, 181n2

rape: of Acholi men and women by NRM/A, 48–9; by husbands, 157; by Joseph Kony, 9, 92; orphans born as the result of, 174

Rawlings, E., 71

recruitment. *See* abductions; child abductees

reflexivity, 26–7

Reisman, W.M., 45

religious indoctrination, 67–9

resilience, 153, 155–6, 164

restitution, 167–8

returning CI soldiers: anxiety of, 152; cleansing ceremony *(yweyo kom)*, 151, 169–70; community rejection/

hostility, 77, 122–3, 154, 158; desire to return to ancestral home, 154–5; forgiveness and, 171; healing, 174; identities, 24, 123, 154–5, 160, 171–2; literacy and education impediments, 172–3; optimism of, 176; physical needs of, 172; reconciliation through cultural resources/rituals, 166–9; reintegration programs and support, 155, 165–6, 172–3; rejection by family members, 159–60; restorative restitution for, 166–8; reunification with families, 172; stigmatization of, 20, 122, 154, 158, 170–1; suffering of, 164, 169, 174–6; survivor-perpetrator dichotomy of, 166; victimization of, 154

Revolutionary United Front (RUF), 46

Richards, P., 70

Rimini, N., 71

ringo koko (running to cry on the grave), 183n4

Rites of Passage (Van Gennep), 75

Ritual Process, The (Turner), 75

rituals: animal sacrifices, 151, 156, 169–70, 181n10; blessing of twins, 98; for the chief-elect (Ndembu tribe), 75–6; cleansing the curse of *kiir*, 166; drinking bitter roots (*mato oput*), 166–9; funeral/burial rites, 17–18, 84; hunting, 143–4; to pacify the spirit of the dead (*cen*), 83–4, 181n10; purification with shea butter (*wiiro kom*), 69, 86–9, 139–40; for returning CI soldiers (*yweyo kom*), 151, 169–70; storytelling, 3, 11

Roco wat i Acoli (Re-Establishing Kinship in Acholi) (Liu Institute for Global Issues et al.), 168, 174, 184n12

Sandywell, B., 26

Schabracq, M.J., 71

Schadt, Christa, 16

Schafer, J., 66

self-production, 22, 107

Shaka, 44, 179n1

Sierra Leone civil war (1991–8), 46, 70

Skowronski, J.J., 30

Smart, Elizabeth, 70, 180n3

Smelser, N.J., 161

Smith, G.N., 68

Song of Lawino (p'Bitek), 18–19, 50, 111

sorcery (*yir*), 79, 99–100

Soskis, D.A., 71

Specht, I., 24

spirits: Acholi belief in vengeful, 84, 143, 519; ancestral, 150, 152, 155; *cen* (evil spirit of the dead), 12, 20, 83–4, 159–60, 181n10; in displaced-persons camps, 162–4; *gemo* (evil spirits), 80; guidance for Joseph Kony, 77–8, 100; *jok*, 13, 162; *Lakwena*, 52, 58; offence of *kiir* (disturbing the spirits), 166; of Pamin-Yai Rock, 12–13

Ssemogerere, Paul Kawanga, 38

state elites, 45–6

stigmatization: of child abductees, 77, 81, 95; and CI soldier identity, 74, 144, 155, 157; of *olum* (those from the bush), 20–1, 81, 113, 158; of returning CI soldiers, 20, 122, 154, 158, 170–1

Uganda People's Democratic
Army (UPDA)
Uganda Patriotic Movement (UPM),
38
Uganda People's Congress (UPC), 38
Uganda People's Defence Forces
(UPDF): abductees killed by, 81;
accountability for war crimes, 168;
failure to protect the Acholi, 62,
130; LRM/A labels for, 95; war
with LRM/A, 6, 11, 117–18, 120,
134, 144–6, 181n3
Uganda People's Democratic Army
(UPDA), 57–8, 114; collapse of, 52;
excused for war atrocities, 59;
peace agreement with NRM/A,
59
Uganda People's Democratic
Christian Army (UPDCA), 59–60
UN Convention of the Rights of the
Child, 183n2
UNICEF, 177n6; report on LRM/A
child abductions, 62, 177n1
United Holy Salvation Army
(UHSA), 58–9
United Nations High Commission
for Refugees (UNHCR), 68

Van Gennep, Arnold, 75
van Manen, M., 28

victimization: of child abductees,
6, 107; of CI soldiers, 153, 175;
narratives of, 154; through rape,
48; of returning CI soldiers, 20,
154, 165–6
Vough, Lester, 183n5

walks, purpose of long, 81–2, 134–5
wang-oyo (bonfire), 11, 42, 90
wan luleb (we of the same tongue), 38
war crimes, 153, 173; of Joseph Kony,
60, 63, 173
Warnock, K., 49
wat (extended family and kin), 127,
156, 160
Wat constitution, 23
wegi ot (father of the house), 92
Wessells, M.G., 70
West, C.D., 30
witchcraft, 64, 79, 99–100
World Vision Center, 16, 172, 177n4
wot ii lum (going into the bush),
80–2, 131
wot ki too (walking with death), 85

yir (sorcery), 99–100
Yow, V.R., 30
Yugoslavia, former, 35
yweyo kom (cleansing the body), 166,
169–70